Measuring and Attaining the Goals of Education

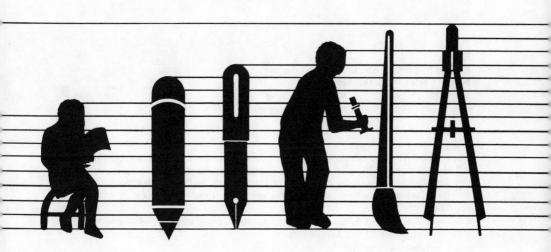

The ASCD Committee on Research and Theory

Wilbur B. Brookover, *Chairman*
Joseph Ferderbar
Geneva Gay
Mildred Middleton
George Posner
Flora Roebuck

Association for
Supervision and
Curriculum
Development

225 North Washington Street
Alexandria, Virginia 22314

Editing:
Ronald S. Brandt, ASCD Executive Editor
Nancy Carter Modrak, Assistant Editor

Stock number: 611-80210
Library of Congress Catalog Card Number: 80-68809
ISBN: 0-87120-102-X

Contents

iii

Foreword

With the current overemphasis on test results, what gets tested often helps determine what gets taught. Unfortunately, most educational measurement concentrates on a narrow band of facts and skills that get measured because they are measurable.

This is not to suggest that these facts and skills are unimportant; on the contrary, reading and computation, for example, are widely recognized as basics. However, there are other aims just as basic—writing, of instance —that are not included in standardized testing programs.

Because a comprehensive testing program may help maintain a balanced curriculum, and because curriculum workers need to know what progress students are making on *all* the goals of education, ASCD asked a group of qualified educators to prepare this report. Beginning with identification and analysis of widely accepted goals of education, they prepared a catalog of instruments currently available for measuring each goal.

Then they went further. Proceeding on the assumption that there is little point in measuring goals if educators can only guess about how to attain them, they devised a model for research on goal attainment.

The research model presented in this book, if used as intended, can contribute substantially to our knowledge about the complex relationships among the goals of schooling, specific outcomes representing those goals, processes of teaching and learning employed by schools, and environmental factors influencing those processes. That will be no small contribution.

BARBARA DAY
President, 1980-81
Association for Supervision and
Curriculum Development

iv

Preface

During the 1970's, citizens and school administrators demanded accountability for student achievement. Teachers throughout the nation were asked to write educational goals which would encompass cognitive, affective, and psychomotor behaviors. Hundreds of goal statements resulted from these demands. However, as school personnel transformed instructional programs to meet the goals and objectives, many questions became apparent. Which goals are really important? Is there a difference between an objective and a goal? How can goal attainment be measured? Are cognitive goals and humanistic concerns incompatible?

These issues led ASCD to create a committee to examine such concerns and suggest ways of responding to them. The Committee, identified as the Working Group on Theory and Research, began work in the summer of 1976. During the three years in which the Committee functioned, it undertook the following tasks:

1. Clarified the purpose of the committee
2. Developed ways of working as a group
3. Collected and examined goal statements from various sources
4. Developed some conceptual parameters on the definition of educational goals and subgoals
5. Wrote a set of goals and subgoals
6. Examined the goals for interrelationships
7. Searched for instruments to measure goals and subgoal attainment
8. Formulated questions and hypotheses concerning the relation of school programs to goal attainment
9. Developed a research model for examining the relation of school to the attainment of educational goals
10. Developed a series of research designs to suggest the kinds of research needed to determine the effectiveness of school programs in achieving educational goals

This publication is intended to give the reader a perception of educational goals and their relationship to cognitive, affective, and psychomotor learning. It identifies and describes the interrelationships of ten major educational goals, suggests ways of measuring goal achievement, and identifies some instruments that measure subgoals. Also provided is a review of the available published and nonpublished instruments for measuring goal attainment.

A comprehensive model for research is included with samples of research designs that suggest hypotheses concerning the relation of selected teaching-learning processes to out-of-school and school variables on one hand and to the attainment of immediate outcomes and desired educational goals on the other. We trust that this publication will assist in improving the efforts of educational systems to attain valued learning outcomes or goals.

The members of the Committee thank all those who assisted in the preparation of this publication:

Kenneth Haskins served briefly as a member of the Committee and assisted in the definition of its task.

Elizabeth Shook and Pricilla Durkin assisted in the examination of goal interrelationships.

Jean King assisted in the search for instruments to measure goal attainment and contributed significantly to the compilation and writing of the instrument review section of this publication.

Hilda Lauber and Deanna Lusk also assisted in the search and review of assessment instruments.

Mauritz Johnson, John W. McFarland, David Aspy, Carl Guerriero and J. Robert Coldiron reacted to and made suggestions concerning the set of goals and subgoals.

The ASCD staff has assisted the Committee throughout its work. Geneva Gay, who first served as staff associate, was later appointed to the Committee. Ruth Long succeeded Ms. Gay as staff associate. Virginia Berthy has managed the meeting arrangements throughout with great efficiency.

The Committee on Research and Theory thanks all of the above, and others who are not mentioned, for their contributions to this task. With some pride in accomplishment, we wish to emphasize that this monograph is a Committee product. No single person should be assigned any responsibility for our mistakes or failures; these must be borne by the Committee alone. Although various sections were first written by individual Committee members, they have all been thoroughly reviewed and often rewritten by the Committee. In view of the disparate backgrounds and orientation to the subject of our endeavor, it is rather remarkable that all Committee members concur in what we have written. Each member has pursued his or her points vigorously and has educated the others while being educated by them. We thank ASCD for the opportunity to learn from one another and we jointly contribute this report of our deliberations.

Chapter 1

Introduction

Since its creation in 1943, the Association for Supervision and Curriculum Development has had an abiding interest in humanistic education. In fact, humanistic education has been a long-standing value commitment of the Association. Not only has ASCD been sympathetic to making education more humane within its own programmatic jurisdiction, it also has been a national leader in this endeavor.

Humanistic education and its advocates have not escaped the skeptical eye of contemporary education critics. Often, the challenge has been made to exponents of humanistic education to clarify the meaning of the concept in terms of pragmatic actions that are useful in everyday school programs. What are the fundamental objectives of humanistic education? How are these to be evaluated? What parts of the school curriculum should be primarily concerned with humanistic education? How does the presence or absence of humane orientation in the school environment affect student performance in the mastery of basic skills, in the terminology of knowledge, and in the development of other intellectual abilities? The list of questions is endless as school practitioners try to make humanistic education meaningful to their functional worlds.

Frequently, humanistic education sympathizers, lacking empirical data to support their ideological and speculative contentions, have been unable to answer these questions to the satisfaction of school practitioners and taxpayers. While many educators may agree with the ideals of humanistic education, this agreement has not weakened their need and demands for ideals to be translated into pragmatic possibilities. Instead, these demands are on the increase. Current concerns for accountability, minimum competency testing, and demonstrated performance of educational programs and priorities, in terms of quantifiable data and cost-effective analyses, are causing even more questions to be raised about the practicality and efficiency of humanistic education.

Nor has ASCD, in trying to live up to its commitment to humaneness in education, remained untouched by the prevailing climate of the national educational community. The frequency with which schools are depending upon one-dimensional cognitive measures as the only devices for assessing student performance has become particularly bothersome to

1

the Association. Such techniques tend to de-emphasize, or ignore entirely, the affective and psychomotor aspects of learning. The fundamental components of humanistic education include cognitive, affective, and psychomotor characteristics. ASCD feels a professional responsibility to caution educators about the distortions caused by single-focused evaluations of student achievement, and to provide some leadership in determining how more comprehensive assessments of student performance in schools might be acquired.

The Committee on Research and Theory was created in June 1976 by the Executive Council of ASCD to (1) "Identify valued learning outcomes which reflect the 'holistic' nature of individuals in terms of the integration of cognitive, affective, and active (that is, to transfer to real life behaviors) dimensions," and (2) "Develop a research design which would have as its major goal the measurement of as many as possible of the valued learning outcomes as identified. . . ."* It was also encouraged to develop an "ambitious" research plan that would "have significant educational implications." Six educators from diverse backgrounds, along with an ASCD staff liaison person, were invited to become members of the Committee. They included Wilbur Brookover (Chairman of the Committee), Professor of Urban and Metropolitan Studies, Michigan State University; Joseph Ferderbar, Superintendent of the Neshaminy School District, Langhorne, Pennsylvania; Geneva Gay, Associate Professor of Education, Purdue University; Ruth Long, Associate Director for Program Development of ASCD; Mildred Middleton, Curriculum Coordinator, Cedar Rapids Community Schools; George Posner, Associate Professor of Education, Cornell University; and Flora Roebuck, Associate Professor of Education, Texas Women's University.

The Committee on Research and Theory began the task by clarifying the charge assigned to it. We recalled the basic tenets of humanistic education, reviewed ASCD's historical association with humanistic education, speculated why most evaluations of student achievement tend to concentrate on mastery of cognitive information in basic skills and subject matter, and observed how an only cognitive-based assessment of student performance approach falls short of the concept of humanistic education.

The Committee asked representatives of the ASCD Executive Council to share their perceptions and interpretations of the mission given to it. After much deliberation, we concluded that the Executive Council, operating on the premise that humanistic education is concerned with *all* aspects of learning and developing the "whole" child, had, in effect, directed us to examine (1) how the valued goals (cognitive, affective learning outcomes

* This statement is from the ASCD Executive Council minutes of June 1976.

and the active dimension of education) were interrelated; (2) the types of school programs and/or experiences that are likely to maximize achievement in all goals; and (3) how educators might design research and evaluation programs to acquire comprehensive measures of student achievement in cognitive, affective, and psychomotor learning.

To accomplish our task, we undertook several activities. The Committee developed a list of goals and subgoals that we believe comprise the kinds of behaviors a well-educated person would exhibit. We developed a set of research questions and hypotheses on goal and subgoal interrelationships. These hypotheses and questions are concerned with the extent to which the achievement of one goal facilitates or interferes with the achievement of other goals, and the relationship of the content and processes within the learning environment to the achievement of multiple goals of education. We have completed an extensive review of available measurement instruments, both published and unpublished, and have made some assessments about their appropriateness for use in determining student achievement of the educational goals specified in this report. Finally, we have developed a research model for use in determining student achievement of the goals of education. The model is used to illustrate the kinds of content and processes within learning environments that are most likely to produce desired multiple goals of education. Each of these activities is discussed in detail in the following chapters.

Chapter 2   **Goals of Education**

Procedure for Identifying Goals

What intellectual, social, and personal behaviors are desirable for individuals who have successfully matriculated through the K-12 educational process? What are the "valued learning outcomes" (goals and subgoals) that have a "humanistic character"? Are there some goals of education that school systems desire to achieve that are inherently contradictory to the principles of humanistic education? How does one determine what is humanistic and what is not humanistic in specifying goals of education? Must any list of goals of education, of necessity, be comprehensive and interrelated to qualify as humanistic? These questions provided the motivational stimuli and orientational direction for us as we began the task of "identifying valued learning outcomes which reflect the 'holistic' nature of individuals in terms of the integration of cognitive, affective, and active dimensions."

The first steps in the development of a set of desired goals of education involved collecting data on existing goal statements and establishing some conceptual parameters on the definition of an educational goal. The data collection process began with a review of the fundamental principles of humanistic education and some preliminary speculations about the kinds of goal statements inherent in these principles. Secondly, we decided to find out from other individuals and organizations involved in the development of educational goal statements what they had discovered about goal inter-relationships. The idea behind this strategy was to avoid reinventing the wheel; it seemed expedient and sensible to identify the best existing sets of "wheels" and endorse those goals as exemplary statements of desired learning outcomes.

Many different lists of goals were readily available since the account-ability, minimum competency testing, and back-to-basics trends were already well under way by the time the Committee on Research and Theory began work on its task. The specification of goal statements has been a priority in these trends. Letters of inquiry were sent to more than a hundred organizations and individuals, including regional research and development centers, testing agencies, and state departments of education, requesting information on their formulations of goals, objectives, learning outcomes, and ways of measuring them. Educational research and development centers were included in the surveys to discover what recent or ongoing research they were undertaking relevant to the relationship between humanistic programs and goals of education. The surveys revealed little ongoing research in humanistic education per se. We also found that no comprehensive knowledge was available on the interrelationship of education goals or on programs that most effectively achieve multiple goals.

Lists of goal statements were collected from such educational agencies as the Educational Testing Service, the North Dakota Study Group on Evaluation, Phi Delta Kappa, National Assessment of Educational Progress, the Learning Research and Development Center, NIE Clearinghouse on Teacher Education, and Research for Better Schools. Among the state departments of education who shared their goals (or "aims," "purposes," "objectives") with us were Michigan, Utah, New Jersey, Texas, Oregon, Pennsylvania, and Florida. A review of their different goals revealed a certain degree of similarity among them: (1) some goal statements appeared, in one form or another, on all lists, (2) the goals aimed to be comprehensive in both breadth of coverage and intellectual demands, and (3) many of the notions we typically associate with humanistic education were included in the goal statements. These inspections also led to two other conclusions: (1) while many of the organizations surveyed had formulated *multiple-dimensional goals,* none of these *integrated* cognitive, affective and psychomotor dimensions of learning; and (2) most of the examined lists of goals were "political statements" that, in their current forms, were extremely difficult to measure. Impressed by Pennsylvania's list of educational goals, and the processes the state was using to continually refine the goals and update its evaluation techniques of student achievement, we decided to use the Pennsylvania list as the primary basis from which to derive our own list of goals.

Definition of Goals

From the outset of the search for goal statements, Committee members were beset by a problem of terminology and some confusion over conceptual parameters. These dilemmas continued to plague us throughout our survey of goal statements. We found that we had to resolve them before we could proceed further with delineating our list of "valued learning outcomes." The major questions seemed to be: What is the distinction between learning outcomes as aims, goals, and objectives? Which of these should be the focus of our attention? Some stipulated definitions and a decision as to our focus were clearly needed. Following the distinctions made by Johnson (1967, 1977) and Zais (1976), we differentiated between teaching-learning events, immediate learning outcomes, objectives, goals, and frame factors, and decided to focus our primary attention on specifying educational goals.

The Committee began the definitional task by describing *teaching-learning events* as occurring when teachers engage in interactions with students for the purpose of producing some learning. That is, they are engaged in the teaching process while the students are engaged in the learning process. These events are expected to lead to particular *learning outcomes,* such as the student believing or knowing that something is the case or knowing how to do something. These learning outcomes may or may not have been intended. If they were intended, they are typically termed *learning objectives* or intended learning outcomes. If they were not intended, they may be termed side effects, or unintended learning outcomes.

Students learn many things, both in school (intended and unintended) and out of school (their "unofficial" education). As students mature, some of the diverse learnings become internalized and integrated so that students, while profoundly affected by some of the things they have learned, may lose the ability to identify the particular learnings that have affected them. We termed changes in students resulting from a combination of maturation and an integration of facts and ideas learned in and out of school an *educational result.* For example, as a result of learning a variety of things both in and out of school, students become more tolerant of people who are different, more law abiding, and more capable of coping with change. As with learning outcomes, some of these changes may have been intended and some unintended. Intended changes of this sort we termed *educational goals.*

Educational goals are the changes in students toward which we want learning outcomes to lead. These goals describe attributes or characteristics of the well-educated person, rather than the specific skills that constitute an education. They represent the cumulative effect or result of many learnings. Educational goals are the intended educational results, just as learning objectives are the intended learning outcomes.

In a sense, educational goals *justify* learning objectives. That is, if one asks *why* a particular learning objective has been included, the answer, in part, must be in terms of the changes in the students toward which that learning is supposed to lead. Likewise, learning objectives help to *actualize* educational goals. In other words, if one asks *how* a particular goal is to be accomplished, the answer is, in part, in terms of the kinds of things students will learn. Figure 1 describes this relationship.

Similarly, learning objectives justify teaching-learning events, while teaching-learning events serve to actualize learning objectives. If one asks *why* particular classroom events were made to happen, the answer, in part,

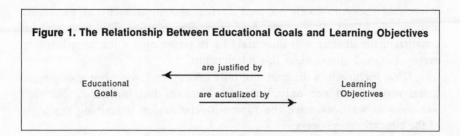

Figure 1. The Relationship Between Educational Goals and Learning Objectives

are justified by

Educational
Goals

are actualized by

Learning
Objectives

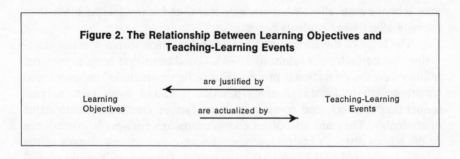

Figure 2. The Relationship Between Learning Objectives and Teaching-Learning Events

are justified by

Learning
Objectives

are actualized by

Teaching-Learning
Events

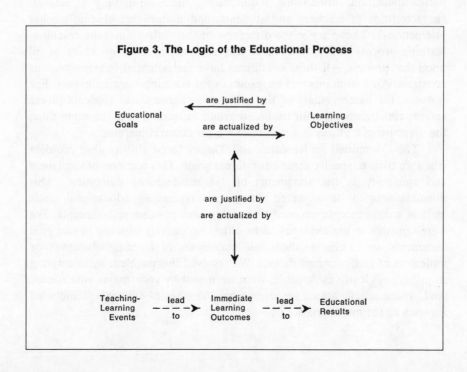

Figure 3. The Logic of the Educational Process

are justified by

Educational
Goals

are actualized by

Learning
Objectives

are justified by

are actualized by

Teaching-
Learning
Events

lead
– – – →
to

Immediate
Learning
Outcomes

lead
– – – →
to

Educational
Results

is because they are likely to lead to the accomplishment of particular learning objectives. If one asks *how* particular learning objectives will be actualized, the answer will ultimately be in terms of the teaching-learning events. Figure 2 summarizes this relationship.

If we include in a diagram not only educational goals but also educational results, and not only learning objectives but immediate learning outcomes as well, we have the Figure 3 relationship describing the logic of the educational process.

The broken lines at the bottom of Figure 3 signify that the element on the left leads to or influences the element to its right. The broken line does not signify a deterministic production process, since many factors other than school events affect what students learn, and many factors other than learning affect what students become.

The logic of the educational process takes place within a set of interactive "frame factors" (Johnson, 1977)—conditions that have a potential influence on the educational process. Frame factors include the school and classroom environment (grouping practices), school input factors (personnel preparation), and community input factors (socio-economic status of students). They are also of an economic nature (per-pupil expenditure or the school district's budget), temporal nature (scheduling, length of the school year, grade structure), spatial nature (the school's architectural structure), and organizational or personnel nature (school size, departmentalization, attendance requirements, decision-making structures, characteristics of teachers and students, and patterns of student-teacher interactions). They vary in the directness of their effect upon the teaching-learning process and may even appear at times to have no effect at all upon that process. All these conditions have the potential to serve both as constraints or limitations and as resources for teaching-learning events. For instance, the heterogeneity of the cultural backgrounds of students places serious constraints on uniform-paced group instruction. At the same time, the diversity of cultures is a rich resource for cultural learning.

The Committee on Research and Theory faced still another problem when we tried to specify some educational goals. This was one of vagueness and ambiguity in the statements of "valued learning outcomes." This dilemma was to be expected. Statements typical of educational goals include such concepts as good citizenship and positive self-concepts. We were sensitive to the tendency to be either excessively obscure in our goal statements, or to change them into statements of learning objectives or indicators of goal accomplishment. We resolved this problem by attempting to justify, as clearly as possible, what we meant by each major educational goal. These specifications we term *subgoals;* a set of subgoals is included for each of the major goals.

Description of Goals and Subgoals

Having stipulated our definitions and determined our focus, we turned once again to our data pool of goal statements. Using the Pennsylvania goals as a starting point, the Committee on Research and Theory set about accumulating, tabulating, assessing, integrating, elaborating, and creating. The result was a list of ten goals, each of which has several subgoals. These goal statements underwent several revisions, based on periodic reviews by members of the Committee as we progressed into new domains of exploration in trying to address the task, and on the opinions of selected individuals who were not directly associated with the study group. The following is our final set of goal statements, describing the kinds of behaviors a well-educated person would exhibit. We believe this list is comprehensive enough to encompass most of the goals the Committee studied.

Goal One: Basic Skills

Subgoals
1. Acquires information and meaning through observing, listening, and reading
2. Processes the acquired information and meaning through skills of reflective thinking
3. Shares information and expresses meaning through speaking, writing, and nonverbal means
4. Acquires information and meaning through the use of mathematical symbols
5. Manipulates symbols and uses mathematical reasoning
6. Shares information and expresses meaning through the use of mathematical symbols

Goal Two: Self-Conceptualization

Subgoals
1. Recognizes that self-concept is acquired in interaction with other people
2. Distinguishes between significant and nonsignificant others and their self-evaluations
3. Takes into account significant others and disregards nonsignificant others in the self-conceptualizing process
4. Distinguishes among many concepts of self in various roles or social situations

5. Assesses own functioning in each of several different situations
6. Perceives accurately, assesses validly, and responds appropriately to others' evaluations in the context of each specific role situation rather than to generalize to all situations

Goal Three: Understanding Others

Subgoals

1. Bases actions and decisions on the knowledge that individuals differ and are similar in many ways
2. Bases actions and decisions on the knowledge that values and behaviors are learned and differ from one social group to another
3. Bases actions and decisions on the understanding of lifestyles or behaviors within the context of the value system of the societies in which they were learned
4. Acts on the belief that each individual has value as a human being and should be respected as a worthwhile person in his or her own right
5. Bases actions and decisions on the understanding that as individuals move from one society to another, they can learn new lifestyles and can learn to behave appropriately in different societal contexts
6. Acts on the belief that human behavior is influenced by many factors and is best understood in terms of the relevant personal context in which it occurred
7. Seeks interactions and feels comfortable with others who are different in race, religion, social level, or personal attributes as well as those who are similar in these characteristics
8. Withholds judgment of another's actions until after trying to understand the personal and social context of that action

Goal Four: Using Accumulated Knowledge to Interpret the World

Subgoals

1. Applies basic principles and concepts of the sciences, arts, and humanities to interpret personal experiences
2. Applies basic principles and concepts of the sciences, arts, and humanities to analyze and act upon public issues
3. Applies basic principles and concepts of the sciences, arts, and humanities to understand natural phenomena
4. Applies basic principles and concepts of the sciences, arts, and humanities to evaluate technological progress

5. Applies basic principles and concepts of the sciences, arts, and humanities to appreciate aesthetic events

Goal Five: Continuous Learning

Subgoals
1. Seeks and values learning experiences
2. Acts as a self-reliant learner, capable of autonomous learning
3. Bases actions and decisions on the knowledge that it is necessary to continue to learn throughout life because of the inevitability of change

Goal Six: Mental and Physical Well-Being

Subgoals
1. Practices appropriate personal hygiene
2. Consumes a nutritionally balanced, wholesome diet
3. Exercises sufficiently to maintain personal health
4. Avoids, to the extent possible, consuming materials harmful to health, particularly addictive ones
5. Performs daily activities in a manner to prevent injury to self and others
6. Adapts to environmental constraints while seeking to change destructive elements in the environment
7. Maintains personal integration while functioning flexibly in varied situations
8. Behaves rationally based upon reasonable perceptions of self and society
9. Perceives self positively with a generally competent sense of well-being
10. Participates in satisfying leisure-time activities

Goal Seven: Participation in the Economic World of Production and Consumption

Subgoals
1. Bases decisions on an awareness and knowledge of career options
2. Interacts with others on the basis of an understanding and valuing of the characteristics and functions of different occupations
3. Selects and pursues career opportunities consonant with social and personal needs and capabilities
4. Makes informed consumer decisions based on appropriate knowledge of products, needs, and resources

Goal Eight: Responsible Societal Membership

1. Acts consonant with an understanding of the basic interdependence of the biological and physical resources of the environment
2. Acts consonant with an understanding of the interrelationships among complex organizations and agencies in modern society
3. Acts in accordance with a basic ethical framework incorporating those values contributing to group living, such as honesty, fairness compassion, and integrity
4. Assumes responsibility for own acts
5. Works in groups to achieve mutual goals
6. Invokes law and authority to protect the rights of all persons
7. Exercises duties of citizenship, such as voting
8. Bases actions and decisions on a sense of political efficacy
9. Exercises the right of dissent in accordance with personal conscience and human justice
10. Assumes responsibility for dependent persons of all ages in a manner consistent with both their growth and development needs, and the needs of society

Goal Nine: Creativity

Subgoals
1. Generates a range of imaginative alternatives to stimuli
2. Entertains and values the imaginative alternatives of others

Goal Ten: Coping with Change

Subgoals
1. Works for goals based on realistic personal performance standards
2. Decides when a risk is worth taking
3. Works now for goals to be realized in the future
4. Entertains new perceptions of the world
5. Tolerates ambiguity
6. Bases actions and decisions on an understanding that change is a natural process in society and one which increases exponentially
7. Bases actions on an understanding that coping with change is a continuous process throughout life
8. Acts with an appreciation that in a changing world, flexibility and adaptability are strengths rather than weaknesses
9. Selects viable alternatives for actions in changing circumstances

These goals do not represent what the Committee believes should be the goals of any particular school system, but any school system should find this listing comprehensive and clear enough to use as a basis for selecting goals suitable for its own particular situation and for assigning the appropriate priority to each goal selected.

The reader should also note that these educational goals are assumed to be appropriate for both elementary and secondary education. However, it should be understood that, depending on the level of schooling, the goals shift in their priority. For example, Goal Seven is more typically stressed in the 11th and 12th grades than in earlier grades and subgoal one of Goal Six is typically given greater emphasis in grades 1-3 than in later grades.

We should also point out again that an educational goal (as we have defined the term) does not describe the content of instruction, but instead, the educational result toward which the learning of the content is intended to lead. Thus, even though historical facts, scientific principles, and interpretations of English literature are not explicitly mentioned in any of the goal statements, all of the goals nevertheless justify the teaching of these content areas. The goals specify what kind of person the student should be as a result of learning the content and not what content they should learn.

The Interrelationship of Goals

In order to ensure that our list of goals was an integrated set that was, in fact, a reflection of the "holistic" nature of the individual, the Committee analyzed the relationships among the ten goals. A matrix of the relationships among all the goals and subgoals was charted. Each goal was analyzed in terms of its relationship to the other goals to determine whether or not its attainment was (1) a prerequisite to the attainment of other goals, (2) an indicator that other goals had already been attained, (3) a facilitator of the attainment of other goals, or (4) an interference with the attainment of other goals.

The resulting matrix was then analyzed by the members of the Committee for directionality of relationships and interdependence among the ten goals. From this analysis a picture of the directionality of dependence within the set of ten goals was derived. Figure 4 depicts these relationships.

The goals seem to fall into four interdependent clusters. Goal One, which encompasses the basic skills, stands alone as a prerequisite for the attainment of all other goals. The next cluster includes Goals Two, Three, and Four, which involve basic understandings of self, others, and the world. The third cluster of Goals Five, Six, and Seven comprises day-to-

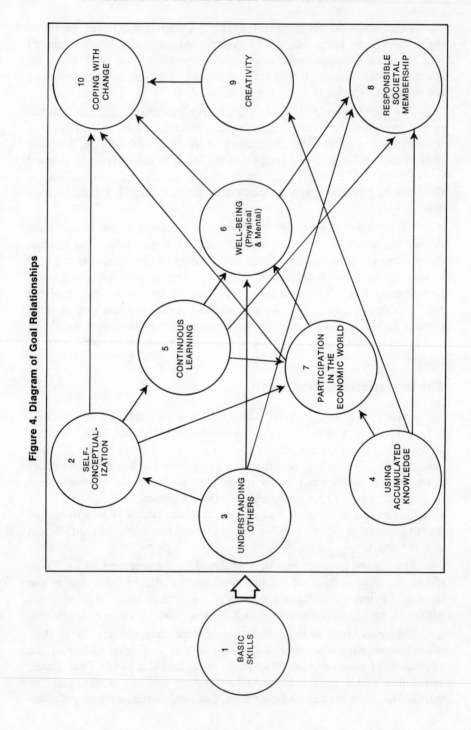

Figure 4. Diagram of Goal Relationships

day living skills. Cluster four, including Goals Eight, Nine, and Ten, have to do with the quality of life of both the individual and society.

A further examination of the goal relationships led to several conclusions from which research hypotheses might be derived:

- A complementary and interactive relationship does exist among the goals and subgoals.

- The achievement of some goals is essential to or facilitates the attainment of other goals.

- Time limitations may dictate the relative emphasis, or lack thereof, on one or more goals at a particular educational level, and thereby restrict respective attainment.

- Basic skills, as defined in Goal One, are prerequisite to all other goals.

- The removal of any goal affects the achievement of other goals.

- The achievement of any one goal does not interfere with the achievement of any other goal.

- The goals concerned with understanding others, self, and the world, facilitate the achievement of subsequent goals.

- All of the goals are characteristic of humane people in a humane society.

In order to ensure that these relationships were natural, the goals were broken apart into subgoals, and the relationships recharted. We discovered that the relationships were not significantly changed when recharted by subgoals rather than by major goals. This discovery led us to conclude that the set of goals is, in fact, integrated and reflective of the holistic nature of the individual.

Two other statements seem appropriate regarding the interpretation of the goal relationships presented in Figure 4. First, Goal One is tied to the other goals in the fashion indicated in the diagram *only* when basic skills are defined as they are in the subgoals of Goal One. That is, only when basic skills are defined as a broad set of functional skills, *not* items of content and *not just* the 3 R's, do they carry a strong prerequisite relationship for the attainment of *all* the other goals. Second, all relationships among the goals are seen as spiral. The prerequisite relationship used for the analysis was *not* one of mastery. Thus, a prerequisite relationship between any two goals does not assume that complete mastery of the prerequisite goal is necessary before the other goal can be activated. Rather, attainment of some aspect of the prerequisite goal makes it possible to begin attainment of other goals; these attainments in turn feed back into previous goals, thus facilitating further learning in a spiraling fashion.

Chapter 3   **Measuring Goal Attainment**

Following the identification of the complex goals of education and their interrelationships, the Committee examined the extent to which instruments were available to measure the specified educational goals and subgoals.

Clearly, measuring the achievement of certain goals and subgoals presents difficulties. First, many goals contain terms such as "self-conceptualization," "creativity," and "basic principles and concepts of the sciences, arts and humanities"—terms which are commonly used in education and may have commonly recognized meaning, but which must now be used for measurement purposes. Published tests do not necessarily seek to measure the same concept as the goal names, nor do they necessarily seek to measure the same concepts identified in the subgoals. Any test selected to measure concepts will be valid only to the extent that the measured concepts are similar.

Second, the goals, worded in behavioral terms, are often unsuited to measurement by paper and pencil tests; in many cases, instrumental or informal observation of student behavior may be the only valid way of determining the extent to which the goal has been achieved. Unfortunately, there seems to be no coherent body of observational instruments that addresses the problem of attainment of goals; that is, assessment of criterion behaviors. Rather, most of the readily available instruments, such as those anthologized in *Mirrors of Behavior* (Simon and Boyer, 1974), are primarily concerned with the process of teaching/learning rather than the outcomes of that process. Thus, there exist instruments such as the *Aspy Process Scales* which, among other things, adequately and reliably measure the teacher's communication of empathy, or Carkhuff's *Detractor-Leader Scale* which measures the degree to which a student contributes to the ongoing learning process. However, no instrument measures, for example, the degree to which a student works for goals based on realistic personal performance standards. Observational instruments designed to measure criterion or outcome behaviors should be as feasible as measures of process variables; in fact, many of the already available and excellent observation instruments could be adapted or extended to measure student learning outcomes as well as teaching-learning processes as criteria. This probably

16

needs to be the next focus of a concerted thrust in measurement methodology.

But, even if observation were feasible, it could prove problematic for those goals where the behaviors identified may be expressed differently in different situations (for example, Self-Conceptualization or Coping with Change). That is, if the self in fact is differently conceptualized in relationship to different reference groups, then measuring it adequately means assessing it in several settings, not just in one classroom. Similarly, measurement of Coping with Change would seem to require assessment of attitudes or behaviors both prior and subsequent to involvement in a change process.

A third measurement problem stems from the long-term nature of certain goals. Must schools wait until a student is 18, for example, to measure subgoal 8.7, "Exercises duties of citizenship," or subgoal 7.3, "Selects and pursues career opportunities consonant with social and personal needs and capabilities"? If not, how shall these be measured? What is needed seems to be instruments which can assess, within the school setting, those behaviors of young people which are reliable predictors of future behavior in an adult context. Needless to say, such instruments are difficult to find.

With these constraints in mind, the Committee began its search for available measurement instruments.

The Search Procedure for Published Instruments

During the first stage of the search procedure, the Committee on Research and Theory used descriptions from two sources: *Measuring Human Behavior* (Lake and others, 1973) and *Fifth, Sixth, and Seventh Mental Measurement Yearbooks* (Buros, 1965) to select the names of published (or commercially available) tests which seemed appropriate for measuring each subgoal. Nonpublished tests (research instruments and others not available from regular publishing sources) were screened through examination of titles and subject classifications in three sources: *Tests and Measurements in Child Development: A Handbook* (Johnson and Bommarito, 1971), *Mirrors for Behavior, III* (Simon and Boyer, 1974), and *Tests in Microfiche* (Educational Testing Service, 1975-1978).

During the second stage, these tests were screened using the following criteria:

(1) Were they aimed at *school-age* subjects (K-12)?

(2) Were they designed for and (if normed) normed to a *normal American* audience (that is, not mentally retarded)?

(3) Were they in-print, published, paper-and-pencil tests *feasible* to administer, score, and interpret in a school setting by *non-clinicians?* (In the case of nonpublished tests, the criteria "in print, published" was interpreted to mean that the text of the test had been reported in the professional literature, in format, and was complete with directions for administration, scoring, and interpretation.)

(4) Were they relatively *recent* (1960-present)?

(5) Were they not based on the concepts of a *specific theorist* (that is, requiring interpretation only from a specific theorist's conceptual perspective)?

(6) Did they report *reliability* coefficient of at least .60 or better?

(7) Did they report high content *validity* and/or at least moderate construct validity?

(8) If published, were they *favorably reviewed* in a *Mental Measurement Yearbook?*

In the final stage, the actual tests and manuals selected in the second stage were examined for the match between what the test measured and what the goal meant. Tests meeting all of the criteria are listed below. The obvious disadvantage of such a search procedure is that some good tests may have been missed in the first stage or rejected in the second or third.

No tests of basic skills were examined by the Committee since many suitable tests are readily available in the form of achievement batteries and are widely used by school districts. The purpose of the Committee's efforts was to identify instruments for potential use as measures of goals currently not being measured by schools.

Review of Available Instruments

This review uses the same format for each of the goals (excluding Goal One, Basic Skills): first, comments on the measurement problems inherent in the goals themselves as related to available tests; second, brief descriptions of the appropriate located tests; and finally, a summary table of information about these tests, including sample items. Two features and one omission on the table require explanation:

1. *Cost.* Rather than give exact figures which may change in these inflationary days, a relative cost estimate—high, moderate, or low—is given. Unless otherwise noted, costs for tests with the Educational Testing Service (ETS) as the source are assumed to be minimal since the ETS microfiche sets are prefaced by the statement, "The materials reproduced

in microfiche may be reproduced by the purchaser for his own use until otherwise notified by ETS or the author." Cost estimates are based on hand-scoring but the availability of machine-scoring is indicated by "m" after the cost estimate in the table.

2. *Subgoals measured.* Unless a subgoal has been footnoted, the test measures the subgoal directly. Footnoted subgoals are either indirectly or only partially measured. The notation "goal number .0" is used for those tests which measure the goal as a whole, rather than individual subgoals.

3. *Reliability and validity data* are omitted from the tables for two reasons: (1) this information has already been used in the selection procedure, and (2) it varied so widely in both type and number that its inclusion would have required a complex and unwieldy encoding procedure that might have produced more confusion than information.

Goal Two: Self-Conceptualization

1. *Comments*

The measurement of Goal Two presents two more problems in defining terms. One difficulty in assessing this goal arises because it focuses on the process of self-conceptualization, rather than on self-concept as a presumably stable characteristic. Each of the subgoals involves an aspect of the process of self-conceptualizing in interaction with other people. Given this focus on the interactive nature of the self-conceptualizing process, most tests currently available are inappropriate. They generally measure aspects of self-concepts that are presumed to be stable human characteristics rather than continuing processes of self-assessment in varying social situations. Although some parts of the tests cited may be relevant in assessing specific subgoals, the test results require careful interpretation if they are to be used for evaluation. The relation of the test results to the subgoals needs careful consideration before conclusions can be drawn.

No instruments specifically designed to measure the self-conceptualization process identified in the subgoals were found, but some of the numerous inventories and scales designed to evaluate various aspects of personal and/or social adjustment and the current state of global or specific self-concepts may vary from one social context to another and from one social role to another. A person's concept of self in the student role may be quite different from his or her self-concept as an athlete. Both may vary with the group relevant to the person at a given time. Observation in various social settings may be useful in assessing students' self-conceptualizing, but this is frequently difficult and subject to the validity problems associated with highly inferential measures.

With these precautions, a few of the instruments available for use with students are cited. Sample items for each test in each goal appear in Tables Ia. through Ig. beginning on page 29.

2. *Appropriate Instruments*

a. The Adjustment Inventory (by Hugh M. Bell; grades 10-12 and college). The manual states that this test provides six measures of personal and social adjustment, submissiveness, emotionality, hostility, masculinity, and femininity. The 200 questions about student self-concept are self-administered; students answer by marking "yes," "no," or "?" on an IBM answer sheet. Although there is no time limit, most students finish in less than 30 minutes. The Adjustment Inventory is scored with stencils.

b. The Gordon Personal Inventory (by Leonard V. Gordon; grades 3-12, college, and adult). The Gordon Personal Inventory consists of 20 multiple-choice items in which students choose from among four phrases the one that is most like them and the one least like them. The four personality traits listed in the manual are "cautiousness, original thinking, personal relations, and vigor." The instrument is self-administered and has no time limit; however, students generally take 10 to 15 minutes to complete it. Stencils are used to correct the inventories. Because of the tenuous relation between the items in this inventory and the subgoals of Goal Two, results require careful interpretation.

c. How I See Myself Scale (by Ira J. Gordon; grades 3-12). Although this instrument is nonpublished, it is one of the few tests which attempts to measure self-concept for younger as well as older students. The scale consists of items in the form of two contrasting statements about self. Between these statements is a five-point scale that the student marks to indicate which of the statements the student feels represents the way she or he is most of the time and the strength of that feeling. The elementary form contains 40 such items; the high school form has 41. Five factors or aspects of self-concept are measured: teacher/school; physical appearance; interpersonal adequacy; autonomy; and academic adequacy. Although hand-scoring is possible, scoring service is available at 25 cents per test. Because the test is not published, its cost is minimal. As with the other tests cited, careful interpretation of results is required.

d. The Mac B Personal Competence Inventory (by Jeanette A. Brown and Mary Ann MacDougall; grades 3-7). Although the Inventory is not yet fully documented, it is included because it attempts to measure self-concept for younger students, as does the How I See Myself Scale. It consists of two indices of affective behavior: the Self-Perception Index and the Peer Acceptance Index. The first, a measure of students' perceptions of the relation of the self to others, to culture, and to itself, contains 33 statements rated on a five-point Likert Scale. The second, a measure of the degree of pupils' acceptance or rejection by their classmates, takes the form of a blank filled in with a student's name and a five-point scale between the phrases "My best friend" and "Never my friend." The Inventory is short and has no time limit. Scoring information is available, but users should be aware that the results will not be a comprehensive evaluation of any of the subgoals of Goal Two.

e. The Tennessee Self-Concept Scale (by William H. Fitts; ages 12 and over). This scale is self-administering, generally requiring less than 20 minutes to complete. A student chooses from one hundred self-descriptive statements "to portray her/his own picture of herself/himself." Separate scores are given in the following areas: self-criticism; positiveness including identity, self-satisfaction, behavior, physical self, moral/ethical self, personal self, family self, and social self; variability; distribution; and time. Scoring requires six to seven minutes per paper.

f. Self-Esteem Inventory (SEI) (by Stanley Coopersmith). This instrument was designed for upper-elementary students, but might be appropriate for older students. Some items are particularly relevant for school situations. Although it reflects the importance of social interaction in self-conceptualization, it does not directly measure the processes identified in the subgoals. It is composed of 58 items.

g. Behavior Rating Form (BRF) (by Stanley Coopersmith). This is a rating form teachers use to observe students in school situations, focusing on the student's behavior in relation to others and the teacher's perception of the student's self-concept. The Form, composed of 13 items, is included to indicate the use of observation in assessing the self-conceptualizing process.

h. Self-Concept of Academic Ability (by Wilbur Brookover). This scale, composed of eight items, has been widely used in research on self-concept and school achievement. It was originally developed for secondary (grade 7-12) students, but elementary and post high-school forms are available. It assesses the student's conception of his or her academic ability in comparison with other students and friends. It does not directly measure the self-conceptualizing process, but reflects the student's self evaluations in reference to others in the student role.

Information about Goal Two instruments is summarized in Table Ia.

Goal Three: Understanding Others

1. Comments

An obvious difficulty in measuring Goal Three stems from definitions concentrating on student behaviors (for example, "Acts on the belief that . . ." and "Withholds judgment . . ."). Proper measurement of such behaviors is not easy because it requires observation of students over an extended period of time. In addition, the behaviors to be observed are related to values and hence may be difficult to define in terms specific enough to be of use in observation.

The nontraditional perspective of Goal Three, focusing on a relativistic value structure, differs in general from that of available tests of interpersonal relations. Most of the tests which were examined concerned students' ability to behave in a school (or middle-class setting) or with students' tolerance for others, but not with their awareness of others' life-styles and values. Only three instruments were found to be at all appropriate, and even these did not directly measure what was intended by the total goal.

2. *Appropriate Instruments*

a. The Children's Scale of Social Values (by Paul M. Insel and Glenn D. Wilson; grades 3-9). Based on the Wilson-Patterson Conservatism Scale, The Children's Scale of Social Values is made up of 50 items, each of which is a short phrase to which students respond by circling "Yes," "No," or "?." Administration of the scale takes approximately ten minutes, and scoring can be done by hand or by computer. The instrument yields scores for the following areas: religious beliefs; enthnocentrism (intolerance of minority groups); preference for conventional art, clothing, and institutions; respect for authority; and insistence on strict rules and punishments. The score for insistence on strict rules and punishments is interpreted as indicative of an antihedonistic outlook coupled with a strict sexual morality.

b. Getting Along (by Trudys Lawrence; grades 7-9). This instrument was designed to evaluate student behavior in everyday situations and to enable teachers to identify students who may need help in improving their behavior. Getting Along has three parts: (1) "Getting Along With One's Self"; (2) "Getting Along With Others"; and (3) "Getting Along in One's Environment"—and consists of 45 items of two or more captioned pictures followed by incomplete sentences with multiple-choice endings. The instrument has two forms, can be completed in 35 to 40 minutes, and is easily scored. Only items in Part 2, however, are appropriate to the measurement of certain subgoals of Goal Three.

c. The Value Socialization Scales (by Richard L. Gorsuch; grades 4-6). These scales, intended for research use only, have been included here because they were designed to reflect the degree to which a child has learned those values necessary to fit into any society or to choose among the sub-cultures available to him or her. There are two scales: one in which the student is asked to rate a series of behaviors reflecting basic, middle-class values; and a second in which the student is asked to indicate how much he or she admires a child who performs various acts.

Administration and scoring are simple, but the results require careful interpretation because of the predominance of middle-class value items.

For information on Goal Three instruments, see Table Ib.

Goal Four: Using Accumulated Knowledge to Understand the World

1. Comments

No appropriate tests were found that address students' use of accumulated knowledge in the way intended by this goal. Available tests measure the amount of students' accumulated knowledge, but do not examine whether they can use the knowledge appropriately. This is clearly an area in which research and development work are needed.

2. Appropriate Instruments

Although unreceived, the American College Testing Program's College Outcome Measures Project (COMP) appears promising for this goal. One of the six areas tested includes "using science and technology." It purports to test the "ability to identify the science/technological aspects of a culture, understand the impact of such activities and products on individuals and the environment, and analyze products for one's own self and the culture." Obviously the test would have to be adapted for a pre-college population if it were useful for secondary schools.

Goal Five: Continuous Learning

1. Comments

Goal Five focuses on students' interest in and capability for continuous learning. The measurement of this goal is a relatively new effort in the field of education. Clearly the notions of continuous learning and the self-reliant learner are in need of definitions in the real world of the school where their achievement is measured. To say that a student values learning experiences can be demonstrated by many different types of behaviors, as can a decision to call her or him a self-reliant learner; these behaviors need to be specified for students at all levels.

Because the interest in examining this aspect of learning is recent, few available tests measure these subgoals. No such tests were located for grades K-2. Tests for older students measured their motivation for learning, rather than their valuing of it, or their current practices in self-initiated learning, rather than their capability. The tests cited, although the best available, require careful interpretation in relation to the subgoals.

2. *Appropriate Instruments*

a. Independent Activities Questionnaire (by Stephen P. Klein; grades 9-13). This questionnaire was designed to assess achievement that may not be reflected by a student's grades in school. Each of the 65 major items has biographical subitems (see Table Ic, below) which deal with student efforts requiring individual initiative. The questionnaire takes approximately 45 minutes to complete and yields scores for 19 areas, including the following: politics, leadership, home responsibility, public speaking, and scholarship. Computer-assisted scoring is recommended by the author. Although this type of instrument measures the goal indirectly, it would serve as an indicator of the student's tendency to learn on her or his own.

b. The Jim Scale, Junior Index of Motivation (by Jack Frymier; grades 7-12). This nonpublished measure, normed on a national sample of 3,189 students, takes about thirty minutes to complete. Fifty of the eighty items are scored, yielding a score which represents the student's motivation for achievement. For each item, the student records a sign and a number from -2 to $+2$ to indicate agreement or disagreement and slight or strong support for the opinion expressed in the item statement. Scoring information is supplied.

c. The Survey of Study Habits and Attitudes (the SSHA) (by William F. Brown and Wayne H. Holtzman; grades 7-12 and grades 12-14). The one hundred items in this survey consist of statements about study habits that students indicate "rarely," "sometimes," "frequently," "generally," or "almost always" apply to them. Separate scores are given for study habits and study attitudes. Students generally take from 20-35 minutes to complete the survey, and hand-scoring is possible.

Information about Goal Five instruments is found in Table Ic.

Goal Six: Mental and Physical Well-Being

1. *Comments*

In contrast to the other goals, the subgoals of Goal Six are relatively straightforward, although they too emphasize student behaviors, rather than mere knowledge. Other than the physical examination by medical personnel in some states, tests of physical well-being for school-age children are not common. Most available tests for mental well-being generally seek to discover students' problems, not their strengths. However, the tests cited for this goal are, for the most part, geared to specific subgoals and measure these directly.

2. *Appropriate Instruments*

a. Health Behavior Inventory, Elementary Level (by Sylvia Yellen; grades 3-6). This inventory consists of 40 illustrated questions to which students respond "Most of the time I do," "Sometimes I do," or "No, I never do." Scores are given for the following areas: personal health, personal cleanliness, nutrition, safety, community health, infection and disease, mental health, and dental health. There is no time limit set, although most students finish in 20 to 30 minutes. Scoring is done by hand.

b. Independent Activities Questionnaire (cited above for Goal Five). Several of the areas assessed in this questionnaire provide information about students' leisure-time activities.

c. Mac B Personal Competence Inventory (cited above for Goal Two). "The Self to Culture" section of this inventory would yield information about a student's perceived relation to his or her culture.

d. Martinek-Zaichkowsky Self-Concept Scale for Children (by Thomas J. Martinek and Leonard D. Zaichkowsky; grades 1-8). Designed to measure children's global self-concept, the Self-Concept Scale is a nonverbal test consisting of 25 sets of pictures. Students respond to each item by marking the picture which is most like them. The following factors are measured: satisfaction and happiness; home and family relationships and circumstances; ability in games, recreation, and sports; personality traits and emotional tendencies; and behavioral and social characteristics in school. The authors state that the test is culture-fair and takes from 10 to 15 minutes to complete.

e. Student Drug Survey (by J. Ray Hays; grades 7-12). Although this survey suffers the limitations of self-report measures, the 88 multiple-choice items may provide information on patterns of drug abuse among secondary school students. Roughly one-third of the questions deal with the frequency of the use of nine categories of substances at three intervals: (1) never used, (2) used in the past six months, (3) used in the past seven days. The remaining questions concern demographic, attitudinal, and factual variables as correlatives of drug use. The survey takes approximately 45 minutes.

f. Thompson Smoking and Tobacco Knowledge Test (by Glen W. Thompson; grades 7-16). The purpose of this test is to measure the smoking and tobacco knowledge of high school and college students. It consists of 25 questions—16 concerning the effects on health of smoking, and nine concerning sociological and historical concepts related to smoking. The test requires approximately 30 minutes to complete, but results indicate students' knowledge, rather than their practices.

Information on Goal Six instruments is found in Table Id.

Goal Seven: Participation in the Economic World of Production and Consumption

1. *Comments*

As was the case for previous goals, the behavioral perspective of Goal Seven makes its measurement with available tests difficult. Currently existing vocational tests are of two types: interest inventories, both personal and occupational; and work value inventories. Neither type of test directly measures the stated subgoals. The definition problem common to the other goals is found here as well; terms such as "informed consumer decisions" and "appropriate knowledge" need to be defined further before the subgoals can be accurately measured.

2. *No Appropriate Instrument Found*

Goal Eight: Responsible Societal Membership

1. *Comments*

The problems inherent in determining whether a student is a responsible member of society relate to the terms used in the subgoals and to the time-delay that may be needed to assess fairly a student's involvement in society. The first frequently mentioned problem is common to all of the goals. Terms such as "values" and "ethical framework" are necessary to the subgoal statements, yet need additional definition for measurement purposes. The second problem is self-evident. How will we know for certain that a student "exercises duties of citizenship" until the student is old enough to vote or participate otherwise as a citizen in his or her society? Many of the desired behaviors are adult and difficult to measure while the student is still in school.

Instruments for school-age children which have been established as reliable predictors of specified criterion adult behaviors would be desirable; however, none were found. The listed instruments were selected on the assumption that the best available estimate of future behavior in an adult setting is similar or related to behavior in the current context. A student who is a responsible member of his school, home, and peer society would more likely continue to be a responsible member of his adult society than would a student who was not responsible in his current contexts.

The problems discovered upon surveying the available tests, again, have been mentioned previously. The available instruments do not measure behaviors, whereas the subgoals focus on the actions of students ("acts," "assumes," "exercises," and so forth). The exception to this general case is the self-report questionnaire, but these may not be accurate appraisals of student behavior since the student does the reporting.

2. *Appropriate Instruments*

a. Biographical Inventory for Students (by Laurence Siegel; grades 12-13). This inventory was designed to elicit factual, biographical information from students through 93 multiple-choice questions, each with five possible alternatives. In Part 1 the student must select only one of the choices; in Part 2 he or she may select as many as are appropriate. The subscale scores include those for political activities, socioeconomic independence, dependence upon the home, and social conformity. Although the measure is self-administering, requiring from forty-five to sixty minutes to complete, the authors recommend machine-scoring.

b. Cooperative Social Studies Tests: Civics (ETS; grades 8-9), and

c. Cooperative Social Studies Test: American Government (ETS; grades 10-12). Each full scale consists of 40 forced-choice (Yes-No) items. Abbreviated scales are available; however, research reported is with the full scale. Each of these tests contains multiple-choice questions devoted to the important concepts, basic principles, and issues of civics and American government, respectively. Charts, maps, cartoons, and graphs are used to test subject matter from the following areas: the Constitution and national government, state and local government, citizenship and political participation, government services, controls and finances, and national defense and international relations. The three skills a student must use to answer the questions are remembering, understanding, and analyzing. There is a time limit of 40 minutes for both tests, and they can either be scored by hand, using stencils, or by machine.

d. Getting Along (cited above for Goal Three). Part III of this instrument is an indicator for the subgoals of Goal Eight, although it does not measure them directly. Furthermore many items on the test do not relate to the subgoals.

e. Nowicki-Strickland Locus of Control Scale (by Stephen Nowicki, Jr. and Bonnie R. Strickland; grades 3-12). The scale consists of 40 questions answered by checking "Yes" or "No." This scale, requiring about 20 minutes to complete, assesses the extent to which reinforcement (the attainment of goals) is attributed to internal or external sources. An abbreviated scale for grades 1-6 is available, but not reported in the research literature. Although the instrument does not directly measure subgoal 5.4, its ease of administration and scoring, coupled with the fact that it does provide an estimate of the factor at work, make it worthy of consideration.

f. Sequential Tests of Educational Progress: Social Studies (ETS; grades 4-6, 7-9, 10-12, and 13-14). The STEP tests in social studies were designed "to measure student development in the broad skills and understandings that every citizen should possess to be effective." Content was taken from the disciplines of political science, sociology and anthropology, economics, history, and geography to test students' ability to organize, interpret, and evaluate information. There are four levels of the test and two forms at each level. The tests consist of multiple-choice questions. The time limits are 45 minutes for the tests given to grades 4-6 and 7-9 and 60 minutes for those given to grades 10-12 and 13-14.

g. Test of Reasoning in Conservation (Conservation Foundation; grades 7-12). This group test, made up of 45 multiple-choice and matching items, was developed to determine students' knowledge of conservation concepts and their implications. Scoring information and keys are provided, although the test may be machine-scored.

h. Value Socialization Scales (cited above for Goal Three). These scales attempt to measure awareness of the ethical framework mentioned in subgoal 8.3.

Information on Goal Eight instruments is found in Table Ie.

Goal Nine: Creativity

1. *Comments*

Despite the fact that the measurement of creativity has been of interest to researchers for years, the available tests lack the reliability and validity necessary for their widespread use as standardized tests. This is due to the varied nature of creativity, both in its expression and in its evaluation. Agreement as to what constitutes creativity has not been reached, and, as a result, measurement remains difficult, if not impossible. This is clearly reflected by the lack of appropriate tests cited for this goal.

2. *Appropriate Instrument*

Independent Activities Questionnaire (cited above for Goals Five and Six, see Tables Id and Ie). Student responses will indicate indirectly whether they are or have been involved in creative activities.

Goal Ten: Coping with Change

1. *Comments*

Coping with change is a necessity in the world today, and Goal Ten marks an attempt to list the behaviors that students need to survive in a changing world. Traditional tests have not as yet attempted to measure these behaviors, and, as with Goal Nine, only one instrument was located which in any way dealt with the given subgoals.

2. *Appropriate Instrument*

Jim Scale, The Junior Index of Motivation (cited above for Goal Five, see Table Ic). Certain items on this scale, which reflect a student's motivation for achievement, point to his ability to cope with change.

Information for Goal Ten is found in Table Ig.

Table Ia. Summary of Instruments Appropriate to Goal 2

Assessed Subgoals	Test Name & Source	Date & Status	Cost	Grade Range	Sample Item
2.0[1]	The Adjustment Inventory Consulting Psychologists Press, Inc. 577 College Avenue Palo Alto, Cal. 94306	1962 p	moderate m*	10-12, college	Do you find it necessary to watch your health carefully? Yes No Do you get upset easily? Yes No
2.0	Gordon Personal Inventory Harcourt, Brace, Jovanovich, Inc. 757 Third Avenue New York, N.Y. 10017	1963 p	low	3-12, college, adult	Prefers to get up early in the morning M L Doesn't care for popular music ___ Has excellent command of English ___
2.0 2.5[2]	How I See Myself Scale Institute for the Development of Human Resources College of Education University of Florida Gainesville, Fla. 71201	1968 n	low m	3-12	Nothing gets me too mad. 1-2-3-4-5 I get mad easily and explode. 1-2-3-4-5 I don't like the way I look. 1-2-3-4-5 I like the way I look. 1-2-3-4-5
2.1 2.3 2.5	The Mac B Personal Competence Inventory (also cited at Goal 6) ETS 007 316 (available in ETS Tests in Microfiche)	1975 n	low	3-7	First index: I have different kinds of friends. Never 1 2 3 4 5 Always Second index: My best friend 1 2 3 4 5 Never my friend
2.0	The Tennessee Self-Concept Scale Counselor Recordings and Tests Box 6184 Acklen Station Nashville, Tenn. 37242	1964 1965 p	high	7-12, adult	I never do things without thinking about them first. Totally false 1 / Mostly false 2 / Partly true & partly false 3 / Mostly true 4 / Totally true 5

[1] Instrument applies to total goal ("0").
[2] Instrument applies only partially or indirectly to subgoal.

Note: p = published, available from commercial source.
n = not published or available from commercial source.
m = machine scoring available (*at extra cost).

Table Ia. *(continued)*

Assessed Subgoals	Test Name & Source	Date & Status	Cost	Grade Range	Sample Item
2.1 2.3 2.5	"Self Esteem Inventory" Stanley Coopersmith, *The Antecedent of Self Esteem* (San Francisco: W. H. Freeman Co., 1967)	1967 n	unknown	3-6	My parents and I have lots of fun together. I like to be called on in class. Kids pick on me often. Like Me / Unlike Me (blanks)
2.0	*Behavior Rating Form* Stanley Coopersmith	1967 n	unknown	teacher observation	Does this child adapt easily to new situations, feel comfortable in new settings, enter easily into new activities? always—usually—sometimes—seldom—never Does this child seek such support and reassurance from his peers or the teacher as evidence . . . or frequently inquires whether he is doing well? always—usually—sometimes—seldom—never
2.0	*Self-Concept of Academic Ability Scale* and	1962 p	low	Three forms: 3-6, 7-12, Post HS	Where do you think you would rank in your class in high school? a. Among the best b. Above average c. Average d. Below average e. Among the poorest How do you rate yourself in school ability compared with your close friends? a. I am the best. b. I am above average. c. I am average. d. I am below average. e. I am the poorest.
2.1	*Self-Concept of Academic Ability and School Achievement* Wilbur Brookover College of Education Michigan State University	p			

Note: p = published, available from commercial source.
n = not published or available from commercial source.

Table Ib. Summary of Instruments Appropriate to Goal 3

Subgoals Assessed	Test Name & Source	Date & Status	Cost	Grade Range	Sample Item
3.2	*Children's Scale of Social Attitudes* ETS 008 449 [2]	1970 n	low	3-9	Which of the following do you favor or believe in? Hanging thieves Yes No Divorce Yes No
3.51 3.61 3.71 3.81	*Getting Along* (also cited for Goal 8) ETS 003 235	1965 n	low	7-9	Caption under pictures: Ruth said, "Today is Saturday. There is housework to do, new records to play, and a birthday party this afternoon." Ruth should . . . a. ask her mother if it is all right to skip the housework this week b. play the records while she does the housework c. do her share of the housework first
3.21 3.51	*Value Socialization Scales* (also cited for Goal 8) ETS 007 592	1970 n	low	4-6	A child is doing the best he can. a. Always admire b. Sometimes admire c. Always dislike

Note: n = not published or available from commercial source.
[1] Instrument applies only partially or indirectly to the assessed subgoal.
[2] ETS numbers refer to tests available in ETS *Tests in Microfiche*.

Table Ic. Summary of Instruments Appropriate to Goal 5

Subgoals Assessed	Test Name & Source	Date & Status	Cost	Grade Range	Sample Items
5.2[1]	Independent Activities Questionnaire (also cited for Goals 6 and 9) ETS 001 518[2]	1965 n	low m	9-12, college	50. Have you ever directed instrumental or vocal music? Yes ___ No ___ If no, go on to question 51. If yes, go to the enclosed question below. (50a. and 50b.) 50a. Have you ever directed music performed publicly and for which you were paid or for which admission was charged? Yes ___ No ___ 50b. Have you ever organized your own instrumental or singing group? Yes ___ No ___ Type of Group ___
5.1[1] 5.2[1] 5.3[1]	JIM Scale (Junior Index of Motivation) (also cited for Goal 10) ETS 004 021	1965 n	low	7-12	Late afternoon is the best time of day. -2 -1 $+1$ $+2$ Most young people do not want to go to school. -2 -1 $+1$ $+2$
5.1 5.2	Survey of Study Habits and Attitudes Psychological Corporation 757 Third Avenue New York, N.Y. 10017	1967 p	low	7-12, college	Having too many other things to do causes me to get behind in my school work. a. rarely d. generally b. sometimes e. almost always c. frequently I seem to get very little done for the amount of time I spend studying. a. rarely d. generally b. sometimes e. almost always c. frequently

Note: p = published, available from commercial source.
n = not published or available from commercial source.
m = machine scoring available and, for this instrument, recommended by the author.
[1] Instrument applies only indirectly or partially to the assessed subgoal.
[2] ETS numbers refer to tests available in ETS Tests in Microfiche.

Table Id. Summary of Instruments Appropriate to Goal 6

Subgoals Assessed	Test Name & Source	Date & Status	Cost	Grade Range	Sample Item
6.1 6.2 6.3 6.4	*Health Behavior Inventory* (Currently being revised) Sylvia Yellen 2744 Angelo Drive Los Angeles, Cal. 90024	1962 1979 p	unknown	3-6	Do you stay at home when you are sick even when you have a cold? Yes ____ No ____ Do you use a hairpin or other sharp object to clean your ears? Yes ____ No ____

6.1[1]
6.2[1]
6.4
6.5[1]
	Thompson Smoking and Tobacco Knowledge Test
	ETS 003 083[2]
		1967
		n
			moderate	7-12
				college
					Part 1
					What are the most important reasons why you started to smoke?
					Please indicate the degree of influence each factor listed had on your behavior.
					Advertising of some type (TV, radio)
					  a. great influence
					  b. little influence
					  c. some influence
					  d. no influence
					
					Part 2
					Since 1950, one professional group has quit smoking in great numbers.
					  a. teachers
					  b. nurses
					  c. physicians
					  d. dentists
					
					Part 3
					The substance in tobacco that causes lung cancer is
					  a. carbon from cigarette paper
					  b. nicotine
					  c. some unknown factor in tobacco
					  d. tobacco tars
					  e. carbon monoxide

Note: p = published, available from commercial source.
     n = not published or available from commercial source.
[1] Instrument applies only partially or indirectly to the assessed subgoal.
[2] ETS numbers refer to tests available In ETS *Tests In Microfiche.*

Table Id. (continued)

Subgoals Assessed	Test Name & Source	Date & Status	Cost	Grade Range	Sample Item
6.4	Student Drug Survey ETS 001 782	1970 n	low	7-12	How many times have you used solvents to get high in the past seven days? a. none b. 1 or 2 times c. 3 to 5 times d. 6 to 9 times e. 10 or more times
6.9	Martinek-Zaichkowsky Self-Concept Scale for Children ETS 007 836	1965 n	low	1-8	Nonverbal. Students select pictures that represent themselves.
6.9	Mac B Personal Competence Inventory (also cited for Goal 2) ETS 007 316	1975 n	low	3-7	First index: I have different kinds of friends Never 1 2 3 4 5 Always Second index: My best 1 2 3 4 5 Never my friend friend
6.10	Independent Activities Questionnaire (also cited for Goals 5 and 9) ETS 001 518	1965 n	low	9-12, college	50. Have you ever directed instrumental or vocal music? Yes ___ No ___ If no, go on to question 51. If yes, go to the enclosed question below. (50a. and 50b.) 50a. Have you ever directed music performed publicly and for which you were paid or for which admission was charged? Yes ___ No ___ 50b. Have you ever organized your own instrumental or singing group? Yes ___ No ___ Type of Group ___

Note: n = not published or available from commercial source.
ETS numbers refer to tests available in ETS Tests in Microfiche.

Table Ie. Summary of Instruments Appropriate to Goal 8

Subgoals Assessed	Test Name & Source	Date & Status	Cost	Grade Range	Sample Item
8.1[1]	*Test of Reasoning in Conservation* Conservation Foundation 1717 Massachusetts Avenue, N.W. Washington, D.C. 20036	1960 p	low m	7-12	In applying conservation practice to his water supply, man is mainly concerned with a. increasing the amount of precipitation b. increasing evaporation from oceans and lakes c. increasing and improving swampland drainage d. delaying the return of precipitation to the oceans.
8.2	*Sequential Tests of Educational Progress:* Social Studies (STEP) Cooperative Test Division Educational Testing Service Princeton, N.J. 08540	1963	Higher	4-6, 7-9, 10-12, College	*Form 4A* (Following a map) On the map above, which continent does the equator go through? a. Asia b. North America c. Africa d. South America *Form 3A (grades 7-9)* The cartoonist is trying to show that the history of a nation . . . a. has no effect on the things it wants to do in the future. b. makes it impossible for the nation to change. c. gives the people something to be proud of. d. Can slow down the nation's process of change. *Form 2A (grades 10-12)* A passage like the one written above would be most likely to appear in a book written by which of the following? a. an anthropologist b. a biologist c. an astronomer d. an archaeologist

Note: p = published, available from commercial source.
m = machine scoring available.

[1] All instruments on this table apply only partially or indirectly to the assessed subgoals, with the exception of subgoals 8.7 and 8.8.

Table Ie. (continued)

Subgoals Assessed	Test Name & Source	Date & Status	Cost	Grade Range	Sample Item
8.31	Value Socialization Scales (also cited for Goal 3) ETS 007 592[2]	1970 n	low	4-6	A child is doing the best he can. a. Always admire b. Sometimes admire c. Always dislike
8.3 8.4 8.5 8.9	Getting Along ETS 003 235	1965 n	low	7-9	Caption under picture: Ruth said: "Today is Saturday. There is housework to do, new records to play, and a birthday party this afternoon." Ruth should . . . a. ask her mother if it is all right to skip the housework this week b. play the records while she does the housework c. do her share of the housework first
8.4	Nowicki-Strickland Locus of Control Scale ETS 006 839	1971 n	low	3-12	Are some kids just born lucky? Yes ____ No ____ Do you feel that you have a lot of choice in deciding who your friends are? Yes ____ No ____
8.5 8.7 8.8	Biographical Inventory for Students ETS 001 515	1955 n	low m	12, College	Part 1 How old were you when you first started earning money? (Don't count money earned from relatives.) ____ younger than 10 ____ 10-12 ____ 13-15 ____ 16 or older ____ I have never earned any money.

Note: n = not published or available from commercial source.
      m = machine scoring available.

[1] All instruments on this table apply only partially or indirectly to the assessed subgoals, with the exception of subgoals 8.7 and 8.8.
[2] ETS numbers refer to tests available in ETS Tests in Microfiche.

Table If. Summary of Instruments Appropriate to Goal 9

Subgoals Assessed	Test Name & Source	Date & Status	Cost	Grade Range	Sample Item
9.1[1]	Independent Activities Questionnaire (also cited for Goals 5 and 6) ETS 001 518 (available in ETS Tests in Microfiche)	1965 n	low m	9-12, college	50. Have you ever directed instrumental or vocal music? Yes ___ No ___ If no, go on to question 51. If yes, go to the enclosed question below. (50a. and 50b.) 50a. Have you ever directed music performed publicly and for which you were paid or for which admission was charged? Yes ___ No ___ 50b. Have you ever organized your own Instrumental or singing group? Yes ___ No ___ Type of Group ___

Note: n = not published or available from commercial source.
m = machine scoring available and, for this instrument, recommended by the author.
[1] Instrument applies only indirectly or partially to the assessed subgoal.

Table Ig. Summary of Instruments Appropriate to Goal 10

Subgoals Assessed	Test Name & Source	Date & Status	Cost	Grade Range	Sample Item
10.1 10.2 10.3	JIM Scale (Junior Index of Motivation) (also cited for Goal 5) ETS 004 021 (available in ETS Tests in Microfiche)	1965 n	low	7-12	Late afternoon is the best time of day. −2 −1 +1 +2 Most young people do not want to go to school. −2 −1 +1 +2

Note: n = not published or available from commercial source.

Summary of the Review of Tests

The adequacy with which the identified tests measure all the goals and subgoals proposed by the Committee on Research and Theory is summarized in Tables II and III. As indicated in these two tables, there are many gaps currently existing in the proper measurement of these goals. The number of appropriate instruments located was small, despite extensive review procedures. Furthermore, many of the identified instruments require cautious use. Not all grade levels are equally covered by appropriate instruments; nor are all subgoals. In particular, only one subgoal (6.9) was assessed below grade three and only one-fourth (15) of the 57 subgoals are assessed at any elementary school level. Just slightly over half (54 percent) of the subgoals are assessed at any level.

Although these results are in one sense discouraging; in another sense, they suggest promising directions for research and development activities. With modifications, numerous tests could be adapted to measure these goals. Operating on the premise that the best available estimate of future behavior in an adult setting is similar or related behavior in the current context, other new tests could be specifically developed with the goals in mind. Still another area for development is in the use of methods other than paper-and-pencil tests to measure the achievement of the goals. Observation instruments, attendance records, and longitudinal surveys are approaches which may be more valid for examining such behavioral goals. The use of "constructed" situations to elicit value-revealing behaviors from students appears to be a promising method for assessing some of the more difficult subgoals. The limited findings of the Committee on Research and Theory can be the first step in a new direction for creative measurement of educational goals.

Additional Test Information

For each goal, two additional test lists are given; the first, tests to consider for further research (along with a brief statement of our reservations) and the second, tests or instruments that have not been examined, but are worthy of attention.

Goal Two: Self-Conceptualization

A. *Examined Tests to Consider for Further Research*
   1. California Test of Personality (CTP), by Louis Thorpe, W. W. Clark, and E. W. Tiegs. New York: McGraw Hill, 1939-1953 (Buros 5:73). Seems appropriate but needs updating since its last revision in 1953.

Table II. Summary of Identified Appropriate Measures by Subgoals and Grade Levels on Which Assessed

Subgoals	Goal 1	Goal 2	Goal 3	Goal 4	Goal 5	Goal 6	Goal 7	Goal 8	Goal 9	Goal 10
					Grade Levels					
1	No tests reviewed	3-7	none	none	7-12 c	3-12 c	none	7-12	9-12	7-12
2		none	3-9	none	7-12	3-12 c	none	4-12 c	none	7-12
3		3-7	none	none	c, a 7-12	3-6	none	4-9	—	7-12
4		none	3-9	none	—	3-12 c	none	7-9	—	none
5		3-12	4-9	none	—	7-12 c	—	7-9 12, c	—	none
6		none	3-9	—	—	none	—	none	—	none
7		—	7-9	—	—	none	—	12, c	—	none
8		—	3-9	—	—	none	—	8-12 c	—	none
9		—	—	—	—	1-8	—	7-9	—	none
10		—	—	—	—	9-12 c	—	—	—	—
Total tests identified for goal		5*	3	0	3	6	0	8	1	1

Note: none = no test found; c = college; a = adult; and —— = not a subgoal of this goal.
* Four of the five tests did not measure specific subgoals but did measure the goal in general.

Table III. Distribution of Appropriate Instruments Among Goals and Subgoals

Goal	Number of Subgoals	Number of Tests Identified as Assessing Goal	Number of Subgoals Measured	Number of Subgoals Not Measured	Percent of Subgoals Measured
2	6	5	3	3	50
3	8	3	6	2	75
4	5	0	0	5	0
5	3	3	3	3	100
6	10	6	7	3	70
7	4	0	0	4	0
8	10	8	8	2	80
9	2	1	1	1	50
10	9	1	3	6	33.3
Totals	57	21*	31	26	54

* Total is for *different* tests; some tests measured subgoals of more than one goal.

2. Chapin Social Insight, by F. S. Chapin. California: Consulting Psychologists Press, Inc., 1967-68 (Buros 7:51). Still experimental, but in presenting students with social situations and options for behavior, it seems on target.
3. Illinois Index of Self Derogation, by Joseph H. Meyerowitz (ETS 005 754). Normed on educable, mentally retarded children in grades 1 and 2, but the author states that it can be used with normal children in pre-school to grade 2.

B. *Unexamined Tests to Consider for Research*
   1. Allport-Vernon Study of Values (high school edition) (Buros 7: 146).
   2. Bledsoe Self-Concept Scale (BSCS). *Self-Concept and School Achievement.* New Jersey: Prentice Hall, Inc., 1975.
   3. Index of Adjustment and Values, by R. E. Bills, E. L. Vance, O. S. McLean, Jr. *Consulting Psychology* 15 (1951):257-61.
   4. Mooney Problem Checklists, by E. F. Lindquist. *Educational Measurement,* p. 722. New York: Psychological Corporation, 1971.
   5. Pennsylvania EQA Tests. *Educational Quality Assessment Inventory.* Harrisburg, Pa.: Division of Educational Quality Assessment, Pennsylvania Department of Education.
   6. Self-Disclosure Inventory for Adolescents, by Lloyd W. West and Harvey W. Zingle. "A Self-Disclosure Inventory for Adolescents," *Psychological Reports* 24(1969): 439-45.

Goal Three: Understanding Others

A. *Examined Tests to Consider for Further Research*
   1. The AB Scales (Attitude-Belief Scales), by M. Fishbein and B. H. Raven. *Human Relations* 15(1962): 35-44.
   2. Affectional and Aggressive Observation Checklist, by M. Johnson and J. W. Bommarito. *Tests and Measurements in Child Development: A Handbook,* p. 452. San Francisco: Josey Bass Publishers, Inc., 1971. If combined with SES characteristics of students, this could be a good estimator of the relational behavior of children.
   3. California Test of Personality. Cited at Goal Two, AI. Seems appropriate, but needs updating.
   4. Cultural Awareness Scale, by Jack Danielson. "Line Simulation of Affect Laden Cultural Cognitions," *Journal of Conflict Resolution* 11(September 1967): 3. Experimental scale measures an "appreciation of the impact of cultural values on psychological processes."

5. Dogmatism Scale and Opinionation Scale, by Milton Rokeach. *The Open and Closed Mind,* pp. 80-87. New York: Basic Books, Inc., 1960. The first scale measures openness or closedness of belief systems; the second measures intolerance.

6. Interpersonal Value Scales, by William A. Scott. *Values and Organizations,* pp. 245-60. Chicago: Rand McNally and Company, 1965.

7. Social Beliefs and Reliefs About School Life. *Evaluations in the Eight Year Study.* Progressive Education Association, 1939.

B. *Unexamined Tests to Consider for Research*
   1. Classroom Social Distance Scale, by M. Johnson and J. W. Bommarito at 281.
   2. College Outcome Measures Project (COMP). American College Testing Program.
   3. Pennsylvania EQA Tests. Cited at Goal Two, B5.

Goal Four: Using Accumulated Knowledge to Understand the World

A. *Examined Tests to Consider for Further Research*
   1. Science Curriculum Assessment System, by Charles C. Mathews. *Mirrors of Behavior III: An Anthology of Observation Instruments.* Wyncote, Pa.: Communication Materials Center, 1974. Observation system for recording and rating the behavior of students in science classes. It might be adapted to this goal.
   2. Tab Science Test, by David P. Butts. *An Inventory of Science Methods* (ETS 007 741). This test actually tries to measure application rather than knowledge.
   3. Critical Thinking Appraisal Test, by Watson-Glaser (Buros 7: 783). Test activities may tap what is desired, but further development is needed.

B. *Unexamined Tests to Consider for Research*
   1. College Outcomes Measures Project (COMP). Cited at Goal Three, B2.
   2. Pennsylvania EQA Tests. Cited at Goal Two, B5.

Goal Five: Continuous Learning

A. *Examined Tests to Consider for Further Research*
   1. Children's Achievement Scale, by Bernard Weiner (ETS 008 47). No statistical information provided in this source.
   2. Intellectual Achievement Responsibility Questionnaire, by Virginia C. Crandall (ETS 006 098). Relatively little developmental work as yet.

3. Pictographic Self Rating Scale. Rockwell Center, New York: Acorn Publishing Co. Dated material, but an interesting cartoon approach to the goal.

4. Value Socialization Scales. See Table Ib, under Goal Three. A scale for subgoal 5.1 might be construed from items on these scales.

B. *Unexamined Tests to Consider for Research*

1. Achievement Motivation Projective Tests, by D. McClelland, J. W. Atkinson, R. A. Clark, E. W. Lowell, M. Johnson, and J. W. Bommarito at 174.

2. Beller's Scale of Independence or Autonomy Among Children, by E. K. Beller. "Dependency and Autonomous Achievement Striving Related to Orality and Anality in Early Childhood," *Child Development* 28 (1957): 287-315.

3. Pennsylvania EQA Tests. Cited at Goal Two, B5.

Goal Six: Mental and Physical Well-Being

A. *Examined Tests to Consider for Further Research*

1. Florida Key, by W. Purkey, R. Cage, and W. Graves (ETS 007 323). A short teacher-inferred self-concept scale based on observation of student.

2. Sears Self-Concept Inventory, by Pauline Sears (ETS 000 701). Designed for use with grades 3-6, the inventory needs further developmental work.

3. Self-Concept Rating Scale for Children, by Lewis P. Lipsett (ETS 007 705). This scale needs further developmental work, but is appropriate for grades 4-6.

4. A Study of Young People (ETS 007 526). This is a self-report of drinking patterns and opinions, but was used for males only and provided little developmental information.

B. *Unexamined Tests to Consider for Research*

1. (1) Dental Health Practices Inventory; (2) Scale for the Measurement of Attitudes toward Healthful Living; (3) Stimulants and Depressants Test; (4) Tuberculosis Information Test, by Marian Solleder. *Evaluation Instruments in Health Education.* Washington, D.C.: American Association for Health, Physical Education and Recreation and the National Education Association, 1968.

2. Health and Safety Education, by Lester D. Crow and Loretta C. Ryan (Buros 5:555). National Achievement Tests.

3. Index of Adjustments and Values. Cited at Goal Two, B3. In the work cited, at page 27.

4. Pennsylvania EQA Tests. Cited at Goal Two, B5.
5. Physical Fitness Tests, by F. J. Hayden. *Physical Fitness for the Mentally Retarded: A Manual for Teachers and Parents*. Ontario, Canada: Metropolitan Toronto Association for Retarded Children. Author states test is useful for grades 1 and 2 non-handicapped children. Canadian norms.
6. *Measuring Human Behavior,* p. 77, by Dale C. Miles, B. Mathew, and Ralph B. Earle, Jr. New York: Teachers College Press, 1973.
7. Things I Like To Do, by J. Anderson. "The Relation of Attitude to Adjustment," *Education* 73(1952): 210-18.

Goal Seven: Participation in the Economic World of Production and Consumption

A. *Examined Tests to Consider for Further Research*
1. Children's Knowledge About Occupations Test, by Richard C. Nelson. (Johnson and Bommarito at 437). Uses colored slides of 16 occupations.
2. Thurstone Interest Schedule, by L. L. Thurstone (Buros 4:745). An old and insufficiently validated test, but uses an interesting approach.

B. *Unexamined Tests to Consider for Research*
1. Making Career Decisions. *A Plan for Evaluating the Quality of Education Programs in Pennsylvania, Vol. I: Basic Program*. ETS, 30 June 1965. A report from ETS to the State Board of Education.
2. Pennsylvania EQA Tests. Cited at Goal Two, B5.

Goal Eight: Responsible Societal Membership

A. *Examined Tests to Consider for Further Research*
1. Allen Scale of Beliefs (ETS 007 044). This test measures agreement or disagreement with American socio-political values, but little developmental work has been done.
2. Florida Key (ETS 007 323). Cited at Goal Six, A1.
3. Intellectual Achievement Responsibility Questionnaire (ETS 006 098). Cited at Goal Five, A2. Relatively little developmental work has been done, but the questionnaire is designed to determine students' perceptions of responsibility for intellectual and academic success or failure.
4. Machiavellianism Scales, by Dale Lake (Lake and others at 36).

Currently for experimental use only, but the approach is interesting.

5. Orientation Inventory (ORI) (Lake and others at 34). Validity is sufficient only for use with groups; with more development, it may be appropriate for individual use.

6. Russell Sage Social Relations Test, by Russell Sage (ETS 001 531). A group measure of children's skills in social relations, it now yields a group score, but might be adapted to give individual scores as well.

7. Social Interest Scale, by James E. Crandall (ED 008 333). The scale is currently normed by adults, but its purpose, to assess a person's interest in the welfare of others, makes it a good candidate for adaptation for school-age subjects.

B. *Unexamined Tests to Consider for Research*

1. Children's Locus of Control Scale, by I. Bialer. "Conceptualization of Success and Failure in Mentally Retarded and Normal Children," *Journal of Personality* 22(1961): 303-20.

2. F-Scale, by T. W. Adorno and E. Frenkel-Brunswik. *The Authoritarian Personality.* New York: Harper and Row, 1950.

3. Interest Index. *Evaluation in the Eight Year Study.* Progressive Education Association, 1939.

4. Interpersonal Competence Scoring System (Lake and others at 31).

5. Orientation Scale, by Milton Rokeach and Ray M. Lorce. *Psychology of Education,* pp. 469-70. New York: The Ronald Press Company, 1970.

6. Pennsylvania EQA Tests. Cited at Goal Two, B5.

7. "Political Efficacy" and "Sense of Citizen Duty," by Angus Campbell and Geral Gurin. In *The Voter Decides,* pp. 187-89 and 194-99. Evanston Illinois: Row Peterson and Co., 1954.

8. Physical Causality Test, by R. E. Muuss. "The Transfer Effect of a Learning Program in Social Causality on an Understanding of Physical Causality," *Journal of Experimental Psychology* 29(1961): 231-47.

9. Scale of Economic Belief. *Evaluation in the Eight Year Study.* Progressive Education Association, 1939.

10. Social Attitudes Scale, by D. B. Marris. "A Scale for Measuring Attitudes of Social Responsibility in Children," *Journal of Abnormal and Social Psychology* 55(1957): 322-36.

11. Stages of Moral Development, by Kohlberg (Lake and others at 80).

Goal Nine: Creativity

A. *Examined Tests to Consider for Further Research*
   1. Biographical Inventory for Students (ETS 001 515). See Table Id, under Goal Eight. It may be possible to get an estimate of subgoal 9.2 from the ratio of creative activities selected (music, literature, art) to other activities although some control of the quality of the activities would be needed.
   2. Christensen and Guilford Fluency Tests, by P. R. Christensen and J. P. Guilford (Buros 6:544). California: Sheridan Psychological Services, Inc.
   3. Denny-Ives Creativity Test, by Denny and Ives (ETS 000 794). This test is restricted to creativity in the dramatic arts; however, it yields scores for fluency, redefinition, originality, and sensitivity.
   4. Gross Geometric Forms, by Ruth B. Gross (ETS 005 614). Currently requires special administration and scoring, but the approach is good.
   5. Pennsylvania Assessment of Creative Tendency (ETS 008 309). This measures creative tendency rather than performance.
   6. Pikunas Graphoscopic Scale (ETS 004 175). This test currently needs interpretation by a highly trained person, but if simplified would be appropriate.
   7. Remote Associates Test (RAT), by Sarnoff A. Mednick and Martha T. Mednick (Buros 7:455). Boston: Houghton Miflin. Adult norms only.
   8. Torrance Tests of Creative Thinking, Research Edition, by Paul E. Torrance. Revision of *Minnesota Tests of Creative Thinking*. Columbus, Ohio: Personnel Press, 1966. The tests look good, but need further developmental work.
   9. What Kind of Person Are You?, by Paul E. Torrance (ETS 007 206). Athens, Georgia: Department of Psychology, University of Georgia. This measures the tendency to function creatively, rather than measuring actual behavior.

B. *Unexamined Tests to Consider for Research*
   1. College Outcome Measures Project. Cited at Goal Three, B2.
   2. Draw-A-Scene Test, by J. H. West. "Correlates of the Draw-A-Scene," *Journal of Clinical Psychology* 16(1960): 1.
   3. Interpersonal Value Scales. Cited at Goal Three, A6.
   4. Novelty Experiencing Scale, by Pamela H. Pearson. "Relationships Between Global and Specified Measures of Novelty Seeking," *Journal of Consulting and Clinical Psychology* 34(1970): 199-204.

5. Pennsylvania EQA Tests. Cited at Goal Two, B5.

Goal Ten: Coping with Change

A. *Examined Tests to Consider for Further Research*
1. The Cassel Group Level of Aspiration Test (CGLAT), by Russell N. Cassel. Los Angeles: Western Psychologic Services, 1952-57.
2. Gordon Personal Profile (GPP), by Leonard V. Gordon (Buros 6:103). Profile could perhaps be adapted for this goal.
3. Survey of Personal Values (SPV), by Leonard V. Gordon (Buros 6:103). Chicago: Science Research Associates, Inc.
4. Thorndike Dimensions of Temperament (TDOT), by Robert L. Thorndike (Buros 7:154). New York: Psychological Corporation. Not quite on goal target, but it could be adapted.

B. *Unexamined Tests to Consider for Research*
1. Do You Agree?, by J. W. Getzels and P. W. Jackson. *Creativity and Intelligence: Explorations With Gifted Students,* pp. 135-36. New York: John Wiley and Sons, Inc., 1962.
2. Pennsylvania EQA Tests. Cited at Goal Two, B5.
3. Rydel-Rosen Ambiguity Tolerance Scale, by A. P. MacDonald. "Revised Scale for Ambiguity Tolerance: Reliability and Validity," *Psychological Reports* 26(1960): 780-89.

Chapter 4

A Model for Research on Goal Achievement

The Committee's work on research and theory emerged from concern over the current, almost exclusive, concentration by the lay and educational communities on a limited range of educational goals commonly identified as basic skills. The achievement of fundamental communication and computation competencies does not guarantee the achievement of other educational goals, nor does their attainment provide much insight into the effectiveness of educational programs in the achievement of other long-range educational outcomes.

As the Committee on Research and Theory undertook to suggest needed research to enhance knowledge of the effectiveness of educational programs in achieving all educational goals, we became increasingly aware of the complexity of the task. It seemed apparent to all of us that most educational research has focused on very limited goals and a very narrow range of learning environmental factors which may affect the achievement of those goals. In this part of our report, we have sought to develop a model to assist in developing research on the relationship between *all* aspects of the learning environment and the attainment of *all* educational goals identified in Chapter II.

We have not reviewed the present state of research relative to the model developed here. From our collective experience, knowledge, and judgment, we conclude that there is relatively little known about the impact of various educational organizations and experiences on human skill in coping with change or participation in the economic world. In like manner, there is little known about the kind of educational environment that is most effective in producing other educational outcomes. We have sought, therefore, to suggest a frame of reference that may assist in identifying appropriate and important questions that need answers. We believe that this model will assist in the comprehensive evaluation of any educational program, humanistic or not. Such evaluation is dependent on the identification and examination of all pertinent educational environment variables which may affect educational outcomes of concern to the investigator.

The purpose of this chapter, then, is to present a research model that identifies several types of educational variables which may affect outcomes and to offer some sample sets of research hypotheses derived from this model.

The Limitations of Current Research

Our efforts to develop a comprehensive model for research on factors affecting the outcomes of schools emerged from recognition of several limitations in contemporary educational research.

Exclusive Focus on Basic Skills

Perhaps the most pressing and obvious limitation of research on school outcomes is its almost universal focus on basic communication and computational skills. *We recognize and emphasize the importance of basic skills but we also recognize that we know little about the achievement of the other nine sets of goals which we have identified.* We find little evidence on which to base conclusions about the effect of school environments and teaching-learning processes on the achievement of either basic skills or other goals.

The variables that are hypothesized to affect outcomes have commonly concentrated on non-school variables or the kinds of inputs that are made into the school environment. It is known that the racial and socioeconomic backgrounds of students are associated with their levels of reading and math achievement. It is also known that the teacher-pupil ratio, educational level of teachers, expenditures for education, and other inputs explain little of the differences in the achievement of the basic skills as commonly measured (Coleman and others, 1966). The family background and school input variables are frequently presumed to represent what occurs in the school. Since the school has little control over the characteristics that children bring there, and other school inputs do not seem to explain the variance in achievement of basic cognitive skills, scholars have frequently concluded that what happens in the schools makes no differences in the learning outcomes. Although this conclusion may be valid, it is hardly appropriate to arrive at such a conclusion without examining the wide range of school environmental factors and teaching-learning processes that may affect both the immediate (Brookover and others, 1979) and long-range outcomes of education.

A number of scholars have examined the long-range outcomes and several have concluded that schooling has little effect on later life roles. (Jencks and others, 1972, Hauser and others, 1976). Others have concluded that the level and quality of schooling make a significant contribution. Jencks and his associates (1979) have modified earlier conclusions about the contribution of schooling to economic success. After reviewing a number of studies, Hyman and his associates (1975) concluded that levels have other significant effects. They indicate that the higher the school levels, the more informed the person is in terms of (1) academic knowledge, (2) knowledge of current public affairs, (3) continuing to read more newspapers, books and magazines, (4) actively seeking to stay informed about areas of vital interest such as health and elections, (5) participating in continuing education, either formal or self-taught, and (6) knowing about popular cultures such as sports or movie stars. These benefits remain as the person grows older (further from schooling). They are not the effect of socioeconomic status inputs, but rather are the direct effects of schooling; for example, the college graduate from a low-income family and one from a high-income family are more similar in benefits than college graduates and high school graduates of high-income families. The same holds true for other factors influencing the effects of education; that is, when the data were controlled for the effects of age, religion, sex, social class, geographical distribution, and current social status, the differences in the benefits of schooling were still maintained.

We do not yet have conclusive evidence on the effects of schooling on adult human behavior, but the pursuit of such evidence is a worthy endeavor.

Disregard of Total Learning Environment and Multiple Goals

Another limitation of contemporary research on the effects of educational programs is the concentration on a specific characteristic or a single outcome of a school program without examination of the context of other school variables within which it occurs. Research on specific materials or methods of teaching a particular skill is extensive, but this is seldom examined in the context of the *total school environment* or the multiple outcomes, intended or unintended, which may result from the particular method or materials of teaching.

An assessment of associated outcomes of a particular method and the conditions under which it is effective or ineffective may lead to very different conclusions. For example, the language experience approach to teaching a reading skill may be very effective in a carefully defined school situation but, when located in a different school social situation, its effectiveness may be significantly different. In the achievement of a particular math skill, the students' understanding of themselves and others may be affected in unintended and undesirable ways. In similar fashion, a particular teaching process may be effective in students acquiring designated knowledge but do little or nothing to assist them in becoming responsible members of society.

Time Limitation

The limitation of time makes research on the effectiveness of school programs in achieving educational goals very difficult. The assessment of the degree to which some goals and subgoals have been achieved is nearly impossible during the school years. Although some indicators of the likely effects of school programs on continuous learning may be possible, the actual evidence on whether the students of a given generation in a given school will continue autonomous learning habits must await post-school years. A few educational projects have now undertaken longitudinal studies, but there is little basis on which particular school learning environments can be associated with the behavioral goals identified for the post-school years. Comprehensive understanding of the relationship between school environment or teaching-learning events and the behavioral goals of education must await comprehensive longitudinal research.

Inadequate Measurement

Although there are many other limitations to educational research, the final one we wish to identify is the inadequacy of the means of measuring or assessing the outcomes, the characteristics of the school learning environment, and teaching-learning processes. Researchers are quite sophisticated in measuring some basic cognitive outcomes, but have much to learn about other behavioral measurements. Furthermore, although much progress has been made in the last decade on the measurement and identification of significant characteristics of learning environments and teaching-learning processes, the major portion of the task remains undone.

Perhaps the educational research community should direct its energies to the development of adequate measures in new areas of both goals and school characteristics rather than multiplying the studies of narrowly defined methods and their effectiveness on narrowly defined skills.

Studies that use the socioeconomic background of students as a proxy for crucial characteristics of school environments that are otherwise undefined and unmeasured contribute little to our knowledge of the effect of various school environmental characteristics.

A Model for Formulating Research on School Learning

ASCD and educators generally are constantly confronted with this question: "What kinds of educational programs and/or processes are most likely to produce the desired behavioral outcomes in the learner?" This seemingly simple and direct question becomes very complex when we consider the full range of factors that may affect learning and the multiple outcomes desired. When confronted by the complexities of the total learning situation, the Committee on Research and Theory sought to develop a format or model to classify the many variables involved and the sets of desired outcomes. Figure 5 (at pp. 56-57) diagrams the model which developed from our efforts to conceptualize the relationship of learning environmental variables and the various types of outcomes. Some explanations of this model and the rationale for it are appropriate.

Out-of-School Factors—Category I

The rectangle at the left of the diagram, identified as Category I, indicates that there are complex sets of out-of-school forces or variables which may affect a school environment and, in turn, the outcomes of the school experience. There is much research on family socioeconomic background, racial identity of families, and aspects of the community in which the school is located which supports a hypothesized relationship with teaching-learning processes and the outcome of schooling. Emphasis on these out-of-school variables have led many to conclude that most of the explained variance in the achievement of basic skills is accounted for by these out-of-school factors. Researchers ignore the possibility that what occurs in the school environment might not reinforce the impact of family background and out-of-school forces on learning outcomes. Contemporary research has also ignored the relationship of out-of-school factors to desired outcomes other than basic skills. For example, we know very little about how family background or community variables relate to continuous learning or skill in coping with change.

The placement of out-of-school factors at the left hand side of the diagram indicates that, to some extent at least, these variables operate prior to and may affect the functioning of school variables identified in Categories II, III and IV.

School Input Factors—Category II

School Input Factors are, to some degree, a transition from the out-of-school factors to in-school variables. Inputs include many of the variables that traditionally have been considered factors that determine the quality of schools. Category II includes the *number of professional personnel, the qualification of these professional personnel,* the *facilities* provided in the school, the length and regularity of *student attendance.* Some of the input characteristics are significantly related to the *expenditures* for education. *Expenditures have therefore frequently been used as a measure of school inputs.*

Much of the research on school inputs ignores the possible relationship of these factors to other types of school variables and the possible relationship to learning outcomes other than basic skills. The location of Category II in Figure 5 suggests the hypothesis that school input factors may be influenced by out-of-school variables and, thus, affect other school variables as well as learning outcomes.

School Environment—Category III

Category III is concerned with school environment factors. The physical environment, such as arrangement of space, is a relevant aspect of the school environment that may facilitate certain types of learning processes or put limitations on various instructional programs. We would emphasize, however, that school learning environment involves much more than the physical characteristics of that environment. The school is not only a physical structure but a social system which encompasses organizational and cultural characteristics. *The social organization of the school involves grade classifications, staff relationships, patterns of authority, status-role definitions, size of organizational units, and numerous other social structural characteristics. Common expectations, evaluations, beliefs and norms of behavior which may be identified as the school culture are also a part of the school social system and a significant part of the school environment.*

The location of school environment in the Figure 5 model suggests the hypothesis that out-of-school and school input factors may affect the school environment which, itself, may affect the teaching-learning processes and school learning outcomes.

There is an increasing body of research on the characteristics of the school social system and its relationship to a limited range of educational outcomes. Very little is known, however, about the manner in which the school environment affects teaching-learning events or the achievement of educational goals.

Teaching-Learning Processes or Events—Category IV

The fourth category of variables is identified as teaching-learning processes or events. The category includes all of the patterns of interaction and communication between teacher-students, student-students, and all of the specific behaviors that occur in teaching-learning situations. Many teaching-learning events are designed to result in specific learning, but others are more or less unplanned processes that occur in the teaching-learning situation. Since teaching-learning processes are the variables which *presumably* affect school learning most directly, the Committee on Research and Theory chose to concentrate on specific types of teaching-learning processes or events as the focus for developing the research designs that follow. We hypothesize that the nature of the teaching-learning events may be affected by school environment, school input, and out-of-school variables. We also hypothesize that teaching-learning processes lead to immediate learning outcomes that in turn may or may not be productive in achieving the desired educational goals.

There has been a great deal of research on some aspects of teaching-learning processes, such as the relationship of reading programs or teaching methods on the achievement of reading skills. These research efforts on teaching-learning processes have frequently ignored the school environment in which they occurred and the other learning outcomes.

Immediate Learning Outcomes—Category V

Category V suggests that immediate learning outcomes result from teaching-learning events and involve many different types of behavior. The immediate learning outcomes may or may not be directly linked to the desired goals of education.

The Goals of Education to be Attained

The goals of education as identified by the Committee and discussed in Chapter II of this report are identified as Clusters A, B, C, and D in Figure 5. The location of basic skills in Cluster A suggests the hypothesis that the mastery of basic communication and mathematics skills facilitates the achievement of the other goals of education. We do not suggest that basic skills are more important than other goals, but perhaps the achievement of these skills is significant in the process of achieving other goals. The Cluster B position simply indicates relationships hypothesized in our discussion of goals and subgoals: that self-conceptualization, understanding others, and use of accumulated knowledge facilitate to some degree the achievement of the goals identified in Clusters C and D. For example, it seems that the acquisition of knowledge and its use is sometimes prerequisite to participation in the economic world or coping with change. In similar fashion, understanding others may be prerequisite to becoming a responsible member of society or a mentally healthy person. The possible interrelationships of the various goals and subgoals identified in Clusters A, B, C, and D have been discussed previously. These are perceived as long-range goals for all educational programs. We, therefore, hypothesize that out-of-school factors as well as the school variables identified in Categories I through IV may affect achievement of the goals identified in Clusters A-D.

The purpose of the research model as diagrammed in Figure 5 is to assist in the identification of out-of-school and school factors that may affect the attainment of educational outcomes. We suggest that the assessment or evaluation of educational programs must recognize the possible contribution of each category of school and out-of-school factors to these educational outcomes. In short, the total educational system involves a complex of many variables that may perform in various ways to produce or fail to produce the goals of education.

Utilization of The Model

Steps in the utilization of the hypothesized model may be identified as follows:

1. Determine the educational problems or research areas of particular concern.
2. Identify the variable(s) of research concern.
3. Classify the variable(s) according to the category or cluster into which it falls.
4. Place each variable into the model at its appropriate location.
5. Work backwards from each variable of concern to identify as many as possible of the relevant variables which impact upon it.
6. Work forward in the model to identify as many as possible of the potential consequences or effects of the variable concerned.
7. Classify the variables identified in steps 5 and 6 and enter them at their appropriate location in the categories or clusters until the full model has been explicated.
8. Once the full model is developed, determine how much of it must (and can) be accounted for in the investigation of the concerned variable and specify hypotheses to be tested.
9. Select or devise ways of gathering data about all the variables in the model (or portion thereof) which are to be investigated.
10. Analyze the data.
11. Interpret the data in terms of the *full* model as specified in Step 7, being careful to consider potential effects of variables in the model which were neither measured nor controlled.

56

Figure 5. Educational Research Model—Basic Structure

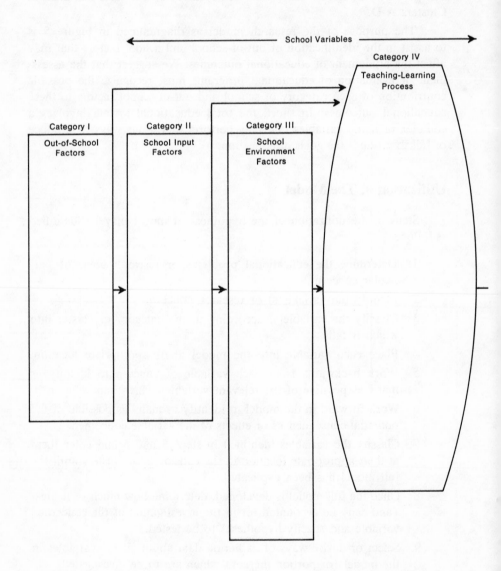

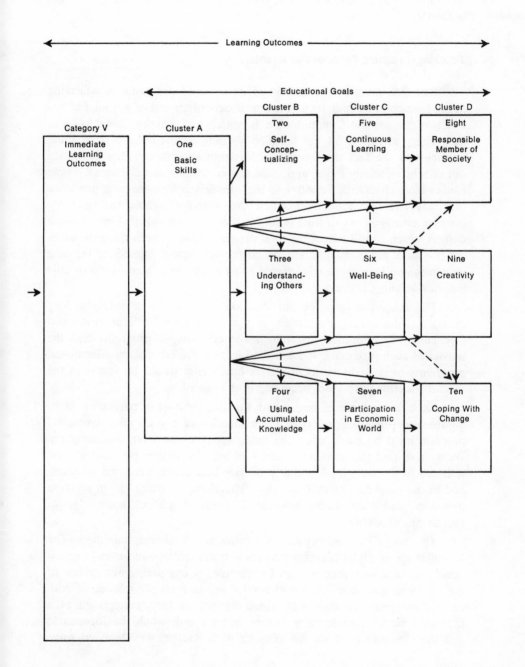

The next section of this chapter presents several examples of the use of the model through Step 8. Chapter Three has already presented recommendations for measures of some outcomes that may be selected for use in Step 9.

Teaching-Learning Processes or Events

Research on the effectiveness of educational programs in achieving desired outcomes could focus on any in-school or out-of-school factors. For two reasons the Committee on Research and Theory chose to focus its primary attention on the teaching-learning events. The first of these reasons was the fact that considerable significant research has examined out-of-school, school input, and some school environmental factors. These studies have given little attention to the specific teaching-learning processes that may relate to school outcomes. We, therefore, chose the teaching-learning events as the starting point for the development of some research designs which would reflect the total process. That is, both the antecedent out-of-school and school variables and the subsequent immediate learning outcomes and long range educational goals would be related to the specific teaching-learning process.

The second reason for our decision to focus on teaching-learning events was the underlying concern of the Association for Supervision and Curriculum Development for humanistic educational programs and the impact of such programs. It seemed to us that the crux of an educational program which might be identified as humanistic would be found in the teaching-learning processes occurring in the school.

Each research model begins with the identification of particular teaching-learning processes or events. The evaluation of any school instructional program must be based upon the outcomes resulting from that program. We believe that the humane qualities of an educational program will be reflected in the teaching-learning processes that characterize the program, and in the outcomes of that program. Therefore, an examination of these processes and their outcomes should reveal significant knowledge of humanistic education.

The range of teaching-learning processes is almost unlimited. The identification of all such events that could occur in the educational process could not be undertaken by this Committee. A comprehensive review of past research and identification of needed research on the relation of educational programs to outcomes would necessitate the development of a taxonomy of teaching-learning events. Such a task would be formidable and the Committee chose not to attempt it. Rather, we identified some types of teaching-learning processes that involve potentially critical dimensions of humanistic versus nonhumanistic educational programs. These are not suggested as being exhaustive or most important by any criteria. They reflect the Committee members' biases regarding significant aspects of teaching-learning processes, but we trust they illustrate the kind of research that needs to be done on the relationships of educational programs to educational outcomes.

The characteristics of the teaching-learning processes used in the development of possible research designs are as follows:

1. Flexibility of student movement and interaction
2. Types of cooperation and competition
3. Content of instruction
4. Patterns of support, encouragement, and reinforcement
5. Patterns of reactions to feelings

By using the model and starting with the teaching-learning processes as the crucial school variable, a number of hypotheses are suggested concerning the relationships of these processes to both out-of-school and other school factors as well as to the immediate and long-range outcomes of schooling.

Sample Research Designs

It should be noted that the sample designs presented in this section are suggestive and not extensive. They identify important areas of needed research on the relationship between school programs and educational goals. They should also suggest the need for ASCD or other agencies to initiate comprehensive programs of research on educational goal attainment.

The following series of hypotheses is concerned with the relation of selected teaching-learning processes to out-of-school and school variables on the one hand and to immediate outcomes and desired educational goals on the other.

Flexibility of Student Movement and Interaction in Teaching-Learning Activities

This teaching-learning process focuses primarily on students' freedom to move about the instructional space and interact with others while engaged in learning activities. However, this degree of flexibility in movement and interaction also reflects the patterns of authority and control exercised by teachers. Student freedom to move about and talk with other students without the teacher's permission indicates that students make decisions about their activities in this domain and perhaps others. This apparently is evidence that authority is shared by the students.

The degree to which students move about and interact with other students has commonly, in recent years, been associated with the concept of open or traditional classroom organization. We do not, however, intend the hypotheses suggested in this research model to encompass all aspects of the open-traditional classroom concept.

In similar fashion there are numerous aspects of flexibility of movement and interaction in the classroom. Some involve cooperation and competition examined in another section. We obviously cannot identify all aspects of movement and interaction, but we have identified a few types of the processes involved in teaching-learning activities:

1. Students move about the classroom freely and are encouraged to talk with each other.

2. Students move about freely and are permitted limited interaction with other students.

3. Students move about the classroom freely, but talk with other students only with the teacher's permission.

4. Students move about the room only with the teacher's permission but are encouraged to talk with each other.

5. Students move about the room and talk with each other only with the teacher's permission.

The following hypotheses suggest possible relationships between flexibility of movement and interaction and out-of-school variables, school inputs, and school environment on one hand and the relation of varying degrees of flexibility and learning outcomes on the other. Figure 6 provides an outline of the hypothesized relationships.

A. *Hypotheses concerning the impact of out-of-school factors on flexibility of student movement and interaction in teaching-learning activities*

1. Middle-class community patrons are more likely to permit and encourage flexible (open) patterns of movement and interaction than lower class community patrons.

2. Ethnic background of the school community affects the degree of flexibility of movement and interaction considered appropriate.

B. *Hypotheses concerning the impact of school input factors on flexibility of student movement and interaction in teaching-learning activities*

1. Teachers trained to tolerate classroom noise are more likely to permit students freedom of movement and interaction in teaching-

learning activities than teachers less tolerant of noise.

2. Teachers trained to permit and/or encourage student-initiated activity are more likely to permit students freedom of movement and interaction in teaching-learning activities than teachers trained to initiate instructional activities.

3. Teachers trained to maintain control of student activities are more likely to restrict student movement and interaction in teaching-learning activities than teachers trained to share control.

4. Administrative definition of teacher authority role affects the degree of flexibility of student movement and interaction in teaching-learning activities.

5. Building structural characteristics regarding space, sound absorption, and visibility affect the flexibility of student movement and interaction.

C. *Hypotheses concerning the impact of school environment factors on flexibility of student movement and interaction in teaching-learning activities*

1. School traditions and norms regarding student freedom of movement and interaction affect classroom patterns of movement and interaction.

2. School norms regarding teacher authority and control affect flexibility of student movement and interaction.

3. Teacher authority role-definitions in the school social system affect the degree of flexibility of student movement and interaction permitted in teaching-learning activities.

4. Principal's definition of teachers' functions in the classroom affects flexibility of movement and interaction in the classroom.

5. Classroom structural and space arrangement (movable chairs, activity centers) affect the flexibility of movement and interaction in teaching-learning activities.

D. *Hypotheses concerning the relationship between flexibility of student movement and interaction and immediate learning outcomes*

1. The degree of flexibility of movement affects students' beliefs about the desirability of physical activity in learning activities.

2. The degree to which students are permitted to talk to each other affects their judgment of the value of such interaction in learning activities.

3. Freedom of interaction among students encourages cooperation in learning activities.

4. Freedom of movement and interaction increases the frequency with which students make decisions.

Figure 6. Flexibility, Movement, and Interaction

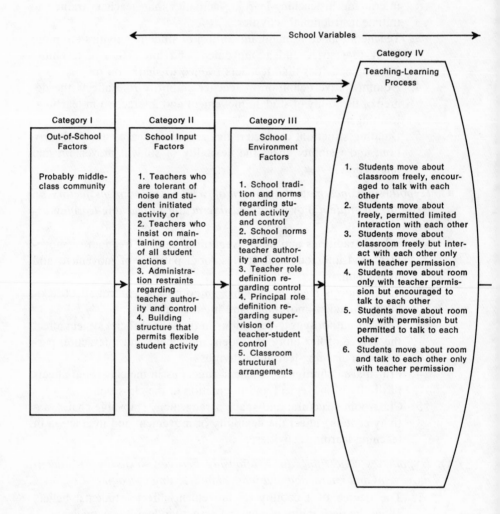

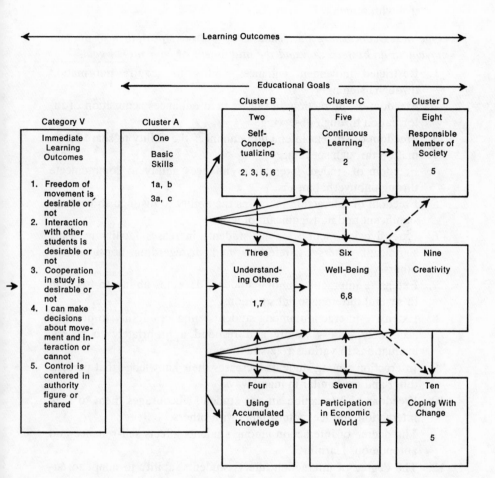

5. Restricted movement and interaction affect the degree of acceptance of teacher authority and control.
6. Freedom of movement and interaction affects the sharing of control with others.

E. *Hypotheses concerning the relationship between flexibility of student movement and interaction and the attainment of educational goals*

1. Restricted movement enhances ability to acquire information through listening.
2. Freedom of interaction and movement enhances acquisition of information through observing.
3. Freedom of student interaction enhances the ability to share information through speaking.
4. Freedom of student interaction enhances ability to communicate through nonverbal means.
5. Freedom of interaction increases the ability to distinguish between significant and nonsignificant others.
6. Extensive interaction among students increases facility in using significant others as referents and disregarding nonsignificant others.
7. Extensive interaction among students develops ability to function in several different social situations.
8. Extensive interaction among students enhances ability to perceive accurately, assess validly and respond appropriately to others' evaluations in various role situations.
9. Interaction among students increases their knowledge that persons differ and are similar in many ways.
10. Freedom of interaction among students encourages them to seek interaction and feel comfortable with others.
11. The degree of interaction among students affects self-reliance and autonomous learning.
12. The degree of interaction affects students' ability to adapt to environmental constraints while seeking.
13. Freedom of movement and interaction enhances ability to maintain personal integration while functioning flexibly in varied situations.
14. Flexible interaction with others enhances rational behavior based on reasonable perceptions of self and society.
15. Freedom of interaction among students enhances ability to work together in groups to achieve mutual goals.
16. Freedom of movement and interaction enhances tolerance of ambiguity.

Types of Cooperation and Competition in Teaching-Learning Activities

The teaching-learning process involves various types of cooperation and competition among students. Cooperation is defined as students working together to achieve certain common outcomes. Cooperation can involve small groups of students or larger aggregates with considerable division of labor in the cooperative process.

Competition is the process in which an individual or group seeks to excel another individual or group. Success in competition is attained by superior achievement of a person's or group's particular outcomes. Success, therefore, may result from the high performance of one competitor or the poor performance of another.

Within any teaching-learning situation, cooperation among individuals may be encouraged or prohibited. The same may be true of competition. Individual competition for specific rewards tends to reduce the cooperation among individuals.

The outline of the research focusing on cooperation and competition in teaching-learning processes is presented in Figure 7. There are many variations in the degree to which students may cooperate and/or compete with each other in teaching-learning activities. A few possible variations in competitive and cooperative processes or the combinations of the two are identified.

The following five points are suggestive of significant differences in the types of cooperation and/or competition in the learning process events:

1. Randomly selected teams working cooperatively in learning activities within each team but competing with other teams
2. Student teams working together on learning activities, but no competition between teams
3. Individual students working alone and competing with other students for differential rewards
4. Individual students working alone with little or no competition and common rewards for all
5. Individual students working alone with no comparison of work achieved

The hypotheses which follow suggest the various types of student cooperation-competition and a series of relationships that may exist between out-of-school factors, school inputs, school environment variables, immediate learning outcomes and educational goals. First, we state possible hypotheses concerning (1) out-of-school variables and student cooperation-competition, (2) the relation between school input and cooperation-

66

Figure 7. Cooperation-Competition

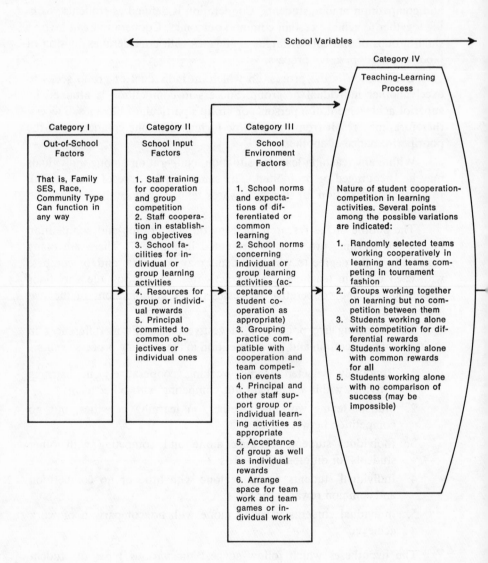

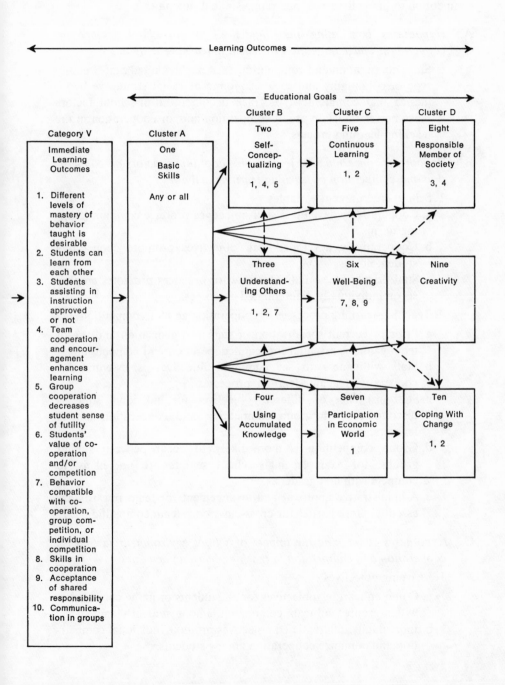

competition, (3) the relation of school environmental factors to cooperation-competition, and (4) the relation of patterns of cooperation and
competition to immediate and long-range student outcomes.

A. *Hypotheses concerning the impact of out-of-school factors on
cooperation and competition in teaching-learning activities*

Since cooperation and competition exist in the United States in any
type of community and socio-economic or racial strata, we hypothesize that community-type, race or other out-of-school factors
place no restraints on use of competition and/or cooperation in the
teaching-learning process.

B. *Hypotheses concerning the impact of school input factors on cooperation and competition in teaching-learning activities*

1. School environment variables
   a. Cooperatively developed staff objectives produce common learn-
      ing norms.
   b. Cooperatively developed staff objectives promote cooperative
      student norms.
   c. Staff orientation to individual reward practices promotes empha-
      sis on individually differentiated outcomes.

2. Teaching-learning processes of cooperation and/or competition

   a. Prior or current socialization of staff in organization and use of
      team games is essential for team cooperation and competition.
   b. Staff willingness to set common objectives is essential for
      cooperative teaching-learning processes.
   c. Staff insistence on different objectives for individual students
      discourages both group competition and cooperation among
      learners.
   d. Group competition is more likely to occur between similar
      groups, for example, high school seniors are not likely to
      compete with first graders.
   e. Administrative approval and arrangement for team rewards are
      essential prerequisites for cross-classroom team competition.

C. *Hypotheses concerning the impact of school environment factors on
cooperation and competition in teaching-learning activities*

1. Learning objectives
   a. Common learning objectives for all students promote cooperation
      within groups and team competition among student teams.
   b. Individually differentiated objectives promote individual competi-
      tion and minimize cooperation among students.

2. Grouping practices
   a. Homogeneous grouping practices promote individual competition within groups and minimize intergroup competition.
   b. Heterogeneous grouping practices facilitate between-group competition and within-group cooperation.
3. Staff commitment to individually differentiated student objectives prevents group cooperation on common objectives and competition between groups.
4. School emphasis on individual work promotes individual competition and prevents within-group cooperation.
5. School norms providing for group rewards promotes within-team cooperation and between-team competition.
6. School norms providing for individual rewards promote individual competition.

D. *Hypotheses concerning the relationship between cooperation-competition and immediate learning outcomes.*

1. Individual competition with differential rewards results in the acceptance of different levels of achievement as desirable.
2. Group competition with group rewards enhances belief that common group achievement is possible.
3. Within-group cooperation and group competition enhances specific immediate learning outcomes.

E. *Hypotheses concerning the relationship between cooperation-competition and the attainment of educational goals*

1. Within-group cooperation and between-group competition in learning activities:
   a. enhances the achievement of basic skills more than individual competition.
   b. facilitates students' interaction with each other and recognition that self-concept is a function of this interaction.
   c. promotes understanding that values and behaviors are learned from others, and that values and behavior differ from one social group to another.
   d. increases the acquisition of the principles and concepts of the sciences, arts, and humanities, and the application of this knowledge.
   e. promotes the acquisition of knowledge about careers.
   f. develops skill in determining when a risk is worth taking.
2. Cooperative and competitive interaction in learning activities:
   a. assists in the perception of self in varied social roles and social situations.

b. facilitates the assessment of self in different situations.

c. results in understanding that individuals differ and are similar in many ways.

d. develops rational behavior based on reasonable perceptions of self and society.

3. Cooperation in learning activities:

a. enhances the likelihood that students will feel comfortable with others in *heterogeneous* groups who are different in race, religion, social strata or personal characteristics and will seek interaction with them.

b. helps students to value continuous learning experiences.

c. develops skill in functioning flexibly in varied situations.

d. promotes positive self-perceptions and sense of well-being.

e. develops persons who act in accordance with a basic ethical framework.

f. develops individuals who assume responsibility for their own acts.

g. enhances willingness to work for goals based on realistic personal performance standards.

4. Develops self-reliant learners with common rewards through individual noncompetitive learning activities.

Content of Instruction in the Teaching-Learning Process

A growing number of researchers are concluding that the crucial variable in predicting learning outcomes is the content studied. What these researchers appear to conclude is that *students learn what is taught and do not learn what is not taught*. Further, they conclude that the *amount of time spent teaching* a topic or skill *predicts* better than any other variable (including teaching methods) level of *achievement*. Of course, these conclusions are commonsensical and one wonders why it has taken 50 years of educational research to conclude the obvious. There are many such common sense notions in education, but only some are true. At any rate, there should be no doubt that the content of instruction and the time allocated to it must be considered crucial determinants of school-related outcomes.

For discussion as a teaching-learning event, content is considered as the result of a process of curriculum decision-making. With this perspective in mind, we can attempt to refine our thinking by considering the dimensions of instructional content. The following dimensions, although not comprehensive, suggest the range of decisions which must be made regarding content.

1. Who makes which decisions?
   a. individual student
   b. teacher-student
   c. teacher
   d. team of teachers
   e. department or administration
   f. agency external to school
2. To whom is the content allocated?
   a. individual student
   b. within-class groups
   c. whole class
   d. all classes in school
   e. all classes in district
3. On what basis is content selected and sequenced?
   a. student interest
   b. student ability and developmental readiness
   c. diagnoses of missing prerequisites
   d. teacher interests and abilities
   e. structure of subject matter
   f. societal problems or expectations
   g. district or state guidelines or tests
   h. textbooks
4. How diverse are the content options available?
   a. highly diverse
   b. highly restricted
5. What is the content emphasis?
   a. cognitive, affective, psychomotor
   b. recall, comprehension application, analysis, synthesis, evaluation
6. How flexible is the pacing of content?
   a. predetermined (before the instructional activity)
   b. situationally determined (during instructional activity)

For illustrative purposes, three of the factors mentioned above were selected to define the parameters of a teaching-learning event to be considered in a research design. They were: (1) content allocation, (2) basis of content selection, and (3) flexibility of pacing. Figure 8 summarizes the levels of the factors considered.

Teaching-learning events described in terms of these three factors define the degree of individualization of content provided within a classroom. Disregarding for the moment all other dimensions of curriculum decision-making, the Committee on Research and Theory selected several types of activity within the teaching-learning process for the development

Figure 8. Three-Dimensional Matrix of Selected Factors Defining Individualization of Content

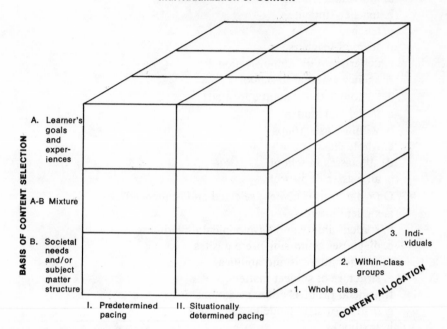

of potential research hypotheses. Each type samples a cell within the three-dimensional matrix above; however, not all cells are sampled.

The cells selected are identified below by a combination of letters and Roman and Arabic numerals which refer to the levels of the three factors of the matrix. For example, the cell on the lower-left-front corner of the matrix is identified as IB1. It represents predetermined pacing of content selected in accordance with societal needs and/or subject matter structure, allocated to the whole class. Similarly, the upper-right-back corner of the matrix is identified as IIA3. It represents situationally determined pacing of content selected in accordance with the learner's goals and experiences, allocated to individuals.

One other distinction needs to be made before the selected cells are discussed. Although treated as a single factor, "Situationally determined pacing," is clearly multidimensional. For example, decisions about pacing of content might be made on the basis of time required for mastery, duration of student interest, or coordination with current events. For purposes of this illustration, only mastery is considered, that is, pacing situationally determined by the amount of time required for mastery of the content under consideration.

The types of activities selected for deriving hypotheses are as follows:

1. *Cell IB1:* This is the "traditional" whole-class, grades instructional method. It represents the predetermined pacing of content selected in accordance with societal needs and subject matter structure, allocated to the whole class. In this cell, the time is predetermined on some basis other than consideration of the particular learners, for example, by dividing the number of units to be covered by the weeks in a school year. When this time has expired, the class moves on to new content, regardless of whether prior content has been learned.

2. *Cell IA-B2:* This might be a variety of the familiar within-class "ability grouping." Typically, there is predetermined pacing of content selected in accordance with societal needs/subject matter structure, allocated to a relatively permanent within-classroom group. Some adaptation of content is done to make it more relevant to the learners' needs, capabilities, interests or background experiences.

3. *Cell IA2:* This is the familiar "interest" group. It might be a skills study unit on map reading. The teacher might decide that a group of students that is interested in "other countries" will spend a week learning to read maps. Each student selects the country whose maps he or she will use to develop map-reading skills. In other words, this cell represents predetermined pacing of content selected on the basis of the learner's needs/experiences, allocated to within-class groups.

4. *Cell IAB3:* This is the "free-time" concept. The teacher sets aside some portion of time, say Friday afternoons, during which each learner can work on a learning activity or project of his or her choice. So, in this case, the cell describes predetermined pacing of content selected in accordance with the learner's goals/experiences, allocated to individuals.

5. *Cell IIB1:* This is a variation of the "traditional" whole-class method. In item 1 above (Cell IB1), the time for the content was predetermined on some basis not involving learners, that is, by dividing the number of units to be covered by the number of weeks in the school year. When this time has expired, the class moves on to new content regardless of whether the prior content has been learned. In Cell IIB1, the difference is that the amount of time spent on the content would be determined by the amount of time required for mastery. In other words, this cell represents situationally determined pacing of content selected in accordance with societal needs/expectations and/or subject matter structure, allocated to a whole class.

6. *Cell IIB2:* This might be exemplified in "skills groups" which are formed on the basis of common skills to be learned as defined by a skill's scope and sequence for the school. Each group is maintained until those particular skills are learned, then regrouped for learning other skills. Thus, there is situationally determined pacing of content selected in accordance with societal needs/expectation and subject matter structure allocated to a within-class group.

7. *Cell IIB3:* A good example of this is "individually prescribed instruction." The teacher selects from a skill's scope and sequence or a curriculum guide the learning activities needed by a particular student, gives her or him the prescription, and allows the student to work at the prescription until it is completed. In this case, content selected in accordance with societal needs/expectations and subject matter structure, is allocated to an individual and pace is situationally determined by the time required for mastery.

8. *Cell IIA-B1:* This is one type of "core" curriculum. The whole class is involved in learning activities around a "core" of content with "project groups" or "study groups" specializing in some area of the content, but everyone is expected to learn certain "key" concepts or skills. New "cores" are not introduced until those required "keys" are mastered. Content is selected upon a mixture of the learner's goals/experiences along with societal needs/expectancies and subject matter structure with pacing situationally determined by the time required for mastery. "Key" content is allocated to the whole class.

9. *Cell IIA3:* This is "personalized" instruction. A good example is a reading approach in which the learners select their own books to read and receive instruction in individual conferences with the teacher as they finish the books they have selected. In this cell, pacing is situationally determined, content is selected on the basis of the learner's goals/experiences and is allocated to the individual.

Figure 9 presents several of the possible relationships between the teaching-learning process (Content of Instruction) and out-of-school factors, school inputs, school environment variables, immediate learning outcomes, and educational goals. These potential relationships are explicated as researchable hypotheses.

A. *Hypotheses concerning the impact of out-of-school factors on source and pacing of instructional content in the teaching-learning process*
   1. The more proficient a student is in oral expression, based upon previous language experiences in the home environment, the more likely that experiences and goals will be accepted as legitimate

    sources of instructional content.

2. If the community is rich in possibilities for many and varied out-of-school experiences for students, the more likely the student's experiences and goals will be accepted as legitimate sources of instructional content.

3. The competency requirements legislated by states act as guides for the teacher's selection of instructional content.

4. The socio-economic level of students affects the variety of experiences students bring to the learning situation.

B. *Hypotheses concerning the impact of school input factors on instructional content in the teaching-learning process*

  1. School Environment Variables

    a. Adopted tests, curricula, and/or scope and sequences of skills might adversely influence the teacher's perceptions of (a) self as a facilitator or guide, (b) the student as an appropriate curriculum decision-maker, and (c) expectancy levels for students.

    b. Time constraints on instructional processes decrease the teacher's expectancy levels for students.

    c. The school's philosophy of instruction influences teachers' perceptions of (a) their role as information giver, guide, or facilitator, (b) student motivation as affected by relevancy of content, and (c) beliefs that the learner's experiences are an important source of comfort.

    d. Staff training in the utilization of personal and community experiences or resources in instruction increases teachers' skills and attitudes in curriculum development and response to students' goals and needs.

  2. Teaching-Learning Process

    a. Adopted texts, curricula, and/or scope and sequence of skills tend to (a) increase the use of fixed time units for presentation of content, (b) decrease the degree to which curriculum decisions are made in response to learners' abilities, goals, and experiences, and (c) reduce the amount of content allocated to individuals rather than groups.

    b. Time constraints on the instructional processes influence the teacher's flexibility in using the learner's abilities, goals, and experiences in making curriculum decisions.

    c. Availability of a wide variety of resource materials tends to increase the teacher's flexibility in (a) using learner's abilities, goals, and experiences as determinants of curriculum decisions and (b) allocating content to individuals rather than groups.

Figure 9. Content of Instruction

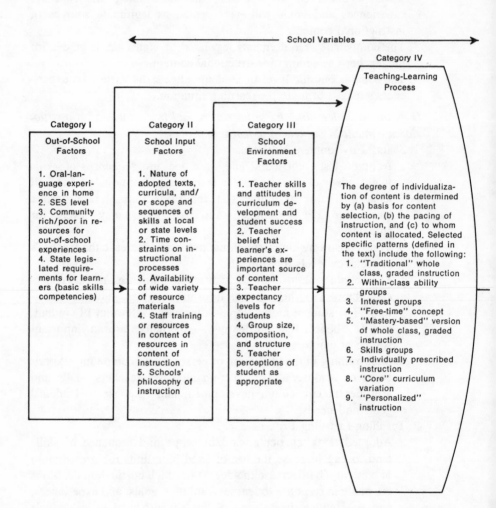

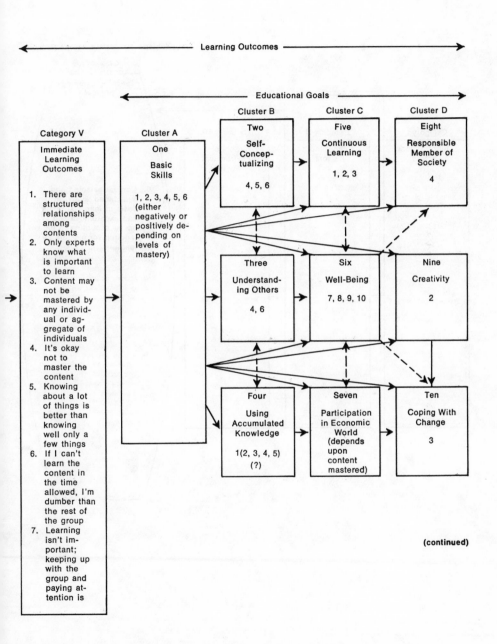

(continued)

78

Figure 9. Content of Instruction (continued)

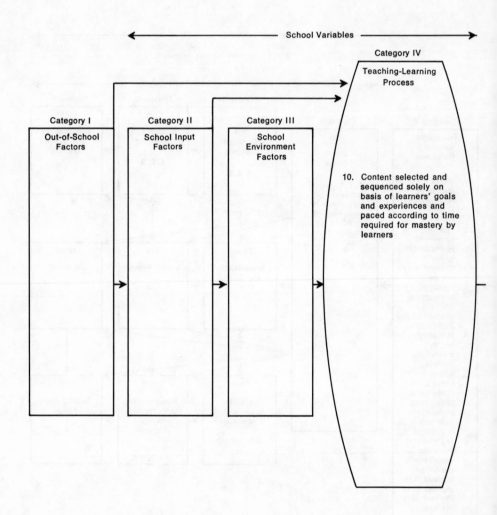

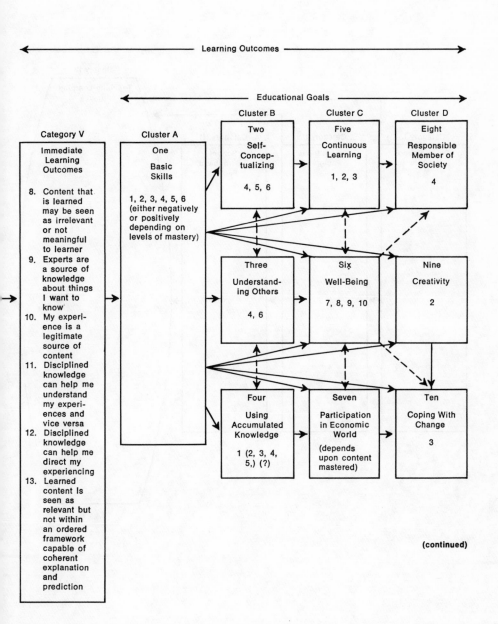

(continued)

80

Figure 9. Content of Instruction (continued)

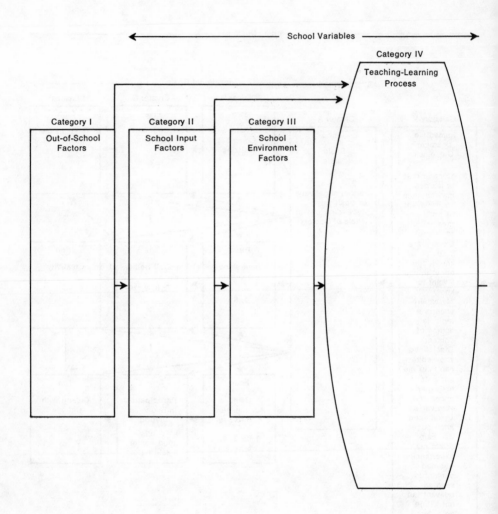

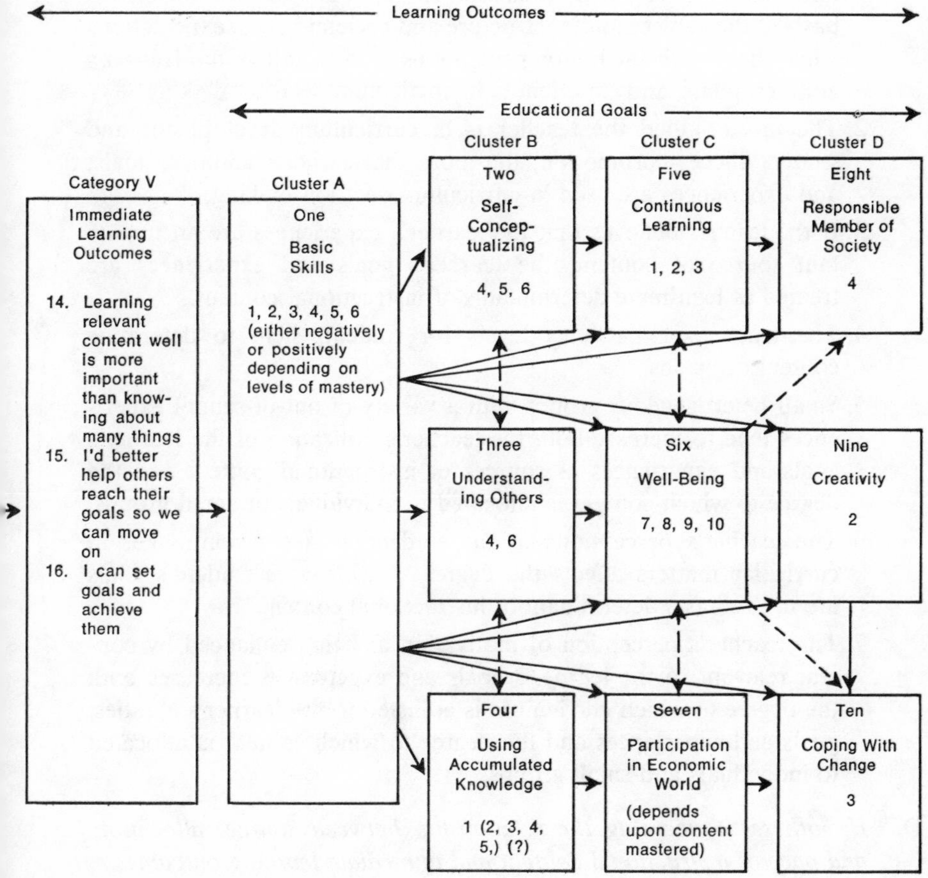
Learning Outcomes
Educational Goals
Category V
Immediate Learning Outcomes
14. Learning relevant content well is more important than knowing about many things
15. I'd better help others reach their goals so we can move on
16. I can set goals and achieve them
Cluster A
One
Basic Skills
1, 2, 3, 4, 5, 6 (either negatively or positively depending on levels of mastery)
Cluster B
Two
Self-Conceptualizing
4, 5, 6
Three
Understanding Others
4, 6
Four
Using Accumulated Knowledge
1 (2, 3, 4, 5,) (?)
Cluster C
Five
Continuous Learning
1, 2, 3
Six
Well-Being
7, 8, 9, 10
Seven
Participation in Economic World
(depends upon content mastered)
Cluster D
Eight
Responsible Member of Society
4
Nine
Creativity
2
Ten
Coping With Change
3

C. *Hypotheses concerning the impact of school environment factors on instructional content in the teaching-learning process*

1. The teacher's perceptions of self as information giver, guide, or facilitator affect instructional content such that teachers who have information-giver perceptions tend to determine curriculum on the basis of the subject matter structure and societal needs/expectations while those with facilitator perceptions tend to utilize the learner's abilities, goals, and experiences in curriculum decision-making.

2. The more skilled the teacher is in curriculum development and student success promotion, the more the learner's abilities, goals, and experiences are used in curriculum decision-making.

3. If the teacher believes that the learner's experiences are an important source of content, the learner's goals and experiences are treated as legitimate determinants of instructional content.

4. The teacher's expectancy levels for students help to determine content decisions.

5. Small heterogeneous groups with a variety of out-of-school experiences tend to increase both the teacher's utilization of the learner's goals and experiences as sources of instructional content and the degree to which content is allocated to individuals or small groups.

6. The teacher's perceptions of the student as a decision-maker in curricular matters affects the degree to which the student's goals are utilized as a determinant of instructional content.

7. The teacher's perception of motivation as being enhanced by content relevant to the learner's goals and experiences increases both the degree to which curriculum is adjusted to the learner's abilities, goals and experiences and the degree to which content is allocated to individuals and small groups.

D. *Hypotheses concerning the relationship between source, allocation, and pace of instructional content and immediate learning outcomes*

1. When curriculum is selected and sequenced on the basis of societal needs/expectations, subject matter structure and pacing is predetermined, and content is allocated to large groups, then the student learns that

   a. There are structured relationships within content areas.
   b. The content may not be mastered by any individual or aggregate of individuals.
   c. It's okay not to master the content.
   d. Knowing about a lot of things is better than knowing well a few things.

      e. "If I can't learn the content in the time allowed, I must be dumber than the rest of the group."

      f. Learning isn't important; keeping up with the group and paying attention is more important than learning.

2. When instruction is selected and sequenced on the basis of societal needs and/or subject matter structure and allocated to large groups but paced in relationship to the time required for mastery by learners, then the student learns

      a. That only the experts know what is important to learn.

      b. To master content even though it may seem irrelevant or not meaningful to the learner.

3. When instruction is selected, allocated, and paced on the basis of both the structure of the discipline and the learner's goals and experiences, then the student learns that

      a. Experts are a source of knowledge about things I want to know.

      b. My experiences are a legitimate source of learning content.

      c. Disciplined knowledge can help me understand my experiencing, and vice versa.

      d. Disciplined knowledge can help me direct my experiencing.

      e. I can set goals and achieve them.

4. When instruction is selected and sequenced solely on the basis of the learner's goals and experiences, allocated to individual or small groups, and paced according to the time required for mastery by the learner, then

      a. Learned content may be seen as relevant but not within an ordered framework capable of coherent explanation and prediction.

      b. The student learns that learning relevant content *well* is more important than knowing *about* many things.

      c. The student learns that "I'd better help others reach their goals so we can move on!"

E. *Hypotheses concerning the relationships between instructional content and immediate learning outcomes leading to educational goals*

   1. When students learn that their experiences are a legitimate source of content and that disciplined knowledge can be applied to help understand their experiencing, there is an increase in the degree to which the learner

      a. Distinguishes among many concepts of self in various roles or social situations.

      b. Is able to assess his or her functioning in each of several different situations.

   c. Is able to perceive accurately, to assess validly and to respond appropriately to others' evaluations in the context of each specific situation rather than to generalize to all situations.

   d. Believes that human behavior is influenced by many factors and and is best understood in terms of the relevant personal content in which it occurred.

   e. Applies basic principles and concepts of the sciences, arts, and humanities to interpret personal experiences.

2. To the extent that students learn that disciplined knowledge can help them direct their experiencing, they will also

   a. Value learning experiences.

   b. Know that it is necessary to continue to learn throughout life because of the inevitability of change.

   c. Participate in satisfying leisure-time activities.

3. To the extent that the student learns that "I can set goals and achieve them," he or she will also

   a. Act on the belief that each individual has value as a human being and should be respected as a worthwhile person in his or her own right.

   b. Be a self-reliant learner who is capable of autonomous learning.

   c. Perceive self positively with a generally competent sense of well-being.

   d. Assume responsibility for personal actions.

   e. Be willing to work now for goals to be realized in the future.

4. When students learn that their experiencing is a legitimate source of content, that disciplined knowledge can be applied to help them understand and direct their experiencing, and that they can set and achieve goals, they will also be more likely to

   a. Behave rationally based upon reasonable perceptions of self and society.

   b. Maintain personal integration while functioning flexibly in varied situations.

   c. Entertain and value the imaginative alternatives of others.

Patterns of Reinforcement, Encouragement, and Support in the Teaching-Learning Process

   A teacher's desire to encourage students, particularly disadvantaged ones, and support their efforts in the teaching-learning process sometimes complicates the teacher's reinforcement behavior in the teaching-learning situation. There are several combinations of teacher support, encouragement, and reinforcement of a student's accurate or inaccurate response. Some of the likely combinations include:

1. Student gives an accurate response; teacher gives positive reinforcement of the response and provides encouragement and support.

2. Student gives accurate response; teacher gives positive reinforcement of response but withholds encouragement and support.

3. Student gives accurate response; teacher gives negative reinforcement of response and withholds encouragement and support.

4. Student gives inaccurate response; teacher gives positive reinforcement of response and provides encouragement and support.

5. Student gives inaccurate response; teacher gives positive reinforcement of response and withholds encouragement and support.

6. Student gives inaccurate response; teacher gives negative reinforcement of response and withholds encouragement and support.

7. Student gives inaccurate response; teacher gives negative reinforcement and provides encouragement and support including reinstruction.

The hypotheses that follow suggest a series of relationships between the patterns of reinforcement, encouragement and support, and out-of-school variables, school input variables, school environmental factors, and immediate learning outcomes and educational goals. All of these hypotheses are derived from the underlying notion that reinforcement is essential in the teaching-learning process, but those affective behaviors (such as encouragement and support) associated with the reinforcement may modify or confuse the learner's response.

A. *Hypotheses concerning the impact of out-of-school factors on patterns of reinforcement and encouragement in the teaching-learning process*

   1. Any pattern of reinforcement and encouragement may occur in any community type.
   2. Positive reinforcement for inaccurate responses is more likely to occur in schools located in poor and minority communities.
   3. Encouragement and supportive teacher behavior associated with inaccurate responses is more likely to occur in poor and minority communities.

B. *Hypotheses concerning the impact of school input factors on patterns of reinforcement and encouragement in the teaching-learning process*

   1. Types of classroom and school facilities are unrelated to patterns of reinforcement and encouragement processes.
   2. Students in special programs for disadvantaged, such as compensatory and bilingual education, are more likely to receive positive reinforcement for inaccurate responses than students not in such programs.

Figure 10. Patterns of Reinforcement, Encouragement, and Support

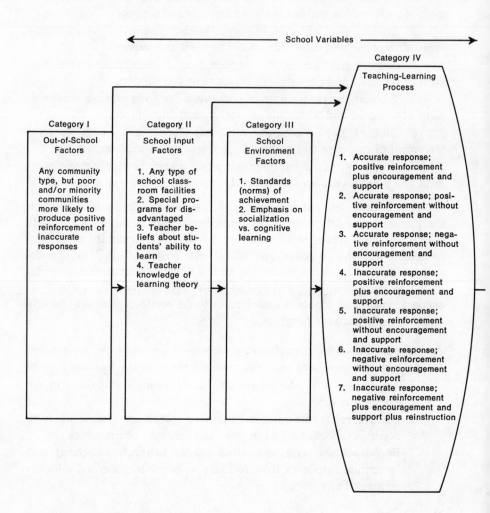

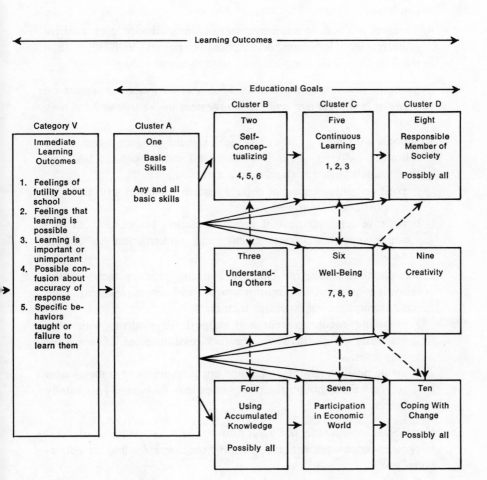

    3. Teachers who believe that some students cannot learn provide more positive reinforcement for incorrect student responses and associated supportive behavior than teachers who believe that all students can learn.

    4. Teachers trained in reinforcement learning theory give positive reinforcement for incorrect student responses less often than teachers with little knowledge of reinforcement theory.

C. *Hypotheses concerning the impact of school environment factors on patterns of reinforcement and encouragement in the teaching-learning process*

    1. Schools with high standards of achievement produce more of the following patterns of reinforcement and encouragement behavior than schools with low standards of achievement:

      a. positive reinforcement of correct student responses with personal support and encouragement.

      b. negative reinforcement of incorrect student responses with personal support, encouragement, and reinstruction to correct errors.

    2. Schools that emphasize effective learning produce more of the following patterns of reinforcement and encouragement than schools emphasizing cognitive learning:

      a. providing encouragement and support for students with little emphasis on positive or negative reinforcement of cognitive responses.

      b. giving positive reinforcement and encouragement to students who respond even though their responses may be partially or totally inaccurate.

D. *Hypotheses concerning the relationships between patterns of reinforcement-encouragement and learning outcomes leading to educational goals*

    1. Positive reinforcement of students' accurate responses with encouragement and support results in:

      a. mastery of intended behaviors.

      b. acquisition of knowledge of basic principles of science, arts, and humanities.

      c. feeling that learning is possible and valuable.

      d. ability to appropriately assess one's functioning in school social situations.

      e. ability to perceive accurately, assess validly, and respond appropriately to others' evaluations.

    f. rational behavior based on reasonable perceptions of self and society.

    g. positive perceptions of self and a sense of well-being.

    h. increased tendency to seek interaction and to feel comfortable with others.

2. Positive reinforcement of accurate responses without encouragement and support results in:

    a. acquisition of intended behavior.

    b. negative self perception and low sense of well-being.

    c. inability to perceive accurately, assess validly, and respond appropriately to others' evaluations in school context.

3. Negative reinforcement of accurate student response without support and encouragement results in:

    a. feeling of futility in school situation.

    b. failure to learn correct behavior.

    c. inability to assess one's functioning in school situation.

    d. irrational behavior based on unreasonable perceptions of self.

    e. failure to value learning experience.

    f. tolerance of ambiguity.

    g. failure to learn basic principles and concepts of science, arts, and humanities.

    h. inability to perceive accurately, assess validly, and respond appropriately to others' evaluation in academic role.

    i. negative perceptions of self and low sense of well-being.

4. Positive reinforcement of inaccurate responses with encouragement and support results in:

    a. learning incorrect behavior in basic skills and other areas.

    b. positive self perceptions and sense of well-being.

    c. inaccurate assessment of one's functioning in school situations.

5. Positive reinforcement of inaccurate responses without encouragement and support results in:

    a. incorrect knowledge, skills, and other behavior.

    b. feelings of futility and hopelessness regarding school.

    c. confused self-assessment and inability to accurately assess one's self in school situation.

    d. inability to apply basic principles of sciences, arts, and humanities.

    e. minimized knowledge of career options.

6. Negative reinforcement of inaccurate response without encouragement and support results in:

    a. failure to learn correct behavior.

    b. assessment of self as incompetent and unable to learn in school situations.

    c. feelings of futility in school situation.

    d. devaluing learning experience.

    e. failure to acquire knowledge of basic principles and concepts in sciences, arts, and humanities.

7. Negative reinforcement of accurate student response with encouragement and support including reinstruction results in:

    a. feeling that learning is possible.

    b. learning of correct behavior.

    c. maintaining personal integration and acquiring reasonable perceptions of self.

    d. accurately assessing one's functioning in school situation.

    e. ability to perceive accurately, assess validly, and respond appropriately to others' evaluations.

Responding to Expressed Feelings in the Teaching-Learning Process

Within the classroom environment, feelings occur and are treated as either legitimate in the educational context or as inappropriate. The response to feelings in the instructional setting can range all the way from helping students learn processes for controlling/changing their internal states to actively discouraging even the recognition that feelings exist. There are several dimensions to be considered in response to feelings: (1) the kinds of feelings, if any, which are made legitimate for expression in the classroom; (2) who may express their feelings; (3) to which stimuli feelings may be expressed, for example, personal content versus school-related content; (4) whether feelings, or actions based on feelings, are evaluated, that is, it's okay to *feel* the way you feel but what you *do* about feelings may be right or wrong; (5) which ways of expressing feelings, are acceptable, for example, verbal versus nonverbal, creative expression in writing or art versus destructive behavior; and (6) instruction in ways of dealing with emotions.

Three dimensions were selected to define a teaching-learning process to be used for illustrative purposes: (a) the teacher's discouragement/acceptance of feelings, (b) the student's expression of feelings verbally or nonverbally, and (c) whether the feelings expressed are those typically classified by most people as unpleasant (sadness, fear, hatred) or pleasant (joy, compassion, caring). The teaching-learning process was stated as "The degree to which the teacher communicates understanding and acceptance of each student's feelings (accurate empathy)." Several points were delineated along a continuum of acceptance and rejection of pleasant or unpleasant feelings which were expressed verbally or nonverbally.

The full spectrum of this continuum could be diagrammed as follows in Figure 11.

Figure 11. Dimensions of Response to Expressed Feelings

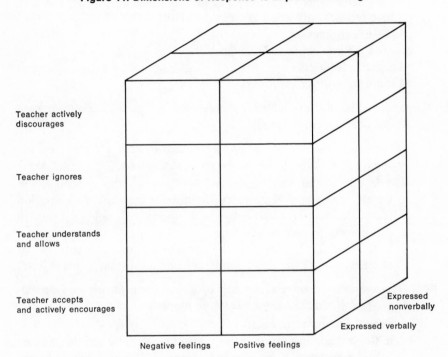

Several cells were sampled from the above figure and were then explicated in a research model. The cells sampled for use in the research model were as follows:

1. The teacher actively discourages student expression of . . .
   all feelings *or*
   negative feelings only *or*
   negative feelings when expressed verbally.
2. The teacher ignores student expression of . . .
   all feelings *or*
   negative feelings only *or*
   negative feelings only when expressed nonverbally.

3. The teacher understands and allows student expression of . . .
    positive feelings only when expressed nonverbally *or*
    all positive feelings *or*
    negative feelings expressed nonverbally *or*
    all negative feelings *or*
    all feelings, however expressed.

4. The teacher accepts and actively encourages student expressions of . . .
    positive feelings only when expressed verbally *or*
    all positive feelings *or*
    negative feelings expressed nonverbally *or*
    all negative feelings *or*
    all feelings, however expressed.

The model which was explicated is represented in Figure 12. Following are hypotheses drawn from the model.

A. *Hypotheses concerning the impact of out-of-school factors on responding to feelings in the teaching-learning process*
    1. The ethnic and social-economic make-up of the community in which the school is located influences central administration restraints, school philosophy, and norms of staff behavior in legitimizing response to feelings.
    2. Ethnic and SES make-up of the community influences the amount of training and experience in interpersonal skills that teachers have.

B. *Hypotheses concerning the impact of school input factors on responding to feelings in the teaching-learning process*
    1. School Environment Factors
       a. Central administration restraints and philosophy and the training and experience of teachers in interpersonal skills influence norms of staff behavior in legitimizing response to feelings.
       b. Class size, age, SES status, and ethnicity of students determine intra-class grouping practices and composition of classroom student body.
       c. Prior training and experience of teachers in interpersonal skills influences both the teachers' beliefs about the place of feelings in schools and the teachers' levels of interpersonal skills.
       d. Central administration restraints and philosophy for selection and training of administrators influence the principal's level of interpersonal skills.
    2. Teaching-Learning Processes
       a. Teachers who have had prior training and experience in the use of interpersonal skills are more likely to understand feelings that

are expressed in nonverbal ways and attempt to communicate understanding and acceptance of students' feelings, however expressed.

b. Smaller class size and freedom from time constraints increase the degree to which the teacher communicates understanding and acceptance of *each* student's feelings.

C. *Hypotheses concerning the impact of school environment factors on responding to feelings in the teaching-learning process*

1. The teacher's interpersonal skills and beliefs that feelings have a proper place within the instructional setting affect the teacher's attempts to communicate understanding and acceptance of students' feelings.

2. The higher the teacher's level of interpersonal skills and use of flexible and varied patterns of intra-class grouping, the more frequently understanding and acceptance of *each* student's feelings are communicated.

3. The higher the level of interpersonal skills utilized by the principal, the more likely the teacher is to communicate understanding and acceptance of each student's feelings.

4. When interpersonal skills training is held constant, and the more closely the composition of the classroom student body approximates teachers' own ethnic and SES backgrounds, the more likely they are to understand the feelings expressed and to accept both the modes for expression of those feelings and the feelings themselves.

5. The younger the age of the classroom student body, the less likely the teacher is to actively discourage the expression of feelings.

D. *Hypotheses concerning the relationship between responding to feelings and immediate learning outcomes*

1. The more frequently and accurately the teacher expresses acceptance and encouragement of each student's feelings, the more likely the student is to learn

a. It's okay to be me.

b. Feelings are important in learning.

c. Understanding others' feelings is important.

d. To associate referents with feelings.

e. To clarify the relationship of feelings to referents.

f. An increased number and variety of labels for feelings.

g. To express feelings more accurately and more freely.

h. To be more able to understand his or her emotional responses to stimuli.

i. To have more control of own feelings.

Figure 12. Responding to Expressed Feelings

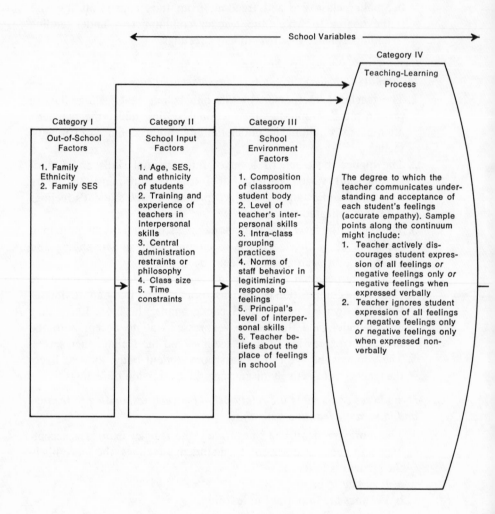

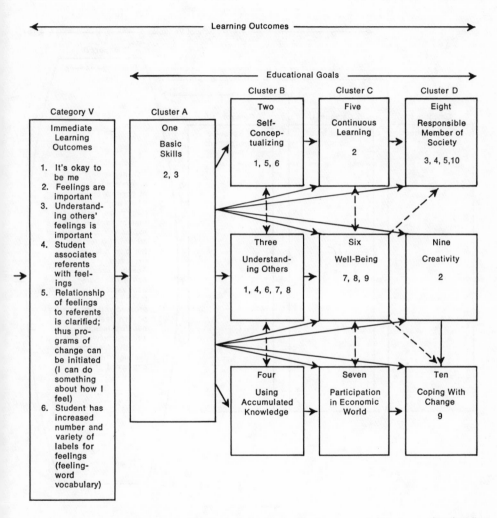

(continued)

Figure 12. Responding to Expressed Feelings (continued)

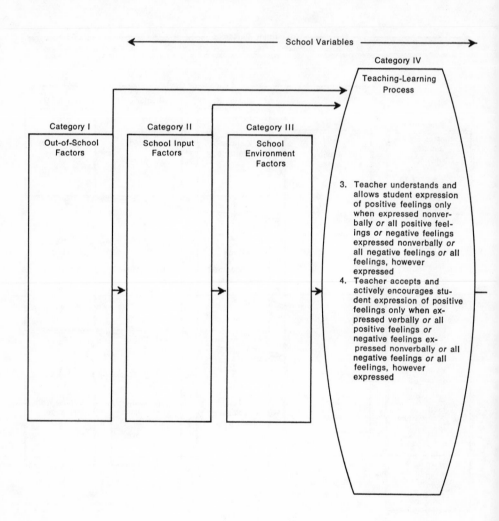

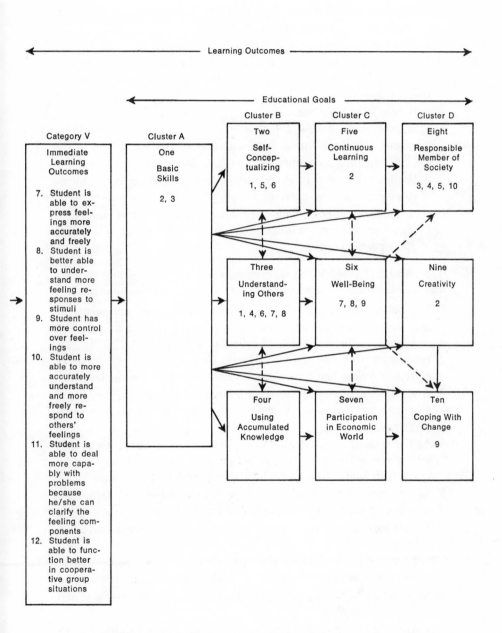

    j. To more accurately understand and more freely respond to others' feelings.

    k. To deal more capably with problems because of an increased ability to clarify the feeling components.

    l. To function better in cooperative group situations.

2. The more frequently and emphatically the teacher actively discourages the expression of student feelings, the more likely the student is to learn

    a. It's *not* okay to be me.

    b. Who I am and how I feel is not worth spending time on in school, therefore I must not be a very worthwhile person.

    c. Understanding how other people feel is not important.

    d. Feelings do *not* play an important role in learning or problem-solving or decision-making.

    e. A much smaller feeling-word vocabulary, lessened ability to communicate own feelings, and poorer skills in understanding other people's feelings.

E. *Hypotheses concerning the relationships between responding to feelings and immediate learning outcomes leading to educational goals*

1. The better students are able to clarify the feeling components of problems, the more likely they are to process acquired information and meaning through skills of reflective thinking.

2. When students learn that "It's okay to be me," they tend to become more *self-reliant* learners who are capable of autonomous learning.

3. When students learn to associate referents with feelings, they begin to recognize that self-concept is developed in interaction with other people.

4. As the student is better able to understand more about his or her feeling responses to stimuli, he or she also becomes more able to assess own functioning in each of several different situations.

5. As students gain skill in accurately understanding and freely responding to others' feelings, they also learn

    a. That individuals differ (and are similar) in many ways, including feelings.

    b. To entertain and value the imaginative alternatives of others, because they understand others' feelings about their creations.

6. As students become able to function better in cooperative group situations, they also

    a. Are more able to perceive accurately, to assess validly, and to respond appropriately to others' evaluations in the context of each specific role situation rather than to generalize to all situations.

b. Are more likely to act in accordance with a basic ethical framework incorporating those values contributing to group living, such as honesty, fairness, compassion, and integrity, because they understand the impact of those behaviors (or lack of them) upon others in the group.

c. Are more likely to work together in groups to achieve mutual goals.

7. As students increase the number and variety of labels for feelings, become able to express feelings more accurately and more freely, and can more accurately understand and respond to others' feelings, they also improve their abilities to express information and meaning through speaking, writing, and nonverbal means.

8. As students learn (1) it's okay to be me, (2) feelings are important, (3) when the relationship of feelings to referents are clarified, programs of change can be initiated, and (4) to be able to accurately understand and more freely respond to others' feelings, they also become more likely to

a. Act on the belief that each individual has value as a human being and should be respected as a worthwhile person in his or her own right.

b. Believe that human behavior is influenced by many factors and is best understood in terms of the relevant personal context in which it occurred.

c. Seek interactions and feel comfortable with others who are different in race, religion, social level or personal attributes as well as those who are similar in those characteristics.

d. Withhold judgment of another's action until after trying to understand the personal and social context of the action.

9. When students know that understanding others' feelings is important and can both accurately respond to others' feelings and function well in cooperative group situations, then they are also more likely to assume responsibility for dependent persons of all ages in a manner consistent with both their growth and development needs and the needs of society.

10. When students have learned to (a) associate and clarify feeling referents so that programs of change can be initiated, (b) better control and more freely express feelings, (c) accurately understand and respond to others' feelings, (d) deal more capably with problems through clarifying feeling components, and (e) function better

in cooperative group situations, then they are also more likely to

a. Maintain personal integration while functioning flexibly in varied situations.

b. Behave rationally based upon reasonable perceptions of self and society.

c. Perceive self positively with a generally competent sense of well being.

11. When the student has learned (a) that it's okay to be me, (b) to clarify the relationship of feeling to referents and initiate programs to change own feelings or referents, and (c) gain more control over own feelings, he or she also will tend to assume responsibility for his or her own acts.

Chapter 5   Getting There

We began this booklet by considering the objectives of humanistic education. We subsequently addressed the following kinds of questions:

"On what sorts of destinations should schools set their sights?"

"How can they find out when they arrive?"

"What sorts of inquiries will disclose better ways of getting there?"

Now it may prove fruitful to extend our travel metaphor in order to make some concluding remarks. Let us consider for whom and for what use this book is intended, and the possible dangers that are inherent in its misuse.

This booklet is not for disinterested visitors to a foreign land. It is for those concerned and acquainted with schools, for those knowledgeable of the topography and, particularly, the prominent features of the landscape. Such persons include those teachers and administrators in touch with the daily functioning of schools and those who are interested in systematically and deliberately trying to improve the chances of school children to attain educational goals. These knowledgeable and concerned school personnel, with input from the community, are in the best position to chart their school's course.

Therefore, rather than attempt to prescribe a single set of educational goals for all schools, the Committee on Research and Theory has provided these professionals with an extensive list that encompasses most of those goals educators consider important. We do not wish to prescribe each school's destination. That is a decision best left to the particular school and community. We do believe that we have provided a guide to the process of goal setting by listing and specifying a wide variety of educational goals.

Any particular school and community can use this list as a resource in setting priorities and choosing from alternatives. The list (in order of priority) developed by each school and community will reflect that community's view of the educated person and the rationale behind that community's support of the schools. In a sense, every educational journey has a different purpose with a correspondingly different itinerary. It would have been presumptuous of the Committee on Research and Theory to decide on one journey for all schools.

101

But exhortations about the importance of setting goals (and even about measuring goal attainment) are not new in educational literature. The gap that has existed is the provision for a *wide variety* of educational goals both in terms of *clear formation* and of *instrumentation for their measurement*. By providing a state-of-the-art assessment of measurement for a wide range of educational goals and suggestions for additional research and development in instrumentation, we are offering not a map of the territory but a guide to map making.

This booklet is, then, intended as a guide for map makers, whose maps of the "terrain" of the educational enterprise help both student-travelers and their teacher-guides in arriving successfully at their destination. Up to now the only maps available have been over limited terrain. As a consequence, teachers and administrators, not wanting students to get lost along the way, have typically stuck to the same itinerary, the widely known and well-worn path of exclusively cognitive skills. Although some travelers will always find this well-traveled route difficult, at least their guides can tell when they arrive and even provide a whole repertoire of techniques for getting them there. To suggest they start out for new destinations, regardless of the desirability of those unvisited places, has been to suggest a journey to the dark side of the moon—no signposts, no map, and no going back.

We recognize that a map, much less a guide to map making, does not constitute a panacea to the problems of educational travel. Much can happen along the way. But the use of our guide to map making, particularly our approach to systematic research on educational inputs, processes, and outputs, will result in direct benefits. The "model" we have provided should help school personnel avoid the "band wagon" approach to innovation of the 1970's. In that approach, educators grabbed at new programs without taking into account the impact any innovation would have on the total school, or if, in fact, the innovation would contribute to goal attainment at all. Particularly in times of severely limited funding available to support schools, we must attempt to utilize our resources wisely. As we plan our educational journeys, we want to provide for the most efficient means of transportation. The days of the gas guzzler are over. Our resources are too precious to waste.

But there is a constant danger inherent in the planning of educational itineraries and the means of transportation; there is much more to a journey than arriving at the destination on time and unharmed. People also embark on journeys for the experience of traveling. A trip through France is not undertaken just to arrive in Paris. The French countryside, the French people, the French wine and food, and the enjoyment of a traveling companion are all as important for the "success" of the journey as the arrival in Paris. Nor should a kindergartener embark on an educational journey merely to receive a high school diploma or to learn only the three R's. Thus, there are compelling reasons for expecting the educational process not only to help children become "well educated," but also to meet a set of criteria relating to the intrinsic, rather than instrumental, aspects of the process. The educational process should not only accomplish goals but also be humane, rational, engaging, enjoyable, and personally gratifying, to mention just a few such criteria. The most compelling reason for this requirement is not that such humane education is most efficient or effective (it may not be), but, instead, that schooling comprises a substantial portion of people's lives and life should be lived in such a humane manner.

One final caveat in using this guide must be mentioned. In all our planning, research, and evaluation it is easy to forget that educational journeys are for the student-traveler, not for their teacher-guides, not for the map-making researchers, nor for the travel-agent administration. The educational travel industry is simply intended to help the student-traveler along on an educational journey; as much as we want to, we cannot make the journey for the student. We can only act as guides. It is in this spirit that this booklet is intended to be used.

References

Brookover, Wilbur B.; Beady, Charles; Flood, Patricia; Schweitzer, John; and Wisenbaker, Joe. *School Social Systems and Student Achievement: Schools Can Make a Difference.* New York: J. R. Bergin/Praeger, 1979.

Buros, O. K., ed. *Fifth Mental Measurements Yearbook.* Highland Park, New Jersey: Gryphon Press, 1965.

_____. *Sixth Mental Measurements Yearbook.* Highland Park, New Jersey: Gryphon Press, 1965.

_____. *Seventh Mental Measurements Yearbook.* Highland Park, New Jersey: Gryphon Press, 1965.

Coleman, James S.; Campbell, Ernest Q.; Hobson, Carol J.; McPartland, James; Mood, Alexander M.; Weinfeld, Frederick P.; and York, Robert L. *Equality of Educational Opportunity.* Washington, D.C.: U.S. Government Printing Office, 1966.

Educatonal Testing Service. *Tests in Microfiche, Sets A, B, C, D.* Princeton, New Jersey: Educational Testing Service, 1975, 1976, 1977, 1978.

Hauser, Robert; Sewell, William; and Alwin, Duane. "High School Effects of Education." In *Schooling and Academic Achievement in American Society.* Edited by W. Sewell, R. Hauser, and D. Featherman. New York: Academic Press, 1976.

Hyman, H. H.; Wright, C. R.; and Reed, J. S. *The Enduring Effects of Education.* Chicago: The University of Chicago Press, 1975.

Jencks, Christopher; Smith, Marshall; Acland, Henry; Bane, Mary Jo; Cohen, David; Gintis, Herbert; Heyns, Barbara; and Michelson, Stephen. *Inequality: A Reassessment of the Effect of Family and Schooling in America.* New York: Basic Books, 1972.

Jencks, Christopher; Bartlett, Susan; Corcoran, Mary; Crouse, James; Eaglesfield, David; Jackson, Gregory; Mclelland, Kent; Mueser, Peter; Olneck, Michael; Schwartz, Joseph; Ward, Sherry; and Williams, Jill. *Who Gets Ahead? The Determinants of Economic Success in America.* New York: Basic Books, 1979.

Johnson, Mauritz. "Definitions and Models in Curriculum Theory." *Educational Theory,* 1967.

_____. *Intentionality in Education.* Albany, New York: Center for Curriculum Research and Services, 1977.

Johnson, O. A., and Bommarito, J. W. *Tests and Measurements in Child Development: A Handbook.* San Francisco: Josey-Bass, 1971.

Lake, Dale G.; Miles, Matthew B.; and Earle, Ralph B., Jr. *Measuring Human Behavior. Tools for the Assessment of Social Functioning.* New York: New York Teachers College Press, 1973.

Pennsylvania Department of Education. *Educational Quality Assessments.* Harrisburg, Pennsylvania: Pennsylvania Department of Education, 1976.

Simon, Anita, and Boyer, E. G., eds, *Mirrors for Behavior, III: An Anthology and Observation Instruments.* Wyncote, Pennsylvania: Communication Materials Center, 1974.

Zais, Robert. *Curriculum: Principles and Foundation.* New York: Harper and Row, 1976.

104

About the Authors

WILBUR B. BROOKOVER, Professor of Urban and Metropolitan Studies, Michigan State University, East Lansing, Michigan

JOSEPH FERDERBAR, Superintendent of the Neshaminy School District, Langhorne, Pennsylvania

GENEVA GAY, Associate Professor of Education, Purdue University, West Lafayette, Indiana

MILDRED MIDDLETON, Curriculum Coordinator, Cedar Rapids Community Schools, Cedar Rapids, Iowa

GEORGE POSNER, Associate Professor of Education, Cornell University, Ithaca, New York

FLORA ROEBUCK, Assistant Professor of Education Applied in Medicine, The Johns Hopkins University, Baltimore, Maryland

ASCD Publications, Spring 1981

Yearbooks

A New Look at Progressive Education
(610-17812) $8.00

Considered Action for Curriculum Improvement
(610-80186) $9.75

Education for an Open Society
(610-74012) $8.00

Evaluation as Feedback and Guide
(610-17700) $6.50

Feeling, Valuing, and the Art of Growing:
Insights into the Affective
(610-77104) $9.75

Life Skills in School and Society
(610-17786) $5.50

Lifelong Learning—A Human Agenda
(610-79160) $9.75

Perceiving, Behaving, Becoming: A New Focus
for Education (610-17278) $5.00

Schools in Search of Meaning
(610-75044) $8.50

Staff Development/Organization Development
(610-81232) $9.75

Perspectives on Curriculum Development
1776-1976 (610-76078) $9.50

Books and Booklets

About Learning Materials (611-78134) $4.50

Action Learning: Student Community Service
Projects (611-74018) $2.50

Adventuring, Mastering, Associating: New
Strategies for Teaching Children
(611-76080) $5.00

Approaches to Individualized Education
(611-80204) $4.75

Bilingual Education for Latinos
(611-78142) $6.75

Classroom-Relevant Research in the Language
Arts (611-78140) $7.50

Clinical Supervision—A State of the Art Review
(611-80194) $3.75

Curricular Concerns in a Revolutionary Era
(611-17852) $6.00

Curriculum Leaders: Improving Their Influence
(611-76084) $4.00

Curriculum Materials 1980 (611-80198) $3.00

Curriculum Theory (611-77112) $7.00

Degrading the Grading Myths: A Primer of
Alternatives to Grades and Marks
(611-76082) $6.00

Educating English-Speaking Hispanics
(611-80202) $6.50

Elementary School Mathematics: A Guide to
Current Research (611-75056) $5.00

Eliminating Ethnic Bias in Instructional
Materials: Comment and Bibliography
(611-74020) $3.25

Global Studies: Problems and Promises for
Elementary Teachers (611-76086) $4.50

Handbook of Basic Citizenship Competencies
(611-80196) $4.75

Humanistic Education: Objectives and
Assessment (611-78136) $4.75

Learning More About Learning
(611-17310) $2.00

Measuring and Attaining the Goals of Education
(611-80210) $6.50

Middle School in the Making
(611-74024) $5.00

The Middle School We Need
(611-75060) $2.50

Moving Toward Self-Directed Learning
(611-79166) $4.75

Multicultural Education: Commitments, Issues,
and Applications (611-77108) $7.00

Needs Assessment: A Focus for Curriculum
Development (611-75048) $4.00

Observational Methods in the Classroom
(611-17948) $3.50

Open Education: Critique and Assessment
(611-75054) $4.75

Partners: Parents and Schools
(611-79168) $4.75

Professional Supervision for Professional
Teachers (611-75046) $4.50

Reschooling Society: A Conceptual Model
(611-17950) $2.00

The School of the Future—NOW
(611-17920) $3.75

Schools Become Accountable: A PACT
Approach (611-74016) $3.50

The School's Role as Moral Authority
(611-77110) $4.50

Selecting Learning Experiences: Linking
Theory and Practice (611-78138) $4.75

Social Studies for the Evolving Individual
(611-17952) $3.00

Staff Development: Staff Liberation
(611-77106) $6.50

Supervision: Emerging Profession
(611-17796) $5.00

Supervision in a New Key (611-17926) $2.50

Urban Education: The City as a Living
Curriculum (611-80206) $6.50

What Are the Sources of the Curriculum?
(611-17522) $1.50

Vitalizing the High School (611-74026) $3.50

Developmental Characteristics of Children and
Youth (wall chart) (611-75058) $2.00

Discounts on quantity orders of same title to single address: 10-49 copies, 10%; 50 or more copies, 15%. Make checks or money orders payable to ASCD. Orders totaling $20.00 or less must be prepaid. Orders from institutions and businesses must be on official purchase order form. Shipping and handling charges will be added to billed purchase orders. *Please be sure to list the stock number of each publication, shown in parentheses.*

Subscription to *Educational Leadership*—$18.00 a year. ASCD Membership dues: Regular (subscription [$18] and yearbook)—$34.00 a year; Comprehensive (includes subscription [$18] and yearbook plus other books and booklets distributed during period of membership)—$44.00 a year.

Order from:

Association for Supervision and
Curriculum Development
225 North Washington Street
Alexandria, Virginia 22314

ARCHAEOLOGIST'S TOOLKIT

Series Editors: Larry J. Zimmerman and William Green

The Archaeologist's Toolkit is an integrated set of seven volumes designed to teach novice archaeologists and students the basics of doing archaeological fieldwork, analysis, and presentation. Students are led through the process of designing a study, doing survey work, excavating, properly working with artifacts and biological remains, curating their materials, and presenting findings to various audiences. The volumes—written by experienced field archaeologists—are full of practical advice, tips, case studies, and illustrations to help the reader. All of this is done with careful attention to promoting a conservation ethic and an understanding of the legal and practical environment of contemporary American cultural resource laws and regulations. The Toolkit is an essential resource for anyone working in the field and ideal for training archaeology students in classrooms and field schools.

Volume 1: *Archaeology by Design* CC83 .B58 2003
By Stephen L. Black and Kevin Jolly

Volume 2: *Archaeological Survey* CC76.3 .C65 2003
By James M. Collins and Brian Leigh Molyneaux

Volume 3: *Excavation* CC76 .C37 2003
By David L. Carmichael and Robert Lafferty

Volume 4: *Artifacts* CC75.7 .E97 2003
By Charles R. Ewen

Volume 5: *Archaeobiology* CC75.7 .S59 2003
By Kristin D. Sobolik

**Volume 6: *Curating Archaeological Collections:
From the Field to the Repository*** CC55 .S85 2003
By Lynne P. Sullivan and S. Terry Childs

Volume 7: *Presenting the Past* CC75.7 .Z56 2003
By Larry J. Zimmerman

ARCHAEOLOGICAL
SURVEY

DATE DUE

ARCHAEOLOGIST'S TOOLKIT

SERIES EDITORS: LARRY J. ZIMMERMAN AND WILLIAM GREEN

The Archaeologist's Toolkit is an integrated set of seven volumes designed to teach novice archaeologists and students the basics of doing archaeological fieldwork, analysis, and presentation. Students are led through the process of designing a study, doing survey work, excavating, properly working with artifacts and biological remains, curating their materials, and presenting findings to various audiences. The volumes—written by experienced field archaeologists—are full of practical advice, tips, case studies, and illustrations to help the reader. All of this is done with careful attention to promoting a conservation ethic and an understanding of the legal and practical environment of contemporary American cultural resource laws and regulations. The Toolkit is an essential resource for anyone working in the field and ideal for training archaeology students in classrooms and field schools.

Volume 1: *Archaeology by Design*
By Stephen L. Black and Kevin Jolly

Volume 2: *Archaeological Survey*
By James M. Collins and Brian Leigh Molyneaux

Volume 3: *Excavation*
By David L. Carmichael and Robert Lafferty

Volume 4: *Artifacts*
By Charles R. Ewen

Volume 5: *Archaeobiology*
By Kristin D. Sobolik

Volume 6: *Curating Archaeological Collections:*
      From the Field to the Repository
By Lynne P. Sullivan and S. Terry Childs

Volume 7: *Presenting the Past*
By Larry J. Zimmerman

ARCHAEOLOGICAL SURVEY

James M. Collins
Brian Leigh Molyneaux

ARCHAEOLOGIST'S TOOLKIT
VOLUME 2

ALTAMIRA
PRESS

A Division of Rowman & Littlefield Publishers, Inc.
Walnut Creek • Lanham • New York • Oxford

AltaMira Press
A Division of Rowman & Littlefield Publishers, Inc.
1630 North Main Street, #367
Walnut Creek, CA 94596
www.altamirapress.com

Rowman & Littlefield Publishers, Inc.
A Member of the Rowman & Littlefield Publishing Group
4501 Forbes Boulevard, Suite 200
Lanham, MD 20706

PO Box 317
Oxford
OX2 9RU, UK

British Library Cataloguing in Publication Information Available

Library of Congress Cataloging-in-Publication Data

Collins, James M.
  Archaeological survey / James M. Collins and Brian Leigh Molyneaux.
    p. cm. — (Archaeologist's toolkit ; v. 2)
  Includes bibliographical references and index.
  ISBN 0-7591-0398-4 (cloth : alk. paper)—ISBN 0-7591-0021-7 (pbk. :
alk. paper)
  1. Archaeological surveying. 2. Archaeological surveying—North
America. 3. North America—Antiquities. I. Molyneaux, Brian. II.
Title. III. Series.
CC76.3.C65 2003
930.1—dc21

2002154548

Printed in the United States of America

∞™ The paper used in this publication meets the minimum requirements of
American National Standard for Information Sciences—Permanence of Paper
for Printed Library Materials, ANSI/NISO Z39.48-1992.

CONTENTS

SERIES EDITORS' FOREWORD

The Archaeologist's Toolkit is a series of books on how to plan, design, carry out, and use the results of archaeological research. The series contains seven books written by acknowledged experts in their fields. Each book is a self-contained treatment of an important element of modern archaeology. Therefore, each book can stand alone as a reference work for archaeologists in public agencies, private firms, and museums, as well as a textbook and guidebook for classrooms and field settings. The books function even better as a set, because they are integrated through cross-references and complementary subject matter.

Archaeology is a rapidly growing field, one that is no longer the exclusive province of academia. Today, archaeology is a part of daily life in both the public and private sectors. Thousands of archaeologists apply their knowledge and skills every day to understand the human past. Recent explosive growth in archaeology has heightened the need for clear and succinct guidance on professional practice. Therefore, this series supplies ready reference to the latest information on methods and techniques—the tools of the trade that serve as handy guides for longtime practitioners and essential resources for archaeologists in training.

Archaeologists help solve modern problems: They find, assess, recover, preserve, and interpret the evidence of the human past in light of public interest and in the face of multiple land use and development interests. Most of North American archaeology is devoted to cultural resource management (CRM), so the Archaeologist's Toolkit focuses on practical approaches to solving real problems in CRM and public archaeology. The books contain numerous case studies from all parts of the continent, illustrating the range and diversity of applications. The series emphasizes the importance of such realistic considerations as budgeting, scheduling, and team coordination. In addition, accountability to the public as well as to the profession is a common theme throughout the series.

Volume 1, *Archaeology by Design,* stresses the importance of research design in all phases and at all scales of archaeology. It shows how and why you should develop, apply, and refine research designs. Whether you are surveying quarter-acre cell tower sites or excavating stratified villages with millions of artifacts, your work will be more productive, efficient, and useful if you pay close and continuous attention to your research design.

Volume 2, *Archaeological Survey,* recognizes that most fieldwork in North America is devoted to survey: finding and evaluating archaeological resources. It covers prefield and field strategies to help you maximize the effectiveness and efficiency of archaeological survey. It shows how to choose appropriate strategies and methods ranging from landowner negotiations, surface reconnaissance, and shovel testing to geophysical survey, aerial photography, and report writing.

Volume 3, *Excavation,* covers the fundamentals of dirt archaeology in diverse settings, while emphasizing the importance of ethics during the controlled recovery—and destruction—of the archaeological record. This book shows how to select and apply excavation methods appropriate to specific needs and circumstances and how to maximize useful results while minimizing loss of data.

Volume 4, *Artifacts,* provides students as well as experienced archaeologists with useful guidance on preparing and analyzing artifacts. Both prehistoric- and historic-era artifacts are covered in detail. The discussion and case studies range from processing and cataloging through classification, data manipulation, and specialized analyses of a wide range of artifact forms.

Volume 5, *Archaeobiology,* covers the analysis and interpretation of biological remains from archaeological sites. The book shows how to recover, sample, analyze, and interpret the plant and animal remains most frequently excavated from archaeological sites in North America. Case studies from CRM and other archaeological research illustrate strategies for effective and meaningful use of biological data.

Volume 6, *Curating Archaeological Collections,* addresses a crucial but often ignored aspect of archaeology: proper care of the specimens and records generated in the field and the lab. This book covers strategies for effective short- and long-term collections management. Case studies illustrate the do's and don'ts that you need to know to make the best use of existing collections and to make your own work useful for others.

Volume 7, *Presenting the Past,* covers another area that has not received sufficient attention: communication of archaeology to a variety of audiences. Different tools are needed to present archaeology to other archaeologists, to sponsoring agencies, and to the interested public. This book shows how to choose the approaches and methods to take when presenting technical and nontechnical information through various means to various audiences.

Each of these books and the series as a whole are designed to be equally useful to practicing archaeologists and to archaeology students. Practicing archaeologists in CRM firms, agencies, academia, and museums will find the books useful as reference tools and as brush-up guides on current concerns and approaches. Instructors and students in field schools, lab classes, and short courses of various types will find the series valuable because of each book's practical orientation to problem solving.

As the series editors, we have enjoyed bringing these books together and working with the authors. We thank all of the authors—Steve Black, Dave Carmichael, Terry Childs, Jim Collins, Charlie Ewen, Kevin Jolly, Robert Lafferty, Brian Molyneaux, Kris Sobolik, and Lynne Sullivan—for their hard work and patience. We also offer sincere thanks to Mitch Allen of AltaMira Press and a special acknowledgment to Brian Fagan.

Larry J. Zimmerman
William Green

ACKNOWLEDGMENTS

JAMES M. COLLINS

I would like to acknowledge the Foundation for Illinois Archaeology/ Northwestern University Archaeological Program (now known as the Center for American Archeology) in Kampsville, Illinois, for kindling the interest that became my career. The field training I received at Kampsville and the appreciation for good field practice instilled there have served me well for a quarter-century. In particular, I am indebted to Raymond W. Perkins for teaching me *almost* all I ever needed to know about archaeological survey.

Since coming to the University of Iowa, involvement with the Iowa Quaternary Studies Program has enhanced my understanding of the natural world and humankind's adaptations to it. Long associations with Rolfe Mandel, Art Bettis, and others have yielded many fruitful insights into Holocene landscape processes. A National Park Service workshop administered by Steve DeVore at Fort Laramie, Wyoming, concerning remote sensing and geophysical techniques for cultural resource management opened my eyes to the potential of noninvasive site survey.

During the past decade, the Office of the State Archaeologist, University of Iowa (OSA), has nurtured my research and nourished my professional development. The OSA has been at the forefront in the development of new survey methods and reporting standards in the Midwest. Many among my cohort at the OSA have generously shared knowledge, information, and skills while I worked on this book. Michele Punke is especially thanked for volunteering her graphic and editorial skills to the production of this volume. Bill Green has been extremely supportive throughout my tenure at the OSA.

Finally, and most importantly, I would like to acknowledge the support of my family, Susan, Kathleen, and Virginia, and my parents, William and Eleanor Collins.

BRIAN LEIGH MOLYNEAUX

Survey archaeology can sometimes provide wonderful silence and a deep respite from the labors of the working world. At times of repose—rare in the turmoil of a deadline-driven CRM project—I sometimes think back to people who helped me along the way: Hamilton Lang, an ornithologist and antiquarian living near Comox, on Vancouver Island, British Columbia, who let a young kid dig holes in his back yard, searching for lost treasure; Selwyn Dewdney, of London, Ontario, who took a raw undergraduate north into the Canadian Shield to look for rock art in the early 1970s; Dr. Joan Vastokas (Trent University) and Professor Peter J. Ucko (Southampton University), supervisors of my graduate theses, who hammered me into a semblance of professional form; Larry Zimmerman and Lawrence Bradley, who gave me a job and let me loose; and many fellow archaeological travelers in Canada, the United States, England, Africa, and South America. I think especially of close friends who have shared the hard work and thrill of discovery.

Most of all, in those distant, mysterious worlds archaeologists inhabit, I think of my mother, my late father, and my own family, Wendy, Freddy, Alex, and Lily. They have gotten me through narrow escapes in the field and kept me going along my chosen path.

1

THE SURVEY LIFE

There is nothing like the vast, empty expanse of a field at the beginning of a survey. Whatever else archaeology is, it begins with
the land. In our search for the human past, we may walk along plowed
fields that were once tundra, pleasant inland ridges that were once the
shorelines of ancient glacial lakes, or grasslands that ten thousand
years ago teemed with giant Ice Age bison. Our quest is for the material remnants of other lives, other times, the evidence that begins the
process of bringing the past into the present. This book gives you the
tools you need for your own journey in archaeology.

A big part of archaeological life is the search for stone tools, ceramics, and other artifacts, but we are not treasure hunters. We are
trying to figure out the lifeways of the cultures who lived on this land
before us. Who were they? Where did they come from? How long did
they live here? How did they get food, make shelter, and pursue their
daily lives? To learn these things, we have to see artifacts as part of a
larger landscape, the natural environment, that supports all living
things. This is because our real goal in studying the scattered remains
of the past is to understand better the mysteries of human origins and
the development of society into what we have today.

So surveyors do not walk a patch of ground aimlessly. Before we set
out, we find out about its natural and cultural history, including its
weather, vegetation, and animal life, and what is already known about
human occupation in the area. After we get back, we take all the information we find—artifacts, photographs, field sketches, and site maps—
and develop a basic picture of life there in the past. This collection of
material and maps is essential information for archaeologists to plan

formal excavations, and our mapping of the prehistoric landscape helps people and agencies plan to protect archaeological sites from damage or destruction by land development.

We do not operate in a social vacuum. Land and people are intertwined, so archaeologists are always on someone else's land and in someone else's community. Landowners, private and public, allow us to survey, and we have to follow their rules and regulations. We must also respect the ideas and attitudes of these communities about the past. For some, archaeology is a window into a wonderful, mysterious world; for others, it is a dangerous threat to the peace of their ancestors. Surveyors not only walk the land but also navigate through the political and social issues of our times. The most difficult relationship, however, is with those people we cannot see—those whose remains we seek. Archaeologists see and use the landscape differently than the people we study. Seeing the world through different eyes, we must be very careful not to put ourselves in their place, to imagine that our way of doing things was their way of doing them. This is the real challenge of a survey, to be able to visualize environments and ways of life that no longer exist, so that we look in the right places for the right things.

In the following pages, we discuss how today's survey life developed through changes in archaeological theory and technology over time. In subsequent chapters, we discuss how to set up and conduct a survey, from creating an initial survey strategy, doing the necessary background research, and readying equipment, to walking the land, conducting subsurface tests and geophysical surveys, to mapping and preparing for the final analysis and interpretation of results.

ORIGINS: SPECULATION TO SURVEY

Modern archaeological survey gets its vision from its own past. This history is one of changes in our perception of the past and what we think is important to know and record.

Imagine what it must have been like when the very first peoples walked into what is now the Americas. The continent had no still-warm campfires, or cast-off tools, or abandoned shelters—no human history. In time, though, human groups began to leave their marks, and other people followed them, taking the same paths and living in the same places. For instance, the town of Vermillion, South Dakota, on the edge of the Missouri River Valley, has been occupied for at least nine thousand years! After European immigrants came, subjugating Native Americans and forcing them into the more remote parts of the West, the rhythm of life changed, and what had been a familiar past was now a mystery.

The roots of survey lie in one of the greatest archaeological mysteries, the origin of the Moundbuilders. Eighteenth-century scholars, sitting in their studies in Washington and Philadelphia, London and Paris, or gathered at learned society meetings, conjured up wild theories about the origin of the Indians. Were they descendants of a second Adam, or one of the Lost Tribes of Israel, or the remnants of the fierce Scythians or Tatars of Asia? These antiquarians were even more fired up by reports from the Ohio and Mississippi Valley of massive earthworks—some burial mounds, others like temples, still others in the shapes of animals. They did not believe that the nomadic hunting and gathering people or villagers occupying these regions at the time of contact could have built them. The Great Serpent Mound in Ohio, for example, was 1,330 feet long, containing approximately 311,000 cubic feet of earth. These mounds had to be the remnants of an ancient civilization, some lost race of the same stock that had produced the most ancient cities of the Old World. It was a rather convenient fiction. Not only did it establish an Old World people as a founding race in the New World, but it justified the genocide of Indians for their destruction of this ancient civilization. Moundbuilders quickly joined giants, Phoenicians, Egyptians, Irish monks, Danes, Welsh princes, and others in popular and scholarly imaginations as original inhabitants of North America.

While these debates raged in the cities, military exploring parties, including scientists and land surveyors, were busy exploring the newly conquered territories and beginning to make systematic collections and inventories of what they found. As they started with a blank slate, the first requirement was to find out what really was there, rather than relying on hearsay. Of course, because the new nation was bent on eliminating the Indians, they were not consulted. In 1787–1788, when General Rufus Putnam established the townsite of Marietta, Ohio, he surveyed the region and found hundreds of mounds, which he mapped and briefly described. It was not until the 1840s, however, that the mounds became objects of a systematic survey. Fascinated by the Moundbuilders, Ephraim G. Squier, a newspaper editor, and Edward H. Davis, a physician, visited hundreds of earthworks, dug into over two hundred, and reported their results in the first publication of the Smithsonian Institution. Although they remained convinced that the Moundbuilders were not Indians, their great work, *Ancient Monuments of the Mississippi Valley* (1848), was a truly archaeological investigation. Rather than plundering a few mounds for their contents, they recorded as many as they could in the hopes of seeing patterns of construction and use. These remain important goals in archaeological survey today.

With the triumph of scientific evolutionism after Darwin, scientific studies based on description and classification replaced the antiquarian delight in mystery. In 1881, the Smithsonian established a Division of Mound Exploration to sort out the Moundbuilder problem and, in 1882, appointed an entomologist, Cyrus Thomas, to conduct the work. There was considerable urgency to this effort. Collectors were rampant, encouraged by a growing market in antiquities. In the spirit of Squier and Davis, Thomas surveyed over two thousand earthworks. In his *Report on the Mound Explorations of the Bureau of American Ethnology* (Thomas 1894), he showed that the mounds contained types of material culture similar to those in the more modest sites attributed to Indians. We know now that most Moundbuilders were Woodland (ca. 800 B.C.–A.D. 1000) and Mississippian (ca. A.D. 1000–1600) Indians. The Moundbuilders took their proper place in mythology. By using the evidence in the ground and understanding that people occupy regions rather than isolated places, Thomas set the standard for the archaeological surveys to come.

Archaeologists were not especially interested in chronology then, as they were in Europe. Swayed by political realities, American archaeologists generally believed that the Indians had simply remained in the Stone Age. The most urgent need was to sort through an ever-growing inventory of cultural material from all parts of the continent.

Over the next two decades, archaeologists discovered that prehistoric cultures were much more diverse than they had first thought. Cyrus Thomas divided North America into three major cultural zones: Arctic, Atlantic, and Pacific. Barely fifteen years and many artifacts later, William Henry Holmes was able to divide it into twenty-six cultural areas. While theorists continued to rearrange cultures on the North American maps, field archaeologists could not ignore the layers of occupations they found in excavations or the differences in stone tools and pottery through time. When Franz Boas argued that prehistoric cultures were really accumulations of cultural traits diffused across time and space, the continent-wide cultural maps seemed empty and pointless. Archaeologists had to study the growth and spread of individual cultural groups, and they could do this only by surveying the regions in which they developed. Alfred Kidder produced the first major regional study in 1924, a survey of nine river drainages in the Southwest. Combining geographic location and chronology, he suggested that there were four periods of cultural development, from the ancient Basket Maker people to the Pueblos of today. From these beginnings, archaeologists began to think of people, through their artifacts, as localized in time and space. The goal was no longer simply the collection of artifacts but collection in specific geographic regions.

Right after World War I, British geographer and pilot O. G. S. Crawford discovered that aerial photographs not only provided a bird's eye view of the terrain but also revealed archaeological features invisible at ground level. Infrared photography, introduced after World War II, increased this remote sensing capability. Archaeologists could now examine more territory than they could on foot and also create more accurate maps, using aerial photographs to verify spatial relationships.

Subsequent developments in survey included both the technological, enhancing the ability to detect cultural material, and the theoretical, changing or refining what we are looking for. During the late 1930s, archaeologists in North America and Europe began to realize that it was the interaction of culture and environment, not the diffusion of ideas and inventions, that gave prehistoric cultures so many common features. Julian Steward applied this new concern for function in a study of the relationship between humans and ecology in the Southwest, and the English archaeologist Grahame Clark did the same in a synthesis of European prehistory. With the development of radiocarbon dating in the late 1940s, archaeologists could date sites more confidently and develop more precise and reliable regional chronologies, giving them better understandings of settlement sequences. Drawing on these ideas, archaeologists such as Gordon Willey, working in the Virú Valley in Peru, broadened their surveys to include data on changes in subsistence, population density, and settlement patterns. Rather than working at the largest sites to extract the maximum data, the new goal of a survey was to identify networks of sites, each contributing to the function of the whole system. As environmental data were now important, archaeology required the work of the natural sciences. When Richard S. MacNeish surveyed the highlands of Mexico in the 1960s in search of the origins of agriculture, for example, his colleagues included botanists, zoologists, and geologists.

THEORY AND PRACTICE TODAY

The idea that culture functions as an adaptive system directed toward the material environment encouraged archaeologists to adopt more consciously scientific methods. In the 1950s, highly detailed excavations in Europe, such as Grahame Clark's study of the Mesolithic site at Starr Carr, England, showed it was possible to identify the seasonal activities of hunters and gatherers. This led to new interpretations of the nature of archaeological sites. In the 1960s, Lewis Binford challenged the archaeological establishment to go beyond artifact description and develop scientific theories of how and why cultures develop and change. This approach, dubbed the New Archaeology, emphasized cultural process. Sites were not accumulations of artifacts and features representing cultures but products of behavior that responded to laws governing the technical and economic aspects of cultural systems.

The assumption that such laws existed affected survey in two ways. First, it legitimized the analysis of the patterns of artifact production, use, and discard among modern hunting and gathering people as a means of understanding past behavior. Archaeological sites represented a variety of different behavioral processes, depending on the nature of the activity in various parts of the lived-in environment (e.g., temporary or longer-term habitation, and food and other resource processing). Second, it changed the nature of surveys. If laws regulated cultural behavior to maintain balance with the natural environment, then it was not necessary to gather all of the artifacts and other information available on a site to understand it. By applying a statistical sampling technique, the archaeologist could use a selection of data from a region or site to stand for the whole. This approach also demanded that archaeologists survey systematically, using a grid system, in place of the traditional intuitive method, in which archaeologists tended to survey what they considered the areas most likely to have the evidence they wanted. Although the idea of balanced systems is now outmoded, the random sampling technique persists in archaeology as a cost-effective, if often theoretically weak, means of getting what is hoped is a representative sample of the site or region.

Dissatisfaction with what some theorists complained was the programmatic and lifeless treatment of the human past began to develop in the 1970s, as part of a general attack on the objectivity of the social sciences. While these disciplines appeared rigorously scientific, they were, and are, naturally fraught with the subjectivism of their practitioners. English archaeologist Ian Hodder brought these criticisms into focus by emphasizing the role of the archaeologist as interpreter. A site was not simply a distribution of easily described and interpreted cultural material but a field of meaning, a "text" to be read, no less subject to the personal biases of the observer than any other phenomenon. The emphasis of this approach on ideas and symbols found much favor in Europe, if only because Old World prehistory covers tens of thousands of years of human culture and more than twenty thousand years in which sites yield evidence of cultural material devoted to ideology, from Paleolithic cave art to Neolithic stone monuments to complex city states. Quickly dubbed postprocessualism, this approach similarly concerned the role of societies and individuals in the formation of the archaeological record, but it rejected the assumption that natural forces were mainly responsible for controlling cultural behavior. Appealing to modern examples, as Binford had done, Hodder pointed out that material culture figures prominently in the construction of social identity and in the representation and control of power relationships. Hence, an archaeological site is a context of social activity, not simply a map of technoeconomic behavior and material formation processes. This approach has had less impact on field survey, in spite of its telling criticism. Although the processual and postprocessual approaches continue to provoke highly politicized theoretical debate, both remind survey archaeologists of the complexity of archaeological sites and the range of potential data.

Archaeology has always focused on the site as the basic unit of survey. A *site* is a place with some explicit evidence of cultural activity that an archaeologist encloses within a boundary. Things are either "inside" or "outside" sites. Drawing boundaries around activity areas makes sense in a world where all land is property, and it makes even more sense when land is managed and cultural resources must be explicitly defined and located, but it is also obvious that people occupy areas rather than places and that cultural material is actually distributed in varying densities over the entire landscape.

To rectify this problem, some archaeologists simply ignore the site concept. In its place, they record all traces of human activity in the landscape, not only the artifacts in the most intensively occupied places. While a comprehensive "nonsite" or "distributional" survey approaches the archaeological ideal, the realities of modern archaeology (cost, access to the land) make it impossible in most parts of the world. However, advances in survey equipment (electronic total stations), locational systems (Global Positioning Systems—GPS), computer mapping (Geographic Information Systems—GIS), and the speed and storage capacity of computer systems have made this type of survey more feasible. It is now possible to record the position of every artifact over a region, so that we can get an impression of human activity across landscapes rather than within sites. The very large scale and highly detailed imagery provided by remote sensing—from Landsat 7, RADARSAT, IKONOS and other satellites, the space shuttle, and high-altitude aircraft—enables vast regions to be explored in a single image and permits identification of environmental and cultural features invisible on the ground. Such technologies increase the range, density, and accuracy of information we can record and decrease the time it takes to record it.

In the end, however, the basic archaeological survey has not come much farther than when Squier and Davis tracked down their mounds. We still have to walk the land, ground-truth our expectations, and record what we find. The difference is that we have the technology to cover more ground and create maps of an accuracy unimaginable only a few years ago. Most important, we now know that the artifacts we find are only a small part of very complex human adaptations to the social and natural worlds around us.

2

THE LAW, THE PROCESS, AND THE PLAYERS

WHY SURVEY?

The vast majority of all archaeological survey undertaken in North America is mandated by the government. To be sure, surveys will always be conducted purely for research purposes, but unless you are one of the lucky few who actually land a faculty position, chances are your survey work will be conducted in accordance with federal and state or provincial regulations governing the identification and protection of cultural resources. The federal governments of the United States and Canada have laws related to heritage protection for federal lands. Federal control also extends to any project, whether private or public, local or national, that uses federal funds. All states and provinces have heritage protection laws and agencies established to manage cultural resources, as well as guidelines that control who can conduct archaeology and how they carry out their projects. Those aspiring to become cultural resource management (CRM) archaeologists should therefore familiarize themselves with the national and state or provincial laws in their region, as success in negotiating through the bureaucracy is the key to a successful archaeological project— whatever you may discover in a survey. Volume 1 in the Toolkit series addresses these issues in some detail as they apply to designing research; here, we discuss a few nuts and bolts of the CRM process as it affects archaeological survey.

REGULATIONS IN THE UNITED STATES

The federal process is governed by several laws and regulations. Government-mandated archaeology may be conducted under many auspices, including various state laws. However, most work derives from compliance with Section 106 and Section 110 of the National Historic Preservation Act of 1966 (PL 89-665), as amended. The rules that implement this law are published as 36 CFR Part 800, "Procedures for the Protection of Historic and Cultural Properties," issued by the Advisory Council on Historic Preservation. As used by these authorities, historic properties (often referred to as cultural resources) include historic and prehistoric sites, districts, buildings, structures, or objects that are potentially eligible for inclusion in the National Register of Historic Places (NRHP). Properties eligible for the National Register must have both integrity and significance.

Exactly what sites may be considered NRHP eligible? The NRHP criteria (36 CFR Part 60.4) state:

> The quality of significance in American history, architecture, archaeology, engineering, and culture is present in districts, sites, buildings, structures and objects that possess integrity of location, design, setting, materials, workmanship, feeling, and association *and*:
> a) that are associated with events that have made a significant contribution to the broad patterns of our history; or
> b) that are associated with the lives of persons significant in our past; or
> c) that embody the distinctive characteristics of a type, period, or method of construction, or that represent the work of a master, or that possess high artistic values, or that represent a significant and distinguishable entity whose components may lack individual distinction; or
> d) that have yielded or may be likely to yield information important in prehistory or history.

Implications of these criteria as they pertain to archaeological survey are addressed more fully in chapters 3 and 5.

Section 106 of the National Historic Preservation Act mandates that federal agencies take into account the effects of their actions on properties listed in, or eligible for listing in, the NRHP. Federal undertakings that often trigger archaeology under Section 106 include construction and other land-altering projects. Section 110 requires federal agencies to locate and protect cultural resources on lands that they own.

Depending on the type and scope of the federal undertaking, provisions of the National Environmental Policy Act (NEPA) may require consideration of historic properties in the environmental impact statement process, especially in large-scale projects that will have a significant impact on the environment, such as highways and reservoirs. The Native American Graves Protection and Repatriation Act (NAGPRA) provides added protection to Native American graves and associated cultural items located on federal and tribal lands. Many individual states and municipalities have also codified protection of historic properties, complementing the federal mandates. Most cultural resource management projects, however, fall under the auspices of Section 106 of the National Historic Preservation Act.

The Section 106 process is intended to identify any historic properties that may be affected by an undertaking and to determine how to minimize adverse impacts to such properties. The insightful review of the Section 106 process by Kathryn Gourley, former Iowa SHPO archaeologist (Gourley 1995), is freely adapted here. See King (1998, 2000) for more details.

Under Section 106, federal agencies must take into account the effect of their proposed undertakings on properties listed in or eligible for the NRHP. The Advisory Council on Historic Preservation has established procedures for compliance with Section 106, published as regulations (36 CFR Part 800). Agencies must allow the Advisory Council a reasonable opportunity to comment before proceeding with the project. The federal agencies are required to do this work before the expenditure of federal funds or the issuance of any licenses or permits.

Once a federal agency has identified that it has an undertaking, the agency must define the undertaking's area of potential effect (APE). The APE must include areas directly or indirectly impacted by the action. For example, the APE for a natural gas pipeline would include not only the actual pipeline trench but also the construction right-of-way, compressor stations, meter stations, staging areas, storage yards, access roads, and other ancillary facilities.

The agency needs to consider the full range of effects that might occur. For example, a construction project might cause vibration impacts to historical archaeological sites that contain structural remains. Or undertakings along in a river valley can impact the view from historic properties on adjacent bluff tops, affecting their historical integrity, so those properties could fall within the APE of the valley undertaking.

The APE is three-dimensional, so every project must include some consideration and assessment of local geomorphology. Years of research provide convincing evidence that certain landscapes have a high potential for containing buried archaeological sites. In others, there may be no potential for cultural resources—for instance, when appropriately aged sediments have been removed by natural or cultural processes. Understanding the landscape history of a project area is vital to understanding the area's archaeological potential.

Once an agency has defined an undertaking and its APE, it is ready to begin Section 106 compliance. The regulations outline a five-step process: (1) identify and evaluate historic properties, (2) assess effects, (3) enter into consultation, (4) allow the Advisory Council to comment, and (5) proceed with the undertaking.

In step 1, the regulations require that the federal agency "make a reasonable and good faith effort to identify historic properties that may be affected by the undertaking and gather sufficient information to evaluate the eligibility of these properties for the National Register." The regulations also specify that "efforts to identify historic properties should follow the Secretary's Standards and Guidelines for Archeology and Historic Preservation" (36 CFR Part 800.4a[2]). As part of the agency's initial identification effort, the agency must seek the views of the State Historic Preservation Office (SHPO) and other interested parties.

The usual procedure is for the agency to begin with a "Phase I" survey. This survey is conducted to identify any cultural resources that exist within the proposed project area. While the majority of resources that surveys find are determined not to be significant, Phase I surveys often identify sites that are potentially eligible for the National Register. Such findings necessitate further study, often dubbed "Phase II" testing, which involves detailed research to determine the significance and integrity of the site(s) in question. If the Phase II testing results in a determination of National Register eligibility for a given property, then the project moves to step 2.

Step 2 involves determination of whether the project will have an effect on the NRHP-eligible historic properties. An effect occurs when "the undertaking may alter characteristics of the property that may qualify the property for inclusion in the National Register." If an effect is found, then the agency and the SHPO consult to determine whether the effect is adverse.

If there is an adverse effect, then the agency and the SHPO consider ways to minimize the impact of the project on the historic property. This constitutes step 3. One way of minimizing the impact is to redesign the project to avoid the historic property. If that is not possible, another way may be to excavate the site. Other alternatives might also be possible.

Once the federal agency and the SHPO have consulted, the project moves to step 4: providing the Advisory Council an opportunity to comment on the undertaking. Once the council's comments have been taken into account, the project moves to step 5 and proceeds.

The sponsoring federal agency is legally required to see that the Section 106 process is completed. If the agency does not fulfill its responsibilities, then any citizen or organization can pursue legal action to make the agency fulfill the requirements.

REGULATIONS IN CANADA

The Department of Canadian Heritage is responsible for policies and programs relating to culture, including archaeology. It administers the Historic Sites and Monuments Act (1952–1953) through the Historic Sites and Monuments Board, whose mission is to "receive and consider recommendations respecting the marking or commemoration of historic places, the establishment of historic museums and the administration, preservation and maintenance of historic places and historic museums." Among Canadian Heritage's many initiatives is the "Access to Archaeology Program," which provides financial assistance to train aboriginal people in archaeological resource protection and to promote awareness of Canada's archaeological heritage.

The provincial, territorial, and federal governments share responsibility for culture. Beginning in the 1970s, provincial governments began to establish agencies responsible for the administration of cultural heritage. Because the provinces had various forms of jurisdiction over public and private property, they were able to pass and enforce legislation extending legal protection to designated properties or sites not owned by governments or subject to federal regulation. In Nova Scotia, for example, the relevant act is the Special Places Protection Act. One of its purposes is to provide for the preservation, protection, regulation, exploration, excavation, acquisition, and study of archaeological and historical remains and paleontological sites considered important parts of the natural or human heritage of the province. Archaeologists must obtain permits to conduct archaeological work, and that work is subject to guidelines established by the province. In British Columbia, the Archaeology Branch of the Ministry of Community, Aboriginal and

Women's Services administers the Heritage Conservation Act. The act, which distinguishes between nondesignated heritage sites and desig- nated provincial heritage sites, covers any land or water in the province that has "a heritage value to British Columbia, a community or an abo- riginal people." As in Nova Scotia and other provinces, it provides le- gal protection for designated sites and incorporates mechanisms for protecting nondesignated sites—places that may be nominated as a re- sult of historical, archaeological, or other heritage-related research. Typically, the Heritage Act deems it an offense to alter a heritage site; hence, the minister may order a heritage conservation inspection or heritage investigation of any property, subject to the rights of private ownership.

Significantly, First Nations communities may enter into agree- ments with the provincial government for the conservation and pro- tection of heritage sites and objects, including those of spiritual, ceremonial, or other cultural value.

WHO SURVEYS?

UNDERGRADUATES

If you are an undergraduate student, you are probably wondering, "How do I get a gig surveying for these cool National Register or cul- tural heritage sites?" Well, perhaps surprisingly, entry-level field technician positions are relatively easy to find. You simply have to be in the right place at the right time. Persistence doesn't hurt your chances at all. Archaeological consulting groups, private or other- wise, continuously hire entry-level staff on an as-needed basis, de- pending on how much work they are able to capture at any given time.

Cultural resource management, sometimes referred to as *applied archaeology* or, more bluntly, *contract archaeology*, now occupies a very competitive niche within the grand scheme of national com- merce and infrastructure development. Prior to 1975, "salvage ar- chaeology," as the field was then more or less appropriately known, was the almost exclusive and usually part-time bailiwick of univer- sity anthropology departments. With the enactment in the 1970s and 1980s of federal regulations governing historic preservation, there was a general upheaval in how and by whom CRM-based archaeology was conducted. Suddenly, there was too much work for academics to perform on a part-time basis. Many universities, museums, and historical societies developed full-time CRM-based programs, and private sector firms proliferated. The legal, political, and intellectual landscape of CRM and academic archaeology changed forever. (See Toolkit, volume 1, chapter 1, and Green and Doershuk 1998 for reviews of the current state of CRM as it relates to archaeology in the United States.)

Many of today's established professionals began their careers in entry-level positions during those heady, early days of modern CRM archaeology in the 1970s. At that time, if you exhibited competence, initiative, and responsibility, you could be quickly promoted from shovel bum to crew chief and then to site director or project director, provided you could maintain an affiliation with a principal investigator who trusted your work. Those days don't exist anymore. Today, if you are a young person aspiring to direct CRM-related projects, you are almost required to possess an advanced degree (M.A. or Ph.D.)— and you cannot become a registered professional archaeologist without one.

GRADUATES

If you are a graduate student, you are probably wondering, "How do I get a gig directing a survey for these cool National Register or cultural heritage sites?" Well, a good place to start is to understand what the minimal professional qualifications are for archaeological consultants as defined by government. In the United States, for example, the Secretary of the Interior's Standards (36 CFR Part 61) read as follows:

> The minimum professional qualifications in archeology are a graduate degree in archeology, anthropology, or a closely related field, plus: (1) at least one year full-time professional experience or equivalent specialized training in archeological research, administration, or management; (2) at least four months of supervised field and analytic experience in general North American archeology; and (3) demonstrated ability to carry research to completion.
>
> In addition to these minimum qualifications, a professional in prehistoric archeology shall have at least one year of full-time professional experience at a supervisory level in the study of archeological resources of the prehistoric period. A professional in historical archeology shall have at least one year of full-time professional experience at a supervisory

level in the study of archeological resources of the historic period. In this definition, a year of full-time professional experience need not consist of a continuous year of full-time work, but may be made up of discontinuous periods of full-time or part-time work adding up to the equivalent of a year of full-time experience.

Where do you get experience? Most archaeologists start with a field school and then get work with a CRM consulting outfit. Private firms, universities, museums, and historical societies do CRM consulting in every state and province. Most SHPOs maintain lists of these consultants. Also, look in indexes such as the *AAA Guide* (issued yearly by the American Anthropological Association) or the American Cultural Resources Association's directory (www.acra-crm.org). Positions are regularly advertised at professional archaeological meetings and on archaeology- and CRM-related websites. Useful places to start are www .archaeology.about.com and www.shovelbums.org.

Call the companies and institutions doing CRM in your area. Sooner or later, you'll get a job. The only way your career will take off from there is for you to exhibit competence, initiative, and responsibility. Those characteristics, *and the ability to write well* (see Toolkit, volume 7), remain in almost universal demand. Ordinarily they will be rewarded by your employer.

CRM CONSULTING

Let's assume that you have just finished graduate school and have accepted your first more or less permanent job with a company or institution doing CRM consulting. Consultants come in a variety of forms. Ordinarily, there will be a director or company president who is mainly responsible for getting contracts from various agencies. Depending on the size of the company or institution, there may be a few or several layers of managers between the director and you, the newly hired project archaeologist.

The CRM consultant fulfills a vital role in the governmental processes outlined earlier. Agencies responsible for identifying historic properties usually assign their responsibility to the local, state, or provincial agencies that will administer the project. Those entities may (rarely) perform necessary initial surveys using their own qualified personnel. Often, they assign the responsibility to the prime engineering contractor for the project, or they may hire your firm as their archaeological or cultural resource consultant. In the cases when the agency assigns compliance responsibility to its engineering contractors, those companies may have qualified in-house personnel, or they may subcontract the work to your CRM consulting firm.

Public agencies or districts within agencies sometimes enter into long-term agreements with individual CRM consultants to perform all compliance work for that agency or district. Just as frequently, agencies will put out a request for proposals (RFP) or a request for quotations (RFQ) inviting qualified consulting groups to bid on an individual project or a package of projects. The agency may select the lowest bid in terms of dollars, but this is not always the case. Many agencies have been burned over the years by selecting strictly on the basis of cost. Contracts often are awarded to the consultant with the highest level of expertise in a given project area, the best personnel and infrastructure, or the best track record for quality work and timeliness of product delivery. The agency can suffer in terms of project scheduling if the consultant it selects cannot provide a competent and timely product that assures the agency of compliance.

The consultant provides the agency with a service (e.g., a survey of a development tract) and a report of the findings of that service. The client (agency) forwards the consultant's product (the report) to the SHPO for review, constituting the beginning of step 3 of the Section 106 process. In practice, while it is the agency and the SHPO that are the main players in the Section 106 process, the consultant as representative of the agency also works with the SHPO to ensure that the work performed will be adequate for a positive compliance review. The reason for this is simply that you do not want to provide your client with a report that the SHPO will find inadequate.

Communication between the consultant, the client, and the SHPO, provincial, or regional archaeologist throughout the course of a project generally precludes nasty surprises at the report review stage. If you provide your client with a report of investigations that is found to be inadequate when reviewed by the state or provincial agency, you have jeopardized your client's project schedule, as well as your employer's future prospects to capture more contracts from that agency. Avoid that situation. Get to know the government archaeologists and what they want to see in terms of fieldwork and reporting standards. In that way you can serve your client's and your employer's best interests, and your own. (See Toolkit, volume 1, for details on the importance of communication with reviewers and sponsors.)

3

 SURVEY DESIGN

In an archaeological survey, you can never hope to find traces of all the cultural activity in a particular place. Surveyors walk in different ways and see different things. Ground visibility changes with vegetation and weather conditions. The ground may be featureless in the flat light of high noon or sharply etched in shadow as the sun rises or sets. Time is always against you. As soil accumulates or erodes with the seasons, it changes the amount of cultural material exposed on the surface. Even if you plan to walk every square meter of land, there will always be more to find. There is never a final survey.

Because the action of these variables and other subtle biases in survey technique affects the quality of the information retrieved in a survey, it is important to develop a research design and survey plan. After all, the results of your survey may determine whether a piece of undisturbed land is preserved or destroyed. The research design is your work plan for the survey, from background research to the writing of the report. To develop it you must know the area you are working in: its geological, topographical, environmental, cultural, and historical features; local and regional research trends and concerns; and previous archaeological research conducted in the project area and the surrounding region. From this background information, you can then estimate the data potential of the project area—whether it has a high, moderate, or low potential for archaeological sites. Of course, you never actually know what might lie beneath the ground surface, but by trying to estimate the potential of a land surface for archaeological sites, you must take into account the physical and cultural factors that generate human activity and consider those factors in the real world of your project area. (See Toolkit, volume 1, for details on developing a research design.)

The type of survey you do depends on whether you are conducting academic research or working under contract as part of a CRM team. Non-CRM surveys follow specific hypotheses to be tested or focus on limited types of information. You may want to conduct a comprehensive inventory, in which you attempt to identify all the cultural resources in the study area, or a problem-oriented survey, in which you search for a predefined set of cultural resources as part of research toward some specific analytical goals. For example, you may be interested only in rock art, Paleoindian environmental adaptations, or protohistoric site distributions rather than all the cultural resources of a landscape.

Problem orientation in a CRM project is a little different. The client, not the archaeologist, defines the study area. Conducting research limited in this way also requires a research design and demands creative thinking: Your interest in settlement patterns in a drainage basin is going to be difficult to accommodate when you have to work within a three-hundred-foot-wide corridor determined by construction needs. A limited survey, however, may yield some useful information if you think of your corridor as a sample of several specific environments such as floodplains, terraces, valley sides, blufftops, and uplands that may, for example, provide data on relative site density for the whole drainage basin.

Once you know what kinds of information you expect from the survey, you must decide how much area to cover. It may seem obvious that you need walk everywhere so that you do not miss any artifacts or sites. Such general reconnaissance surveys range from preliminary exploration, when you search intuitively, concentrating on likely spots, to total area surveys, covering 100 percent of the ground. The value of this approach is that you, the archaeologist, are walking in the same way as the people who walked there before, crossing similar terrain, perhaps through similar vegetation, with nothing between you and the ground—no survey theory or procedures to get in the way of what you seek. This directness of encounter and openness to the environment can help make you aware of qualities in the physical landscape that people in the past also sensed—viewshed (what you can see from a particular place), slope, exposure to sun and weather, and good places to work or camp.

But what do you do if the study area is hundreds of acres, and you have limited money, time, and personnel? Even if you can survey where you want, you may have to introduce your own constraints.

The solution is a systematic sampling survey. In this approach, you predetermine where to walk and how much ground to cover, either by establishing a grid and exploring a portion of the grid squares or by setting out transects (lines, at a set distance apart, along which surveyors will walk). Clearly, you are taking a risk here, as a significant portion of the land will go unsurveyed, so if you want to conduct this kind of survey, you will have to trust probability theory's claim that an appropriate sample will represent what you would come up with if you surveyed the entire area.

You may be somewhat suspicious of statistical claims, but this systematic method does eliminate some of the subjectivity in a survey by ensuring coverage across all areas, no matter how unpromising they look. Now it might seem like a waste of time to struggle up and down steep rocky slopes, crash though dense brush, or slog through wetlands, but biases in your technique might cause you to miss important information. For example, archaeology in the northern forests of Canada and Alaska has a strong seasonal bias: Fieldwork is possible only in the summer. Because the terrain is so rugged, with impenetrable bush and impassable muskeg bogs, surveyors tend to search along the same lakes and rivers that the native peoples inhabit. Yet, the native peoples live year-round in this environment, and their winter adaptation, settlements, hunting patterns, travel routes, and other activities may be quite different because the ground is frozen and travel overland is therefore easier. Each individual and cultural group sees the land and its potential differently. What seems uninviting to us may have been ideal in the past, when conditions and cultures were different.

When you plan a probabilistic survey, you must first divide the study area into nonarbitrary or arbitrary sample units. *Nonarbitrary units* are features with clearly defined natural boundaries, such as terrain types or ecological zones, or cultural ones, such as architectural features. *Arbitrary units* are squares (also called *quadrats*), grid intersections (fiducials or points, which become the center of a circular sampling unit), and transects. Since a simple random survey using an arbitrary method takes no account of ground-level conditions and hence cannot accommodate physical factors affecting distribution, you may want to divide the study area into natural zones and then apply the random sampling technique.

Then you have to decide on the sampling strategy. Generating random numbers to select the sample units to be surveyed is simple, but estimating the sample size is much more difficult. Ideally, the amount you survey should relate to the kind of information you expect to find. If you think you are dealing with a uniform scatter of similar sites or artifacts, you may be able to survey less to get a representative sample than you will if the density and types of sites or artifacts are variable. Unfortunately, what works well on paper may be impossible to achieve in the field because of cost. You may end up sampling much less than 10 percent of the total ground surface, with no confidence in the accuracy of this method.

A carefully planned sampling strategy, informed by background research that can help you define a set of expectations related to the nature, distribution, and density of cultural resources in the study area, might yield a good estimate of the average distribution of cultural material in the region. But you must remember, too, that there is only one Stonehenge. Not all data are susceptible to statistical analysis nor should they be. Your challenges are to determine whether the risk of a probabilistic survey is greater than the appearance it gives of scientific rigor and whether a probabilistic survey will satisfy both the agency's compliance needs and your research design.

The results of a survey are only as good as what you put into it. Finding everything you can on a plot of land may be valuable as an inventory for cultural resources management, but this information is useless unless it is part of a larger research plan.

4

 PREFIELD STRATEGIES

IMPLEMENTING THE RESEARCH DESIGN

Thousands of small-scale archaeological surveys are performed each year without an explicitly defined research design. However, most surveys that are competitively bid via an RFP require a formal research design as part of the bid proposal. Depending on the size and structure of your consulting group, you may or may not be involved in the bidding process or the development of the survey research design. If your boss (normally the principal investigator) assigns the project to you (the project archaeologist), it will be your responsibility to fulfill the particulars of the research design.

Local or regionally based CRM consultants may have an advantage in developing project research designs because they may already be familiar with the project landscape and the important anthropological and archaeological questions pertinent to the region. The expertise they already possess in the region allows for quick preparation of a proposal. Trouble often arises in the compliance process when firms with no established track record in a given state, province, or region land contracts in those areas. They lack understanding of the local geography, cultural-historical sequence, relevant research problems, and idiosyncrasies of local politics and bureaucracy.

Typically, the proposal for a survey project is a relatively simple document that is geared specifically to fulfill the requirements of the scope of work (SOW) provided in the client's RFP. The responsive proposal's research design must demonstrate (1) an understanding of data categories that can be anticipated in the project area; (2) familiarity with source materials pertaining to relevant research and general theory in the social and natural sciences and the humanities that may be pertinent to the region and the project area; and (3) knowledge of previous relevant research, especially research previously conducted in the immediate project area, as well as other research on topics germane to the purpose of the survey. The survey strategy must recognize the project area's data potential.

Research problem domains should be explicitly stated. The research design must outline the survey strategy—that is, how you will approach the project in terms of research-oriented field methods. The capabilities of your consulting institution or firm must be defined, so that the client is assured you have the capability and experience to perform the work. Key personnel must be identified (hopefully, that will include you), with vitae provided. Finally, the proposal and research design must address issues of schedule and budget.

THE TWO-HEADED MONSTER

Schedule and budget—time and money—is the two-headed monster that just became your constant companion. When you enter the workaday world of CRM, concerns related to that two-headed monster are never far away. Your mission as project archaeologist and leader of the survey team, should you choose to accept it, is to do the best anthropological research possible given the constraints imposed on you by this new friend. The balance of this book is devoted to providing you the wherewithal to do just that. You have just entered the real world. Your boss just dropped a folder on your desk and said, "Sink or swim."

What are the mechanics of archaeological survey in the real world? Ordinarily, the process begins when a client or sponsoring agency forwards a set of plans to the archaeological consultant or contractor. The project plans are what just landed on your desk. Depending on the size and design stage of the given project, these plans vary greatly in their detail. Sometimes they are not plans at all but rather sketches, or simply legal descriptions, and sometimes the proposed project area is shown on aerial photographs or maps of various scales. Occasionally, the plans are quite detailed, as in the case of CADD-generated project plans that show the exact location of most natural and cultural features (e.g., streams, tree lines, transportation right-of-ways, utility lines, houses, etc.) and their relationship to the survey area.

GETTING STARTED: MAP IT

As the archaeologist in charge of the survey, your first task is to re-view the plans you receive from your client and determine where the project is located. This review begins by consulting available state, provincial, or county transportation maps and the appropriate index of topographic quadrangles. U.S. Geological Survey (USGS) 7.5-minute, 1:24,000 scale, National Topographic Service of Canada (NTS) 1:50,000 scale, or provincial quads (e.g., in Ontario, 1:20,000 in the north and 1:10,000 in the south) are standard.

Once the appropriate topographic quadrangle or group of quadran-gles is identified from the index, the map(s) should be ordered from a convenient state, provincial, or local map repository. Visit edcwww.cr.usgs.gov/Webglis/catindex.html or http://cartes.nrcan.gc .ca/main.html to see what is available regarding map indexes, cata-logs, and vendor information. Depending on the project, it may be necessary to order multiple sets. You will probably want to keep at least one clean set. These you will use as base maps when you prepare your project report. You'll also need one or more additional sets that will be taken to the field by the project archaeologist, crew chief(s), and perhaps individual members of your crew.

Prior to fieldwork, you should transfer the information from the project plans onto the field copies of your USGS, NTS, or provincial topographic maps. Double-check this work for accuracy. Lacking very detailed project plans, the topographic map will be your only refer-ence to the landscape, your beacon in the wilderness. Develop your map-reading skills until you can read a map as well as the written word. Unless you do this, you may quite literally find yourself lost. Orienteering is now a major aspect of your work.

Large consulting firms and institutionally based archaeological con-sultants will often have in-house map libraries. For small survey proj-ects, you may be able to get by with photocopies of the appropriate topographic maps for field and cartographic purposes. For larger proj-ects, the benefit of actually having copies of the USGS, NTS, or provincial quadrangles for use in the field is almost always worth the cost of procurement. At the conclusion of your project, these maps and your narrative field records will represent your "memory" of the fieldwork. Your maps are likely the only constant during a survey project that will be on your person every time you step out of your ve-hicle, so cram as much information onto them as you can—site loca-tions, landowner names, the dates you acquired permission to access

property, phone numbers, local oral history, crop cover, and so forth.
If your map isn't dog-eared and scribbled all over at the conclusion of
fieldwork, you aren't using the resource to its full potential. Don't
worry, the USGS, NTS, and the provinces make quality products that
will stand up to months, even years, of rough use.

BACKGROUND RESEARCH

THE PHYSICAL SETTING

Once you have plotted your survey area on the appropriate quadrangle, regard the map carefully. Note the type(s) of terrain in the project area. Are you dealing with uplands, shorelines, floodplains, forest,
range land, agricultural fields, or urban areas? The answer will help
you choose your the survey strategy and techniques. Observe the location of fence lines and houses as they relate to your project area so
you can determine how the land is used and who possesses it. In most
cases, when you get to the field you'll need to contact these people for
permission to enter their property (more on that subject later).

Next, determine the area's regional and local geologic and physiographic record. Most states and provinces have studied, mapped, and
published pamphlets or books defining the geologic history and major
landform regions within their borders. Ordinarily, the archives or library at your company or institution will have these materials. Review
these documents to determine what bedrock geology and Quaternary
landscape features might be encountered and how they might affect the
character of the local archaeology. For instance, local bedrock outcrops
may contain chert, a magnetlike resource for prehistoric populations.
In the Northwest, tephra beds are often used as stratigraphic markers
in Quaternary landscapes. Carry this knowledge into the field.

The Quaternary record governs the types of surficial deposits and
often the vegetation you will encounter. For example, older, loess-
mantled drift plains often supported savanna prior to European settlement in many parts of the Midwest, whereas late Pleistocene
glacial drift often supported pothole terrain in which wetlands and
prairie predominated. Obviously, one would expect aboriginal use and
concomitant settlement patterns to have differed from one landform
region to the other.

Holocene environments have been extremely dynamic over the last
ten thousand years. Much of North America's Holocene environmen-

tal history is told in the climatic record. North American populations clearly responded to climatic fluctuations, just as our children and grandchildren will be forced to adapt if our colleagues are correct about global warming. Inferences about prehistoric responses to climatic and environmental change can be derived from settlement location data. Survey data are essential for such studies, but you must first understand the climatic record. Learn about regional paleoclimates from research papers by geologists and botanists.

Perhaps no portions of the Holocene landscape have had a more dynamic history than valley margins and floodplains. Colluvial aprons and alluvial fans, which develop at the base of valley walls, often bury or contain archaeological sites. By definition, the floodplain environment is constantly in flux. Episodes of stream incision and valley filling, often as a complex response to climate change, continually create and bury, and often destroy, habitable surfaces. Geomorphologists study these processes, and you should keep abreast of the latest geomorphological literature and landscape models. Review the pertinent regional geomorphological literature, as it relates to your project area, prior to fieldwork. Field trips organized by the Friends of the Pleistocene and other geology groups are great ways to obtain a hands-on understanding of earth-surface history and processes.

Holocene lithostratigraphic models can be used to predict where archaeological sites might be found on or buried within the modern landscape and the potential age of such sites. Because archaeological materials have primary context in the natural landscape, geologic processes forming the landscape determine the conditions of the archaeological record. Geomorphological information contributes essential data to determinations of significance regarding the age, preservation, and integrity of sites in colluvial and alluvial settings. Your survey strategy must account for these dynamic environments and the often-invisible (buried) surfaces they contain. If you don't understand geologic processes—and it is a sad fact that most graduate programs wouldn't have asked you to learn about them as a requirement for your M.A. in anthropology—it might be a good idea to consult with a geomorphologist familiar with your survey area before you go much further in your background preparations. Contact another archaeologist familiar with your survey area or the SHPO or provincial archaeologist to help you locate a competent consulting geomorphologist.

Once you get a handle on the general physiography of your study area, more specific information can be gleaned from the county soil

survey. In the United States, the Department of Agriculture, in cooperation with state agricultural experiment stations and other federal
and state agencies, has been making and publishing soil surveys since
1899. Agriculture Canada is responsible for soil surveys in Canada in
cooperation with provincial departments of agriculture. These surveys furnish soil maps and interpretations needed by farmers and
ranchers as well as planners and researchers. Uniform scientific and
technical standards are used in soil classification, nomenclature, interpretation, and publication.

Although the information in county soil surveys is generally accurate and undeniably useful, these publications were not made with
the archaeologist in mind. Their primary purpose is to assist evaluation of the land's agricultural potential. Until recently, soil surveyors
did not consistently note buried soils. Recent surveys, recognizing
the broader uses of the data, do a better job of identifying these hidden former surfaces, which is helpful to the archaeologist. In general,
if you come across a term such as *mixed alluvium* in the definition
of a floodplain soil series, be aware that buried surfaces might be present, and design your survey strategy accordingly.

Your firm may have a collection of county soil survey publications.
You can also get them from county USDA offices or provincial departments of agriculture or order them directly from federal, state, or
provincial publication outlets. For a list of available soil survey publications, ordering details, and other related information, explore
www.statlab.iastate.edu/soils/nsdaf/. The Canadian Soil Information
System (part of Agriculture Canada) provides paper and online GIS
map products relating to agriculturally significant soils. It may be
reached at res.agr.ca/cansis/.

Prior to fieldwork, many archaeological surveyors visit a university
map library to examine aerial photographs of their project area. Since
1936, USDA has been making aerial photographs of most of the country at intervals of about every six to eight years. Canada has a similar
aerial mapping program, with images dating back seventy years, and
these are available from the National Air Photo Library. These photographs often reveal startling changes in land use patterns that affect
the context of the archaeological sites you encounter. You can also
follow patterns of natural or human-induced vegetation change. Beyond that information, careful examination of aerial photos can
sometimes identify archaeological sites and individual features.
Many archaeologists have found palisade lines, rows of houses, and
even individual features within Mississippian sites, earthworks

within Woodland sites, fortifications on military sites, and stone fences delineating historical period fields or property lines on aerial photos prior to setting foot in the field. Air photos also serve as excellent base maps for marking sites, features, and finds. They often permit more accurate plotting of survey results than topographic maps do.

Many U.S. aerial photos can be picked up at USDA county offices and can be ordered at edcwww.cr.usgs.gov/products/aerial.html in printed or digitized formats. Terraserver, a commercial enterprise, provides worldwide air photo coverage through www.terraserver.com.

Despite their value, aerial photos remain an underutilized resource in support of archaeological survey. See Deuel (1969) for a comprehensive and highly readable discussion.

Ordinarily, a background review such as that outlined here will give you enough information about the physical setting of your project area to get you into the field. You should know about the age and character of the regional landscape; potential subsistence resources available to its inhabitants through time; and the most recent diachronic models regarding regional climate, vegetation, and geomorphology. Your review of local soils data will have given you an idea of what to expect when you get to the field and how you may want to sample the project area. Aerial photographs may help you identify specific targets to investigate when you get into the field.

THE CULTURAL SETTING

Just as you must know the important characteristics of the physical landscape, you must also know your project area's cultural background. This knowledge is best obtained through systematic review of archaeological planning documents, site records, and historical archives.

The fact that you have your job more or less implies that you are aware of the important CRM and archaeological research questions pertinent to the area where you will work. This assumption is often unfounded. You may be new to the state or region, or perhaps you simply lack experience. Never fear—a statewide or regional planning document or master plan probably exists, containing the accumulated wisdom regarding cultural resources and pertinent research directions. Although always incomplete and outdated, such documents help you place your survey work within the larger CRM and cultural historical picture. You should be able to get a copy of the documents used in your area from your SHPO or provincial archaeologist. Most planning documents are divided into sections that synthesize geographic and cultural historical data. Read sections pertinent to your study area prior to doing anything else.

Archaeological site records are managed differently from state to state, province to province. They might be housed at the SHPO, the state or provincial archaeologist's office, the state Department of Natural Resources or provincial ministry of culture, a university, or a state or provincial museum. Archaeologists learn how to deal with site records simply by dealing with site records. Your boss and colleagues should be able to tell you how it's done where you will be working.

You can delegate the records search to a competent staff member, but usually it is most useful for you to conduct the site records search yourself. Many states and provinces have procedures whereby site-records personnel can conduct the search for you, usually for a fee. Some files such as Arizona's are now searchable remotely via the web. Data on many Canadian sites are available through Artefacts Canada at daryl.chin.gc.ca/Artefacts/e_MasterLayout.cgi?db=3. However you obtain the data, you must learn about any recorded sites relevant to your project area. Copy any pertinent site records and maps, and plot the locations of any nearby sites on your project maps. Ordinarily, a repository of CRM reports ("gray literature") is housed at the same agency as the site records. Examine any literature (gray or otherwise) mentioned on the site forms or that may pertain to your study area. Such works can include published articles as well as previous CRM-generated survey and excavation reports. The National Archaeological Data Base is an online guide to many of the U.S. reports (www.cr.nps.gov/aad/TOOLS/Nadb.htm).

Also review historical records pertinent to your project area. Your state or provincial historical society is an invaluable resource, as are county or other local historical societies. Make friends with the people at these places. It is their business to help you find what you are looking for, and like almost all librarians and archivists, they often possess great knowledge about relevant materials and are normally very good at their job.

Examine all available regional atlases, plat maps, and rural directories. These resources provide a wealth of information about historical land use and sometimes the locations of Indian settlements, rural homesteads, farms, ranches, schools, churches, commercial enterprises, cemeteries, and even whole townsites that may be invisible save for their archaeological signatures. Plat maps and rural directories often contain useful information about demographic and economic trends and property ownership. Cross-check information from the atlases and other documents with any published county histories. The county histories usually will contain biographical information about early settlers and leading citizens. The historical and biographical information provided in the typical old-fashioned county history warrants a degree of skepticism because biographies were normally written for subscribers, and publishers were not in business to alienate patrons. Yet these publications are not without merit and can provide important information.

Other excellent sources of historical information are military maps from the colonial and territorial periods, and, in much of the United States, the notes and plat maps derived from the General Land Office (GLO) surveys. GLO records are often available on microfilm at state historical societies. According to the system inaugurated by the Ordinance of 1785 and permanently established by Congress in 1796, the General Survey of Public Lands physically determined the boundaries of congressional townships, which were then subdivided into thirty-six sections of land one mile square. Instructions to the GLO surveyors were explicit (sidebar 4.1). Notes of the field survey were to form a full and perfect history of operations in the field.

The typical GLO surveying party consisted of a surveyor, two chain carriers, an ax man, a flag man, a hunter, and a camp keeper. These crews left a remarkable record of the American frontier that is both useful and worthy of emulation by all modern surveyors, including those of us who survey for archaeological resources. Serendipitous discovery is often the dividend accrued from a thorough review of historical period records; overlook these resources at your own peril (figure 4.1).

You never know what you might learn by reviewing historical records. It is a great advantage to be aware of the presence of potential historic-era sites before going to the field. Actually finding evidence on the ground for significant sites that you identify through background research is even more rewarding. When you find archaeological evidence of, for example, a "deadstead" (the site of a former farmstead), in many cases you will already have an idea of its occupation span, owners or occupants, and when the place was razed.

The point is simply this: Based solely on preliminary historical research conducted prior to your CRM survey project, it is possible to

4.1. ENUMERATION OF GLO RESPONSIBILITIES

Congress commissioned GLO surveyors to enter in their field notes of the survey a particular description and the exact location of the following:

1. The length and variation or variations of every line you run
2. The name and diameter of all bearing trees, with the course and distance of the same from their respective corners
3. The name of the material from which you construct mounds, with the course and distance to the pits
4. The name, diameter, and exact distance to all those trees that your lines intersect
5. At what distance you enter, and at what distance you leave every river, creek, or other "bottom," prairie, swamp, marsh, grove or windfall, with the course of the same at both points of intersection
6. The surface, whether level, rolling, broken, or hilly
7. The soil, whether first-, second-, or third-rate.
8. The several kinds of timber and undergrowth, naming the timber in the order of its prevalence
9. All rivers, creeks, and smaller streams of water, with their actual or right-angled widths, course, banks, current, and bed, at the points where your lines cross
10. A description of all bottom lands—whether wet or dry, and if subject to inundation, state to what depth.
11. All springs of water, and whether fresh, saline, or mineral, with the course and width of the stream flowing from them
12. All lakes and ponds, describing their banks and the depth and quality of their water
13. All coal banks, precipes, caves, sink-holes, quarries, and ledges, with the character and quality of the same
14. All waterfalls and mill sites
15. All towns and villages, houses, cabins, fields and sugar camps, factories, furnaces, and other improvements
16. All metalliferous minerals or ores, and all diggings therefore, with particular descriptions of both, that may come to your knowledge, whether intersected by your lines or not
17. All roads and trails, with the courses they bear
18. All offsets or calculations by which you obtain the length of such parts of your lines as cannot be measured with the chain
19. The precise course and distance of all witness corners from the true corners that they represent

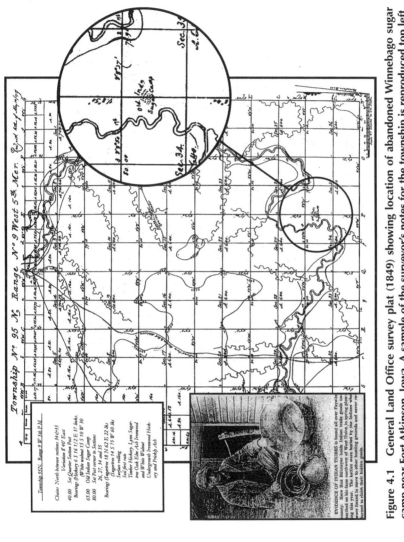

Figure 4.1   General Land Office survey plat (1849) showing location of abandoned Winnebago sugar camp near Fort Atkinson, Iowa. A sample of the surveyor's notes for the township is reproduced top left. Landowner interviews and further background research yielded the newspaper photograph reproduced bottom left. The kettles shown were found at the sugar camp site in 1949.

"discover" sites that may hold great research potential. You might also be able to predetermine that some sites are clearly not eligible for the National Register or for nomination as national or provincial heritage sites because of their age or other reasons, saving some steps in field evaluation. Do your homework before you go to the field. It is really amazing how often it pays off in a useful or effort-saving way.

5

GETTING INTO THE FIELD

Now that you are familiar with the physical, cultural, and historical background of your project area, it is time to contemplate the logistics of fieldwork. As project supervisor, you are responsible for the overall project, which includes the day-to-day, even minute-to-minute, work of every member of your survey party. Among your primary concerns will be how you manage the sometimes mundane details of transportation, equipment, property access, lodging, and meals while in the field. Your skill in managing logistical concerns and project personnel usually determines the project's fiscal success or failure. Success is measured by your ability to bring the project to a professionally competent conclusion, on time and within budget. Failure is easily quantified by missed deadlines and cost overruns.

As you begin your career, you may have little or no experience at managing anything beyond the details of your own life, but when you become the leader of a survey party, your responsibilities increase exponentially according to the number of persons on your crew. You must think not only about what tasks you will perform during the course of a project but also about the tasks every member of your crew will perform. It is generally your responsibility to keep track of their hours, get them their per diem money and paychecks, find them a place to live, provide transportation to and from the project area, and keep them productive during working hours. Depending on the initiative and character of your crew, your responsibilities may extend to deciding where they'll eat their meals, waking them up in the morning, or bailing them out of jail. Delegate responsibility whenever you reasonably can, but always remember that it's your project, and ultimately you are responsible for it.

PERSONNEL

There is only one hard and fast rule for filling crew positions: Hire intelligence and experience, in that order. From a list of experienced persons, always pick the smartest (we assume them to be physically fit if they aspire to be field archaeologists). It is easy to train an intelligent person to do archaeological survey; others are more difficult. An intelligent crew will almost always serve you better than one that is merely experienced. Experience is a generally useful secondary screen, but most really good, experienced field personnel are already employed. Unless you are very lucky and happen to catch some experienced field hands between other projects, most often you will be hiring students or people who were recently students. Select for brains and endurance rather than brawn. The benefits of this selection process are at least fourfold: You can delegate more tasks with the expectation they will be performed as you want them to be, you can influence the careers of some people who might be rising stars, it is far less likely that you will be completely sick of your crew after two weeks in the field, and you might learn something from these bright young people.

A second consideration regarding personnel is crew size. Your crew should include the absolute fewest persons necessary. Smaller crews are invariably more efficient than larger crews. If you can handle the project yourself, by all means do so, although safety considerations sometimes warrant traveling with a sidekick. Two people, you and your sidekick, can handle many projects very efficiently. Unless you've gotten yourself into a hole in terms of time, or if you have a very large or particularly labor intensive survey (e.g., shovel testing through thousands of acres of timber), we can't imagine why you would want a crew larger than five persons, including yourself. Larger groups tend toward cliquishness and other forms of interpersonal dementia; smaller groups promote camaraderie and a positive work ethic. Managing fewer people will be a blessing to you throughout your project, and the resulting efficiency will be manifest in both your bottom line and peace of mind.

The fact that you have now become a manager should not be construed as a license to be an ass. Respect every member of your crew as an individual, and don't play favorites. Let their abilities sort out the pecking order of responsibilities. Just as the individuals on GLO survey crews had specific duties, you should assign specific duties according to each individual's strengths. Yes, everyone will be performing the same tasks a lot of the time—everyone digs and screens, but some individuals will show a higher aptitude for, say, organization. Put that individual in charge of checking bags and paperwork at the end of the day and making sure that things are stored or filed appropriately. Some people will be really good at mapping, photographing, or describing soil profiles. At the end of the day, some people may simply be best suited for repairing, cleaning up, or packing away the equipment. It all has to be done, so make use of the talents individuals possess.

Make clear what you expect from each person. If you yourself are organized, you can also insist that your crew be disciplined in terms of the daily organizational details that you establish. Pretty soon, a comfortable and efficient routine is established for break-out and pack-up chores, lunch, and so on, and there won't be a lot of the goofing off and butt scratching so typical of many poorly managed crews. People will know where to find what they need when they need it, because your supplies and equipment are organized. Supplies and equipment are organized because you have delegated that responsibility to people who have the talent to make it so.

Assess your crew members' strengths and delegate assignments accordingly. You don't have to be a jerk to achieve organizational discipline, but you do have to make clear how you want things done. Establish a workable routine immediately, and stick to it or modify it as necessity dictates. Treat everyone with due respect, and usually you will have a happy, productive crew.

How do you find crew members? One of the best ways is to post a flier at the anthropology department of a nearby college or university or at professional meetings. Your best prospects will be among those people who are finishing their undergraduate degree and want to take a break from school before going on to graduate work. These people are generally smart, eager to work, adventurous, willing to learn field methods, adaptable, have the requisite interest, and are fun to be around.

You can also post employment notices online with archaeological e-mail disscussion groups such as HistArch, Arch-L, and ACRA-L or with the website www.shovelbums.org. This is kind of a grab-bag approach, so screen applicants carefully. Ask for résumés and references. There's not a thing wrong with hiring professional shovel bums—the more the better—unless they are grumpy, jaded, and too set in their ways to take direction.

More than one archaeologist has filled out a crew by walking into a local watering hole and offering patrons the alluring prospect of travel, per diem, a few steady paychecks, and the romantic notion of archaeology. You take your chances here (recall the earlier reference to posting bail), but sometimes it works out.

EQUIPMENT

Always use the best equipment at hand or that you can talk your boss into buying. If you can score a total station, a GPS unit, a laser range finder, a set of VHF five-watt two-way radios, a quality metal detector, and a power winch for your vehicle, go for it. Fluxgate Gradiomter? More power to you!

If you know how to use the instruments, technology will serve you well and usually save you time. Unfortunately, over the years we've seen an awful lot of people pretend expertise with certain instruments only to end up wasting time and effort and in a few cases actually ruining their high-end equipment and their budget.

You're an archaeologist. How do you acquire expertise with technical equipment more commonly associated with engineering and the geophysical sciences? Some field schools offer advanced instruction in the technical tools of the trade. Also, because your employer will have a vested interest in your competency, he or she may sponsor in-house workshops or send you to a course on the use of the high-end field equipment. The U.S. National Park Service sponsors workshops in remote sensing and geophysical techniques for CRM. These intensive, hands-on courses are highly recommended. Also, you may be able to find a mentor who is willing to tutor you. If you're still in school, it might be a good idea for you to go over to engineering, geology, or physics and burn some elective credits. Or, sometimes, as when you require the services of a consulting geomorphologist, you'll just want to subcontract the work.

Your company's technical expertise and the sophistication of its equipment may determine the size and nature of the contracts it can secure. And the size and nature of your project usually determine the level of sophistication required of your equipment. While it is generally true that archaeological survey is trending toward high-tech field methods, fieldwork for most projects still can be adequately completed without the frills.

Regardless of your budget, almost everything you need for fieldwork can be ordered from Forestry Suppliers, Inc. (www.Forestry-Suppliers.com) or Ben Meadows Company (www.benmeadows.com). Sign on to their mailing lists the day you begin your career. Outfitters, hardware stores, farm suppliers, and lumber yards are also good sources for field equipment (sidebar 5.1).

We don't belabor every piece of field equipment you might need or find useful, but here are a few tips concerning your field notebook. Having experimented with dozens of types and styles of field books over the past quarter-century, it is our humble opinion that the "Rite in the Rain" All-Weather FIELD Spiral Notebook, Model No. 353 (www.riteintherain.com), is the best all-around notebook you can carry. You can do your own experimentation; some people prefer a book with a bound spine. Whatever field book you decide on, go ahead and doctor it up to suit your individual needs. Tape your logistics checklist onto the inside front cover for easy reference (see Toolkit, volume 1, chapter 6). Tape copies of table 1 (types and classes of soil structure) and appendix 4 (New Designations for Soil Horizons and Layers) from the *Glossary of Soil Science Terms* (Soil Science Society of America 1987:25, 42) into the back of the notebook (carry a copy of the complete glossary in your portable field file; it can be ordered from the Soil Science Society of America, 677 South Segoe Road, Madison, Wisconsin 53711; www.soils.org/). You may want to carry the Munsell charts you use most often in your notebook for quick reference. Rig up a place (e.g., a tape and paper holster) to keep a small ruler; you get the idea. Always tape your business card in the front. If you lose your notebook, heaven forbid, at least there will be a chance that someone will find it and return it to you. But *don't lose your notebook!*

As project archaeologist, organization will be your key to a simpler life. Your vehicle will be your office and command center. In it you'll keep your plans, maps, notebooks, plat books, soil survey publications, any necessary reference literature, personnel and excavation forms, photo log, copies of your project SOW and contract, computer, phone, cameras, instruments, and the myriad other necessities of working on the road. Acquire a tough portable file box, a good camera bag, a functional and durable briefcase, and something to protect your computer and other instruments. Devise a system to maintain an orderly space within this mobile office. Try to secure everything so that

5.1. BASIC EQUIPMENT FOR A CREW OF FOUR

Item	Quantity
10×12×18–inch metal toolbox	1
3-meter tapes	4
30- or 50-meter tapes	2
Trowels	4
Pipe wrenches	2
Line levels	4
Hammer	1
Mallet	1
Hatchet	1
Flathead screwdriver	1
Phillips-head screwdriver	1
Pliers	1
Channel-lock pliers	1
$\frac{7}{16}$-inch box/open-end wrench	1
Root-cutter	1
Bastard file	1
Plumb bob	1
Wire brush	1
Whisk broom	1
Small paintbrush	1
Dental picks	2
Screening blocks	2
Roll of string	1
Hub stakes	4
Chaining pins	20
Roll of flagging tape	1
Sharpies (indelible markers)	4+

items such as your thirty-pound file box don't become deadly projectiles in the event of an accident. Impress upon your crew that unsecured shovels and other equipment can be pretty dangerous in the event of a rollover or collision. They may scoff, but we've seen people scalped. You're on the road—accidents happen.

On small projects, your command car will double as the general field vehicle. In that case, you'll also have to store your field equipment on board. For larger, longer-duration projects, it is almost always a good idea to reserve your command car for mobile office duty, and keep the field equipment in the other field vehicle(s). Just as your

Item	Quantity
Pencils	8
Shaker screens	2–4
Shaker screen bolt and wing-nut replacements	5
Vial of wood screws	1
Vial of nails	1
Vial of survey tacks	1
Plastic vials	4
Roll of aluminum foil	1
Assorted sizes of zip-top bags	Discretionary
Assorted sizes of paper bags and storage container	Discretionary
Oakfield soil-probe	1
Tile probe	1
Scissors-type posthole digger	2–4
Seymour bucket-augers	2–4
Bucket auger extensions	3–6
Machete	1
Standard shovels	4
Short-handled, square shovels	2
Sturdy boxes for artifact storage	2
Clipboards	4
Five-gallon plastic buckets	1–4 (optional)
Munsell soil color chart book	1–2
Tobacco and/or other votive items*	small quantity

*Native groups may request that a small offering of tobacco and/or other votive material be made when archaeologists encounter mounds or cemeteries.

permanent office is normally separate from your laboratory, it is often sufficiently important to keep the details of project administration segregated from the hubbub of general field operations, equipment management, and so forth. Don't confuse this as merely a status issue—keeping administrative materials segregated from tools and constant human traffic is really a practical logistic strategy, although in practice it does afford you a certain modicum of privacy that your crew might not share. On the other hand, it also affords them ample opportunity to critique your performance—which they will do in any case.

LOCAL RELATIONS

Doing archaeological survey requires you to place a premium on public relations. No matter how much you might wish to remain an industrious, nose-to-the-grindstone archaeologist, project public relations are now your very real concern. On small, short-duration projects, you have a chance to remain relatively anonymous out there. However, it is impossible to bring a crew of archaeologists into the field, stay for any period of time, and not be highly scrutinized by the local populace. Simply put, you will be a topic of local conversation. Try to make the best of it. Remember, if you are doing CRM archaeology, those citizens are at least indirectly paying the tab. Whether you like it or not, you have a responsibility to be an ambassador for your discipline. You'll have many opportunities.

No matter the size of your project, you'll have to make certain local contacts prior to getting started. If you'll be working on private land, you must secure permission from the landowners to survey and dig holes on their property. Nothing ruins an archaeologist's day faster than being run out of a field by an irate landowner. If you're working on public or tribal lands, there will be permitting issues, and you'll need to make contact with the appropriate agency or tribal office even after you have obtained your permit.

For larger projects, budget some time for you and perhaps a sidekick to make local contacts prior to bringing your full crew to the field. Depending on the size of the project and the number of required contacts, you may need several weeks. Don't have your full crew twiddling their thumbs in the field vehicle while you're chewing the fat with local farmers or ranchers about access to their property. On smaller projects, with smaller crews, such contacts are usually subsumed in the general course of fieldwork, and with much less legwork.

Let's assume, for the sake of discussion, that your project is a moderate- to large-size survey project—say for a forty-mile highway corridor on new alignment traversing private land. Once you've lined up your crew and equipment, how are you going to get started? Well, obviously, a lot of private landowners are going to be affected by the project. Very likely, you will have to personally negotiate access to each and every owner's property.

One way to get the ball rolling is to place an announcement about your project in local newspapers after checking with your client (sidebar 5.2). The newspapers may follow up with some kind of story for which you will be interviewed. Most local people will notice, and at least those who will be affected by the project will be expecting to hear from you. Given such forewarning, when your crew shows up, the locals might not be so quick to mistake them for the Fabulous Furry Freak Brothers (figure 5.1).

But before you bring your whole crew to the field, reconnoiter the project area yourself. This is an appropriate time for a "windshield survey." Your sidekick can drive while you juggle maps and navigate. Learn the landscape, natural and cultural—access points, roads, stream crossings, and the like. You should repeat this tour for the benefit of your crew, but you need to know the terrain before they arrive.

Your client may be able to provide you with the names and addresses of people who will be affected by the project, but more likely you'll have to locate these people yourself. Go to the county courthouse, or purchase a plat book or rural directory. Also, score a copy of the phone book(s) that covers the service area for your project area. Back at your home office, in your motel room, or at some other place where you can spread out your stuff, cross-reference your project plans, USGS, NTS or provincial maps, and the plat books or directories. The plat books and

5.2. NEWS RELEASE

XYZ Consulting to Conduct Archaeological Survey

XYZ Consulting will conduct an archaeological survey this summer along the proposed alternate alignments for the relocation of [insert highway identification] in [insert county name] County. The [insert client or agency name]-sponsored project will extend from [insert general project description].

The purpose of the project is to locate and evaluate all archaeological sites within each proposed alternate. The archaeologists expect to find evidence of prehistoric and historic Indian sites, as well as historic Euro-American [or -Canadian] sites. The information will be used by the [insert client or agency name] when selecting the final highway alignment.

The project is part of a phased upgrading of [insert highway identification] scheduled for completion within the next [insert general project schedule years if known]. State [or Provincial] and federal historic preservation [or heritage] laws require archaeological surveys on road projects.

Contact: [insert your name and phone number]

Figure 5.1   Survey crew, a.k.a. the Fabulous Furry Freak Brothers.

rural directories show who owns each parcel of land. The more useful maps show dwellings and their occupants. The latter may be
landowners or renters, but at least you can tell who lives where. Write
the pertinent information onto your field maps. Then use the tele-
phone books to determine the addresses and phone numbers for
landowners along your corridor. This list should be fairly complete
save for absentee landowners. Necessary information about the absentee owners may require another trip back to the recorder's office.
Regardless, you should be able to generate a working list of landowners' addresses and phone numbers fairly quickly. Once your list is
made, you have several choices of how to proceed.

For relatively large projects similar to our hypothetical corridor
survey, try mass mailings to affected landowners. These mailings at
once announce the particulars of the project, request permission to
enter the property, solicit information about local sites, and offer
landowners a chance to discuss their collections with a professional
archaeologist (sidebars 5.3 and 5.4). Include a self-addressed, stamped
envelope. Historically, the technique has been worthwhile, generating a positive response rate of approximately 60 to 70 percent. However, almost everyone will still want to talk to you face-to-face
before you start fieldwork.

5.3.
SAMPLE LETTER INTRODUCING PROJECT TO LANDOWNER

XYZ Consulting Letterhead
Month/Day/Year

Title/First Name/Last Name
Address
City, State/Province, ZIP/Post Code

Dear Title/Last Name:

XYZ Consulting has been selected by [insert client or agency name] to perform an archaeological survey of alternative alignments proposed for the [insert highway identification] highway relocation project. Our responsibility will be to locate, record, and evaluate the significance of all archaeological sites within each alternate. We expect to find archaeological evidence for prehistoric and historic Indian mound and habitation sites, as well as historic Native and Euro-American/Canadian sites. The [insert client or agency name] must consider this information when the final alignment is selected.

It is our understanding that a portion of your property lies within or near one of the possible roadway alternatives currently under consideration. This letter is to inform you that we will be in the area and to explain our survey methods. We hope that you will grant us permission to conduct our survey on your property.

We will employ a crew of [insert number] individuals to conduct the field survey. Each person on the crew has a minimum of [insert number] years of archaeological experience. If you have questions about artifacts you may have found or archaeological sites on your property, any one of us will be happy to discuss them with you. Any information you can provide to us will be greatly appreciated. We will be recognizable by our vehicles which display XYZ Consulting decals.

Our survey methods are nondestructive. The crew spaces itself at regular intervals and walks along the proposed road corridor, scanning the ground surface for evidence of past human activity. To test for the possibility of buried sites and to evaluate the condition of the sites we find, we often will dig small holes with shovels or posthole diggers. The small test holes are always filled back in immediately. Care is taken not to trample or disturb crops in any way. Gates, fences, and livestock will not be disturbed.

Our ultimate goal is to understand and conserve important resources of [insert your state's name's] past. I look forward to talking to you personally in the near future.

Sincerely,

[insert your name]
Project Archaeologist

5.4. SAMPLE LANDOWNER QUESTIONNAIRE

XYZ CONSULTING ARCHAEOLOGICAL SURVEY PERMISSION FORM
XYZ CONSULTING
XYZ CONSULTING COMPANY ADDRESS
XYZ CONSULTING PHONE AND FAX NUMBERS

Please check the appropriate line, sign, and return in the self-addressed, stamped envelope.

____ I grant permission to XYZ Consulting to conduct an archaeological survey on my property.

____ Please talk to me personally before conducting an archaeological survey on my property. The best time to contact me is_____.

____ I own an archaeological site and/or artifacts that I would like to discuss with a [insert your company's name] archaeologist.

    Signature: _____
    Name: _____
    Address: _____
               _____
               _____
               _____
    Telephone: _____
Comments:

XYZ Consulting requests this information for the purpose of obtaining permission to conduct an archaeological survey on your property. No persons outside our organization are routinely provided this information. Completion of this form is optional.

A second method is to pretend that you took that job with the insurance company after college instead of becoming an archaeologist. Get on the phone and start cold calling. We don't recommend this technique except when you simply can't contact people any other way. It is very difficult to explain to people over the phone what you do, what you want to do on their property, and how they might be affected by the project. Some people will confuse you with a telemarketer and hang up. Others won't know an archaeologist from a podiatrist, especially if you start blurting jargon such as "We'd like to do a pedestrian survey for cultural resources on your property."

No, you have a much better chance of explaining what you want to do if you emulate the old Fuller Brush Man and go knock on people's doors. Have your props handy—maps, plans—and be prepared to explain methodically what you propose to do and why. It is at this stage of the project that you will come face-to-face with what it means to be a salaried employee. Naturally, you'll be able to meet with some people only at night. You might be able to catch farmers only between 12:00 and 1:00 P.M. Depending on the season, if you catch them in the field, they may want to talk fast—or slow. Expect a certain percentage of people to grant you access within minutes; others will want to talk over the situation for hours. Landowner contacts for a large project can be exhausting. All of your diplomatic and social skills will be called upon. Often you'll have to negotiate a truce with a dog before you get to its owner's door. Be leery of places that seem wrong—there are a lot of meth labs in the country and a lot of twitchy people. Some people will scare you, and you'll frighten others.

There are also a lot of truly fantastic people out there, the salt-of-the-earth types. You'll literally meet all kinds. Don't be in too great a hurry to get away from these interviews; relax and enjoy the conversation. Make friends with the landowners during these contacts. You never know how they might be able to help you later on—tractors come in handy when you bury your vehicle in mud. If you've done your background research well, you'll have some idea of the history of the area, and you can use this information to prime the pump, so to speak, and get people to open up about what they know about significant historical events, local archaeological sites and collectors, and their neighbors. People may be able to produce useful artifact collections or photographs. Always ask whether they have a collection or have ever found artifacts in the neighborhood. Photograph these collections (figure 5.2), and ask to borrow historical photographs for copying whenever you can (be sure to return them promptly). You may be asked to reciprocate by presenting a talk to the person's Rotary Club or whatever. If you can work it into your schedule, do it; we owe such service (see Toolkit, volume 7).

Occasionally, you may be the first person to inform a landowner that his or her property is scheduled to be affected by the project. This can be very difficult duty, so approach it professionally and sensitively. Some people may get the idea that they can influence the outcome of your client's project to their advantage by "salting" artifacts on their property. Such people almost always tip their hand in one way or another. Sometimes they'll subtly float the idea to you during

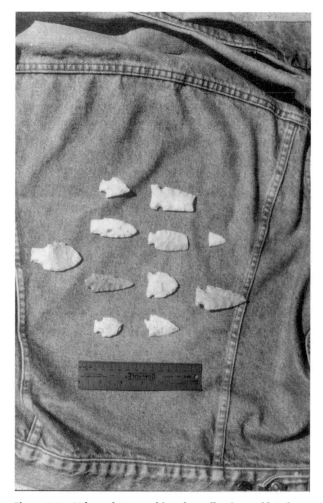

Figure 5.2 When photographing the collections of local residents, place the artifacts on a solid background, such as the back of a denim jacket, and don't forget to put a ruler, coin, or some other object into the frame for scale.

conversation in order to gauge your reaction. If they actually do try to fake a site, they might forget to wipe off the glue that had once held the artifact in its frame, or they'll tell their neighbors, who might tell you. Relatively few archaeological sites of any kind force a significant project modification, and salted sites are even less likely to be considered—spread this news as appropriate.

Keep your notebook handy and record useful information during your landowner interviews, but be prepared for anything. Once a landowner, an otherwise total stranger, told an archaeologist that her son had just committed suicide, and she wanted to talk about it. She felt that if only he had found something interesting in life, like archaeology, things might have somehow turned out differently.

Aside from landowners, it is often useful and always a welcome courtesy to contact local members of your state or provincial archaeological society, the local historical society, and archaeologists residing or working near the project area. Conversations with such interested people provide useful information about sites, landowners, recent unpublished research, and how the project is viewed locally. If you have the need or inclination, you may also solicit crew members or volunteers among these persons.

NATIVE AMERICAN, CANADIAN FIRST NATIONS, AND ETHNIC COMMUNITY ISSUES

It is especially important to find out through the contracting agency or institution sponsoring your survey whether the local or regional Native North American community has been informed or consulted about the planned archaeological work. Similarly, any recognizable ethnic community may have a stake or at least an interest in your work. Consultation is not only a courtesy and, in some areas, a legal requirement, but it opens up lines of communication that may provide valuable information about the traditional use of the land you are surveying. Many archaeologists seek to avoid direct contact, usually out of fear of the unknown or for political reasons. Indeed, some archaeologists spend their entire careers studying people of the past without ever consulting with their descendants. It seems foolhardy, however, not to consult people who have a direct, long-standing interest in the land and oral traditions that may shed light on archaeological problems.

Having said this, the process is not simple, and if you are not familiar with the community, you may find it very frustrating. If you are a member of one of these communities, you may be familiar with rules and norms. However, you may think, for example, that archaeology and its scientific knowledge of the past are essential, but such studies are not considered essential by all people. Native people have their own histories and their own priorities, and you should therefore understand their lack of interest or enthusiasm in yours. If you do consult with Native Americans or Canadian First Nations people, or ethnic community members, prepare yourself first by understanding their rules of decorum, as you should when dealing with any people of other cultures. In general, it is always best to respect your elders (and theirs), and do much more listening than talking. You may very well learn something useful.

TRADITIONAL CULTURAL PROPERTIES

Traditional Native American and Canadian First Nations cultural properties are a concern for those performing archaeological survey. In the United States, National Register Bulletin 38 (*Guidelines for Evaluating and Documenting Traditional Cultural Properties*) defines a traditional cultural property (TCP) as one eligible for inclusion in the National Register because of its association with cultural practices or beliefs of a living community that (1) is rooted in that community's history and (2) is important in maintaining the continuing cultural identity of the community. TCPs can include any type of historic properties, including cultural landscapes, which have significance in a community's or ethnic group's historically rooted beliefs, customs, and practices.

Special emphasis is often placed on American Indian communities and historic properties, but all groups may have TCPs. The identification of TCPs within a project area may require a systematic study to determine significance. A "reasonable effort" to identify TCPs should be implemented for areas that have the potential to contain such properties as determined by conducting background research on the history of the area and by identifying the cultural groups who either are living there or formerly lived there. Consultation with the identified groups should be implemented early in the planning process to determine whether the groups have any concerns about the project or activity.

CONSULTING WITH OTHER SPECIALISTS

If your project requires a consulting geomorphologist—and it does if you don't know much about soils or Holocene landscape development—have your consultant meet you in the field at the very beginning of the project. The geomorphologist should have sufficient regional knowledge and should use that knowledge to develop an appropriate investigative strategy. This approach will make the most out of the geomorphological data, providing you with information on the depositional contexts of the project area before you commit your crew to the field, and allowing you the flexibility to revise and refine the information during the course of your project.

Frequently, your geomorphologist will perform solid core sampling within the portions of your project area that hold the potential for containing deeply buried archaeological sites. This coring is typically accomplished using a Giddings or similar hydraulic drill rig (figure 5.3). You should assist the geomorphologist so that you can understand potential landscape/cultural relationships and so that you will

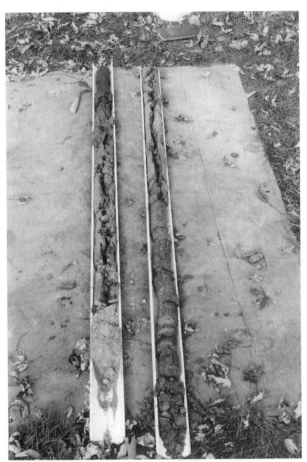

Figure 5.3   Your consulting geomorphologist may use a Giddings or similar rig to pull solid core samples from places that may contain buried archaeological sites.

be able to integrate the geomorphological data into your report. Your geomorphologist should address: the natural stratigraphy; the distribution of landscape-sediment assemblages; the environments of deposition and ages of the deposits (dated or inferred); the presence or absence of buried stable surfaces (soils), nonconformities, or gaps in the Holocene record; the nature of secondary alterations of the deposits (weathering and bioturbation); the degree of disturbance by people; and the distribution and thickness of historic age deposits across the project area.

Using this information, you won't waste time digging 60-centimeter-deep shovel tests in 120-centimeter-thick historic period alluvium. You'll know whether an upland surface is hopelessly deflated. You will understand whether and where, in your project area, you might discover the next Koster or Ozette site. These are good things to know.

On large infrastructure improvement projects, your archaeological crew may be only one of several teams of specialists (e.g., architectural historians, biologists, and zoologists) studying the cultural and environmental impacts of the project. You'll probably bump into these other crews in the field, if not at your motel or a local bar. These people will be working the same circuit that you are, so the opportunities for collaboration or mutually beneficial data sharing are great. Develop these professional relationships whenever possible. Trade information and literature. These sources will serve you well during fieldwork and when you write your report. Your relationship with these scientists also may lead to more work down the road in the form of joint ventures, contracts, or research opportunities.

SURVEY METHODS

As CRM developed, archaeologists and agencies increasingly grappled with standards and guidelines for archaeological investigations, especially surveys. In some states and provinces, guidelines have become mandates that prescribe in great detail acceptable and unacceptable field practice (e.g., requiring shovel test units every five meters in areas of low visibility, mandatory fifteen-meter intervals for survey transects). While such requirements are not universal, most states and provinces have developed some form of written guidelines for field methods. Familiarize yourself with the guidelines; be sure to get a copy from the SHPO or provincial archaeologist. Your employer also may have developed a manual of field procedures that you should read and apply.

While there is no shortage of guidelines and advice, in most places determining appropriate field methods for any given project remains, as it should, the prerogative of the project archaeologist. The reason for this is simply that no two survey projects are ever exactly alike. You have to read the landscape and determine what methods will be most effective in assessing its archaeological potential and how to go about finding sites. Rote compliance with any preordained set of generic guidelines is generally counterproductive because no set of guidelines can anticipate the specific field conditions you will encounter. Use your head, solve the problem, and do the work as efficiently as possible on a case-by-case basis. That is what you are being paid to do. (See Toolkit, volume 1, *Archaeology by Design*.)

You will have to describe and justify your field methods in your report. It is always easier to write about techniques that are conceptually systematic than it is to describe erratic, ill-conceived, or idiosyncratic methods. Be consistent in your field methods and your material recovery techniques unless you have a good reason to deviate from the norm. Avoid spur-of-the-moment decisions, such as telling one crew member to dig shovel test units in twenty-centimeter levels and another to dig in ten-centimeter levels. If you have reason to change methods, do so, but be prepared to explain why and how you did so. Always give yourself the time to make a rational decision. Bad choices will haunt you throughout the remainder of the project.

In other words, don't go off half-cocked. Survey leaders who don't have a plan waste time and effort: The crew stands around waiting for their leader to decide what they should do, or the leader, not knowing exactly what he or she wants done, impulsively rushes the crew into some unproductive task. Such "leadership" will elicit two equally unpleasant outcomes: Your crew will quickly realize you don't have a clue, and both your budget and schedule will suffer. You must have a plan for your crew each day before you even get to the project area. You can then jump out of the truck every morning and say, "OK, let's go do this thing," and your crew won't be left to scratch their butts and wonder how in the world you were ever put in charge.

In CRM-driven archaeological survey, your mission is essentially discovery and evaluation—fairly simple concepts. You use appropriate methods, governed by field contexts, to discover sites. Factors affecting selection of appropriate field method include vegetation, or lack thereof, and the geological contexts within the project area. Then you use appropriate techniques to evaluate the sites you discover in terms of their integrity and significance. Before getting into site evaluation techniques, let's outline the most common methods for site discovery.

SURFACE DISCOVERY TECHNIQUES

Almost all archaeological survey projects incorporate some form of pedestrian surface survey. Pedestrian survey is simply a walking survey of the project area. You walk along looking at the ground surface until you discover an arrowhead, a scatter of artifacts, or a foundation. But there is more to it than that. While you're looking for arrowheads, you must also, at all times, know where you are on the landscape, where your crew members are, and where your project boundaries are, all in reference to your project maps because your project area will rarely be well delineated in the field.

When is pedestrian survey an adequate technique for the discovery of cultural resources? Two main factors apply: ground cover and landscape stability and/or change.

For those who grew up on the Canadian Shield, the Pacific Northwest, or the Eastern Woodlands, it may be difficult to appreciate the fact that the ground surface is exposed to view, unobstructed by vegetation, across a large portion of North America. This was not always the case, of course. It would have been pretty difficult to see the bare ground surface in native prairie. But given postcontact of land clearance and intensive agriculture, during much of the year the land surface is all but naked in the Northeast, Midwest, Great Plains, and arid western states. There, survey seems simple: Look at the ground surface, and you are likely to see archaeological evidence from whatever groups may have previously occupied that landscape. Well, not so fast. Perhaps it isn't quite *that* simple.

The possibility of finding a site on any given surface depends completely on the age of the surface and how that surface may have been modified through time. Archaeological sites are depositional features within a dynamic natural landscape. Few landscapes, even upland landscapes, have been as stable during the past twelve thousand years as we might wish them to have been. Long considered stable or erosional throughout the Holocene, uplands are now being scrutinized more closely as areas where sites might be buried by local eolian, colluvial, and pedogenic processes (Bettis 1995; Bettis and Hajic 1995). You won't find any prehistoric sites by walking over fifty-year-old alluvial floodplain surfaces either. You must know the age and depositional environment of your survey landscape in order to determine whether pedestrian survey is a viable or adequate site-finding technique.

Circumstances when pedestrian survey is a preferred method, regardless of ground cover or landscape stability issues, include surveys geared toward the discovery of mounds, rock shelters, ruins, or petroglyph sites. Many historical period sites also exhibit ground surface features such as foundations, stone walls, cellars, or fortifications. Obviously, ground cover is not quite so material to the discovery of these types of sites, and one of the best ways to find them is to search on foot.

Look for rock shelters, caves, and rock art wherever bedrock outcrops along acute slopes, bluffs, mountains, and canyon lands (figures 5.4 and 5.5). Climbing and caving skills are extremely useful for such rugged, even dangerous, survey work. Never survey in such terrain without experience and proper tools: climbing rope, chocks, pitons, and carabiners, in case you need to tie safety ropes. If the rock is loose, wear a safety helmet. Caves and rock shelters can contain spectacular glyphs and other archaeological features, but watch for snakes and hornet's nests. Always check crevices, even those that seem too narrow to hold a site, as these were viewed by many native cultures as the homes of spirits or portals to the underworld and may contain ritual images or offerings.

Figure 5.4   Look for rock shelters wherever bedrock outcrops in bluff lands and mountains.

Figure 5.5   Check in and around rock crevices for petroglyphs and pictographs.

Don't ignore graffiti. You may be tempted to see it negatively, but it is really just a modern way of marking a special place. Names and dates left by explorers and other travelers may have historical significance. Try to look through, or past, historical period glyphs for the art of earlier peoples that may be camouflaged by the more recent graffiti. It is likely that a suitable geological medium will have been used for millennia.

An extremely effective method for finding and recording petroglyphs is working at night, using side light from a flashlight or lantern. You will be astounded at how much detail emerges in the light and shadow, so much so that you will forget the bugs and bats the light may attract.

There are two general rock art recording methods: photography and direct tracing. Use the best equipment and films for the photographs, as these photographs, not the images themselves, will be the evidence you will analyze later in the lab. If you plan to trace the images, you must be careful not to damage the rock surface. It may be fragile, and if you contaminate it with foreign substances, such as tape or chalk, you may affect the chemistry of the paint or surface, either destroying valuable information or hastening its destruction. A safe recording method is to press Mylar against the rock and trace the images with a fine-tipped black pen. (For details, see Whitley 2001.)

You may treat cave floors as you do other surfaces in a survey, but cave deposits may be much more complex to test and interpret because of their complicated stratigraphy and formation processes. Inspect any deposits in front of the shelter and confine your initial investigations inside the shelter to small samples, as the entire deposit may be relatively small. A shelter is more than a protected floor, so you will have to record its basic interior shape—a tricky job for archaeologists used to planar surfaces, but one accomplished in the same way, with measurements in all three dimensions.

If you find offerings in caves, crevices, or shelters, it is best to leave them untouched and, perhaps, undescribed, except in very general terms. Such offerings may be sacred to the people who left them, and you must respect their privacy. In the interests of protection, however, you should note their location as you would any other cultural resource.

When performing a pedestrian survey, be systematic about covering the ground. Work along contours in bluff lands and mountains. In more open landscapes, most people work in linear transects spaced close enough together so that it is unlikely that a significant site would be undetected between any two transects. Generally, pedestrian survey transect intervals vary from five to twenty-five meters, rarely wider. This is a somewhat subjective call, and you are the one who has to make it and, if necessary, defend it. What kinds of sites are you looking for? How large or small are they likely to be? These questions, and a large literature on survey and sampling methods, will help you design your survey transect plans (see, e.g., Zeidler 1995).

Your crew will take their lead from you. Take a simple example: a square, forty-acre borrow area. Start in one corner, spacing your crew at the determined appropriate interval, and walk parallel transects to the opposite end of the borrow area. There the person farthest from the starting point (call this person the anchor) holds his or her ground, while the other members of the crew walk past the anchor and establish the appropriate spacing again on the anchor's opposite side. Once everyone else is situated at the appropriate transect interval, the anchor walks past the rest, to one interval beyond the last person in line. The crew then walks parallel transects back to the starting baseline. This is repeated in both directions until the entire borrow area is covered. Unless people have convenient crop rows or another grid-like pattern to follow, they inevitably wander off track while walking their transects. Although you may encourage a certain amount of meandering along the transects, you must maintain the general integrity of the transect intervals by monitoring the progress of the entire party. It helps if you place yourself on a transect near the middle of the pattern and ask your crew to occasionally monitor their distance from you. This tip seems very simple, but you will be surprised how often people, head to the ground, wander astray.

It is even easier to wander off course in more irregular survey areas, such as highway or transmission line corridors that may themselves occasionally be somewhat serpentine. However, the principle is the same. Using basic orienteering skills and the landmarks shown on your topographic quadrangle map, you will navigate an appropriate course along the project corridor, and your crew will maintain appropriate parallel transect intervals relative to your lead transect. You must adequately survey your own transect and monitor the transect intervals of the rest of your crew, while performing map navigation along an unfamiliar and unmarked landscape. It isn't hard, but you have to be able to read a map. When it comes to herding your crew around, it doesn't hurt if your gene pool includes a bit of border collie.

Upon finding an artifact or feature along a transect, the lucky crew member generally hollers, "Flake," or "Point," or "Unexploded ordnance," or whatever is applicable to the situation, thereby alerting you and the rest of the crew that the game is afoot. At this point it is a good idea to convene the crew at the site of the discovery and perhaps mark the spot with a wire flag. Deploy your crew at narrow (two- to five- meter) transect intervals, and perform a methodical walkover of the area near the find. Crew members might verbally announce the discovery of other artifacts along their transects, or have them use wire flags to mark each artifact location. This method tends to use up flags pretty quickly, but it is helpful if you plan to piece-plot each artifact or photograph the scatter.

A variation on this technique is to have your crew walk along their transects until they are well beyond the site scatter, turn back, and flag the first artifact they encounter upon reentering the site. This results in delineation of the perimeter of the artifact scatter or site upon completion of your walkover. Once the perimeter is defined, you can then accurately measure the site by pacing, taping, or using a range finder. Draw a sketch of the site and any prominent nearby landmarks (distance to water, fences, etc.) in your field notebook, and write a narrative description of what you did and what you found. Using available landmarks and topography, plot the site location on your air photo and topographic quadrangle map. Obtain several GPS readings to aid in mapping and revisiting the site. Take some photographs, if there is something worthwhile to show. Collect any diagnostic artifacts you encounter; perhaps make a collection of representative material classes. Sometimes all surface artifacts will be collected during a survey, but remember, they'll all have to be curated. Make sure the benefits of making a total surface collection are justified by your research design and budget. Collection procedures may be spelled out in your research design. It is always a good idea to be consistent from site to site because it will allow you to make legitimate intersite comparisons during analysis.

At this point, you may have the choice of evaluating the site immediately or continuing with the survey, to return later to evaluate the site. Because site evaluation entails an array of equipment and a level of effort beyond what is usually necessary for pedestrian survey, we usually opt for the latter. Another reason for continuing with the rest of the survey immediately is that surface conditions may change radically during the course of a long survey project. Hopefully, you will have had the luxury of starting your survey in the spring of the year when surface conditions are optimal—but crops grow. Where crops don't grow, rank vegetation often does. You should complete as much of your pedestrian surface survey as possible when the surveying conditions are good. Ground cover is usually a less critical factor in site evaluation. However, if you are incorporating intensive surface collection techniques in your survey or evaluation design (e.g., surface collection in 2×2–meter units), you may want to go ahead and finish your surface collection immediately upon identifying site limits. (Site evaluation techniques are discussed in detail later in this chapter.)

Cultivated agricultural fields, badlands, and sagebrush flats aren't the only types of terrain that afford good surface visibility for pedestrian survey. Always, *always* inspect any stream cutbank you encounter. Don't just inspect the exposures; scrutinize them in the finest detail. Get right in and wade the stream. If a site is present, you may find artifacts sticking out of the cutbank or exposed in slumped deposits at the base of the exposure. Take a shovel, scrape a clean profile, and examine it (figure 5.6). On high or unstable sections, sometimes it is best to scrape the cutbank down in stepped sections, each a meter or so in height. Considerable digging may be involved, requiring the effort of your whole crew.

Work safely, though. Be sure the cutbank exposure is stable and won't slump while you're working on it. Dirt trickling down the face of a cutbank is one sign of instability. Dirt is heavy; you don't want to find yourself at the base of a cutbank in the middle of nowhere with four hundred pounds of it on your legs.

Identify discrete landform sediment assemblages and buried surfaces. Archaeological sites often are associated with buried soils that are invisible on the current floodplain surface. Sites in buried contexts often hold high research potential because they may be relatively undisturbed. Whether you find a site or not, draw and describe the cutbank soil profile. Minimally this will prove to your reviewers that you at least made the effort to identify buried soils and any associated sites. The more soils you describe, the more adept you will become at the task.

Mapping and describing soils are critical skills you must develop. We highly recommended that you squeeze in a soil genesis class while you're still in school. If you don't, you'll have to pick up an understanding of soils the way most archaeologists do: by paying attention when you have a geologist in the field, and through experience, lots of experience. A good place for the novice to start accumulating soils wisdom is Schoeneberger et al. (1998).

Figure 5.6 The archaeologist examines alluvial stratigraphy along a cutbank. Trowel marks spot where ceramics were found. Note dark soil band between shovel handles indicating a developed soil related to a former buried surface.

Shorelines, whether along a sea coast, lake, river, or man-made impoundment, generally provide good visibility for pedestrian, canoe, or boat surveys. Waves tend to erode beach lines, leaving lag deposits of deflated artifacts together with other flotsam and jetsam along the shore. Follow these lag deposits inland, beyond the destructive influence of the waves, and you may find relatively undisturbed portions of the sites that you first discover along the strand line.

Lakes and rivers were and are major transportation routes for most of the year. Pay close attention to the nature of the shoreline, looking for sheltered coves, portages, good fishing spots, and other natural resource areas that may have attracted occupation nearby, or features such as fish dams and weirs (figure 5.7). In areas such as the vast Canadian Shield, Algonkian peoples regarded the massive granite outcrops along lakes and rivers as the homes of spirits. Many of these striking formations have rock paintings and offerings, and there is much left to explore.

You may assume that the best water craft for a survey is a motor boat, because of its speed. But speed and noise reduce your ability to read the landscape. If you travel as the original inhabitants did, by canoe, you will begin to see as they saw, and this may lead you to a deeper understanding of how they used shorelines.

Perhaps it should go without saying, but don't forget that water can be dangerous. Two archaeologists once conducted a shoreline survey along the upper Mississippi River. They had just pushed off from where they had parked their john boat along the shore, below a U.S. Army Corps of Engineers lock and dam, when the locks unexpectedly opened and a giant whirlpool, big enough to swallow

Figure 5.7   Many archaeological sites are directly related to rivers and streams, such as mill sites, dams, and weirs. A fish weir near Amana, Iowa, is pictured here.

their boat, appeared about twenty feet away. One sat nervously, watching the vortex with dread, as his buddy fiddled to get the outboard started. Luckily, they escaped, but more than one archaeologist has drowned while doing survey, so be sure to take all necessary precautions for water safety.

Wherever you survey, don't ignore the smaller patches of bare ground afforded by cow paths, rodent holes, soil slumps, around tree trunks, and so forth. Many an arrowhead has been found in the middle of a cow path, and you never know when you'll find a trade bead or some other artifact on the piles of dirt around a rodent burrow, crawfish chimney, or anthill. It does happen!

SUBSURFACE DISCOVERY TECHNIQUES

When your project area affords limited or no surface visibility, you must make a good-faith effort to discover sites that may be present on the obscured surface. If an area has been plowed in the past, it may be worthwhile to have a fallow field plowed prior to your survey. Obviously, this method is contingent on landowner cooperation, but in situations where you are dealing with large tracts of functionally condemned land, such as in the case of reservoir construction, replowing your survey sample units may make very good sense.

By far, the most common survey method used in ground-obscured conditions is some form of shovel testing. This technique is suitable for situations where archaeological sites are expected at or near the surface, although its effectiveness has been intensively scrutinized and hotly debated (e.g., Kintigh 1988; Krakker et al. 1983; Lightfoot 1986, 1989; McManamon 1984; Nance and Ball 1986, 1989; Shott 1985, 1989; Zeidler 1995). Essentially, everyone realizes that shovel test sampling has severe limitations as a site-finding technique. In particular, it has been demonstrated that shovel test sampling is biased against the discovery of small sites or sites with few artifacts. Nevertheless, with few exceptions (discussed later), practical and economical alternatives for everyday CRM survey work have not been forthcoming, and shovel testing remains the technique most often used to find near-surface sites in low surface visibility situations.

Although shovel-testing techniques vary widely within and among regions, most archaeologists recognize a distinction between lower effort types of shovel testing, often identified as *shovel probes*, and higher effort, generally larger shovel test units. In general experience, shovel probes are expedient excavations of one, two, or three shovels full of dirt that are then hand sorted with a trowel. The higher effort units are more like miniexcavation units, generally between thirty and fifty centimeters square, and normally excavated in arbitrary levels deep enough to penetrate the B soil horizon. Fill from these more formal shovel tests is usually screened through quarter-inch hardware cloth using shaker-type screens. A given project's research design and specific field conditions normally determine the level of effort employed.

Any subsurface sampling strategy is most effective when done systematically. You must determine unit intervals and transect spacing appropriate to the sometimes-conflicting considerations of site discovery probability, scheduling requirements, and budget. There is no question that excavation of larger units, on tighter grid intervals, with fill screened through quarter-inch hardware cloth, will result in discovery of more sites, smaller sites, and sites of lower artifact density than a less intensive survey will find. Remember, though, your mission as a CRM survey archaeologist is, as the U.S. regulations state, to "make a reasonable and good faith effort to identify historic properties that may be affected by the undertaking and gather sufficient information to evaluate the eligibility of these properties for the National Register" (36 CFR Part 800.4a[2]).

Consult with your SHPO or provincial archaeologist to determine whether any guidelines exist relating to the level of effort required for shovel test surveying in your state. Unit and transect intervals of between ten and twenty meters seem to be most common. It has been demonstrated that use of a staggered or offset grid, rather than a square grid (figure 5.8) is most efficient for site finding (Krakker et al. 1983; Shott 1985; Wobst 1983). Be organized. You can assign letter designations to transects and number designations to units along those transects (e.g., transect A, shovel test unit 1; or transect C, shovel test unit 5). These designations can be referred to as unit A1 or C5. Sketch your project area in your field notebook and show the location of all transects and units, along with whatever designation you assign to each. Be sure to make note of any positive test unit on your sketch. You may also want to plot your transects and shovel test units directly on your project maps or aerial photos.

When you find artifacts (sites) by shovel testing, the logistics of artifact bag control are critical. Be sure that everyone on your crew is labeling their bags in the same way throughout the project. Use a Sharpie or some other indelible marker to label your bags, and on

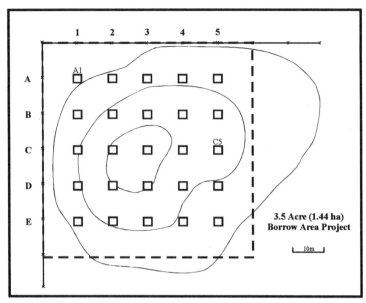

10 Meter Square Grid Pattern

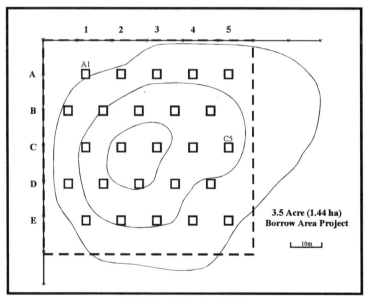

10 Meter Offset Grid Pattern

Figure 5.8   Schematic diagram showing square versus offset shovel test grid patterns.

every bag write all pertinent provenience information so that it can be cross-referenced with the data entered into your field notebook. Prevent hassles later in the lab by including the following data on every bag:

project number;
project designation;
county or township name;
survey parcel designation (landowner's name or legal description of parcel) or field site number (official site numbers usually are obtained from the appropriate state or provincial archaeologist's office immediately upon completion of fieldwork);
date;
excavator's name or initials;
transect or unit designation (e.g., shovel test unit D15);
level or depth (e.g., twenty to thirty centimeters); and
contents of the bag (e.g., all artifacts, projectile point, etc.).

Multiple bags (e.g., levels) from a single unit should be enclosed together within a unit bag, appropriately labeled. Periodically during the day, or minimally at the end of each day, all bags from that day's work should be logged on a bag list and stored appropriately for transport to the laboratory. If practical, store all the unit bags from a single site in one large bag, appropriately labeled. The extra effort will pay off in fewer headaches during analysis.

Normally, if you find artifacts during shovel test sampling, you should tighten the transect and unit intervals around the positive unit to try to define the site's horizontal limits. Carefully map the locus and record the circumstances regarding the change in grid interval. One way to allay confusion is to identify any such satellite excavations by a lowercase letter designation (e.g., shovel test unit G2a, G2b, etc.), and map them on an independent grid relative to the original positive unit, in this case G2 (figure 5.9). Try to put in enough units around the original positive unit to be confident that you have identified a sterile, nonsite buffer around all the positive units. This can be quite difficult, but often sites are confined by landscape characteristics (e.g., terrace scarps, bluff edges) that can be read intuitively. Experience in the field helps in this regard.

Shovel test survey through dense vegetation, such as second-growth forest, is among the most physically and technically demanding of archaeological survey techniques. Transect intervals have to be

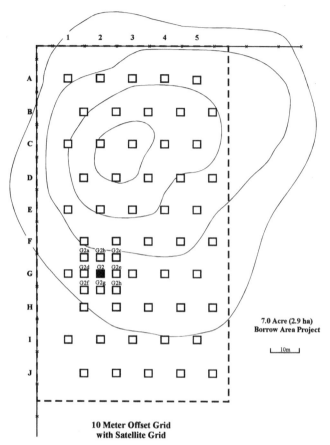

Figure 5.9 Schematic diagram showing typical offset grid with satellite grid around positive unit.

close enough for crew members to remain in visual contact, and great concentration is required to maintain grid integrity. It is advisable for every member of the crew to carry a compass, using it to stay on the appropriate directional tangent you wish to follow.

Shovel test profiles can be relatively easily drawn and described. The excavator should record soils data and any other pertinent data. Crew members can record this information in their own field journals, but it is easier if you develop a simple form that can be attached to a clipboard, with single or multiple generic, scaled, blank unit profiles on which the excavator can simply record the date and provenience data and sketch pertinent depths of soil horizons, soil colors, presence or absence of artifacts, and so forth (figure 5.10). The forms can be collected and filed at the end of each transect or at the end of the day, and they are easily reconciled with data you record in your field book.

Other near-surface testing methods popular in various regions include posthole testing and bucket auger testing (Abbott and Neidig 1993). The bucket auger is also a very useful tool for deep subsurface testing (see our discussion later). Both methods follow essentially the same logistical procedures (grids, screening, etc.) outlined for shovel test survey. Both methods are also useful for quickly evaluating sites you discover during your survey.

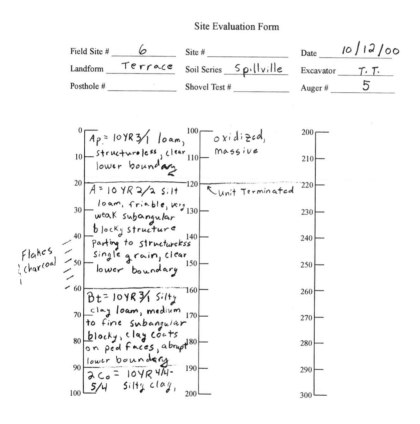

Site Evaluation Form

Field Site # _____6_____   Site # _____   Date __10/12/00__

Landform __Terrace__   Soil Series __Spillville__   Excavator __T.T.__

Posthole # _____   Shovel Test # _____   Auger # __5__

Remarks: Unit exhibits Late Holocene sediments (0-90cm) inset over truncated Early - Mid Holocene sediments (90-120 cm). Flakes and charcoal recovered from the 40-60 cm level near the interface of A/Bt

Figure 5.10   Example of multifunctional subsurface evaluation form.

Posthole testing employs a standard scissors-type posthole digger. These tools have a cylinder-shaped bit that recovers a plug of earth fifteen centimeters in diameter and twenty centimeters in depth. Marking the side and handle of the tool with a ten- or twenty-centimeter scale using an indelible marker helps with vertical control. Excavators can comfortably excavate to a depth of about one meter in standard ten- or twenty-centimeter levels using a posthole digger. Posthole diggers are particularly well suited for quickly determining the degree of plow disturbance on sites and for locating near-surface buried soil horizons. Their limited volume per level makes them less useful than shovel testing for artifact recovery, and the smaller-diameter hole precludes detailed examination of side-wall profiles. However, it has been argued that posthole testing provides better systematic control than shovel probing (Abbott and Neidig 1993:42), and it is common experience that when the tool is in the right hands (there is a knack to it), the technique is more time- and cost-efficient than shovel testing.

It is important to match your subsurface investigation methods to the requirements of the landscape. Not long ago, archaeologists routinely limited their site discovery techniques to pedestrian surface survey or shallow shovel or posthole testing of their project areas. Through blissful ignorance, cynical disinterest, or simply a lack of adequate methods for subsurface testing, they paid little regard to the age or depositional environment of the surface being traversed. In most places, those days are over.

With the growing sophistication of geoarchaeological landscape settlement models (e.g., Bettis 1992; Bettis and Hajic 1995), archaeologists now realize that survey must be conducted in three dimensions. In response to the need to test certain landforms more deeply, many archaeologists now routinely use bucket augers as a primary subsurface testing tool.

The bucket auger is a manual digging tool that rotates horizontally as it penetrates the ground and collects excavated soil in a bucketlike bit (an excellent model that can be ordered through your local lumber company is made by the Seymour Manufacturing Company, Seymour, Indiana). The cylinder-shaped working end is twenty centimeters in diameter and roughly twenty centimeters in depth. The design of the tool facilitates recovery of controlled twenty-centimeter plugs of soil that can be extracted and screened in normal archaeological fashion.

The tool is particularly effective for sampling alluvial deposits and documenting the presence of buried archaeological remains. The handle and shaft of the bucket auger is 110 centimeters long and can accommodate a number of extensions of similar length. Alluvial fan deposits have been probed to depths exceeding six meters using a bucket auger with multiple extensions. Bucket augering is a particularly effective technique when your project traverses alluvial bottomland, as in the vicinity of most bridge replacements. For long traverses across bottomlands, simply excavate bucket auger units at appropriate intervals and to appropriate depths along one or more transects that parallel the traverse of your right-of-way. Transects such as these provide geological and cultural data that can be easily mapped for your report. The technique is useful for surveys of highway corridors, pipelines, levees, and many other types of projects.

In some parts of the country, bucket augering is considered the premier method for the discovery of buried sites in alluvial settings. The technique has a proven track record and can be used in any situation where a local landscape sediment assemblage requires a deep-testing survey strategy. Buried archaeological sites are often associated with buried, formerly stable surfaces in alluvial settings. Bucket auger testing can detect these buried surfaces and can document the presence of archaeological components that may be associated with them. Large projects with extensive deep-testing needs may benefit from use of a gasoline-powered drill rig such as a Giddings coring system. Sediment cores ten to twenty centimeters in diameter can be extracted, and deposits can be described, sampled, and collected quickly. You can also use a gas-powered screw auger for rapid subsurface testing.

Under careful, controlled, and safe conditions, backhoe trenching is a useful method of site survey, although some landowners will not allow it. Usually with your consulting geomorphologist, you can use a backhoe to explore terraces, floodplains, and alluvial fan deposits in order to identify and investigate depositional history and stratigraphic relationships. When buried soils are encountered, so too might be cultural materials or features associated with those soils. Such materials and features can be easily mapped along with the stratigraphic profile.

Backhoe trenches are inherently dangerous. Archaeologists in the United States must be aware of, and comply with, Occupational Safety and Health Administration (OSHA) regulations on excavation safety to ensure the safety of themselves and their crew members, and also to avoid fines and lawsuits if someone is injured. The supervisory archaeologist, or someone else on site, must be qualified as a "competent person" according to OSHA standards. See Mickle (1995) for a concise review of regulations concerning excavation safety and a pamphlet issued by the Trench Shoring and Shielding Association (1994) for a discussion of shoring techniques. More detailed information and sample plans for excavation safety is available on the websites of OSHA (www.osha.gov/) and the National Institute for Occupational Safety and Health (www.cdc.gov/niosh/). In Canada, the Canadian Centre for Occupational Health and Safety serves as a clearinghouse for information on relevant federal and provincial legislation and procedures (www.ccohs.ca/). It will be useful for you to review several safety plans before initiating your survey, especially if your work will take you to remote areas. Also, several archaeological excavation safety plans designed to meet OSHA standards have been published (e.g., Merry and Hedden 1995).

Learn about safety requirements before you commit yourself to a field program that includes backhoe trenching. In many cases, protective shoring systems will be required. Working in a backhoe trench is among the most deadly of occupational situations. Try to avoid becoming a statistic.

As noted earlier, cutbanks are valuable in survey. They offer greater exposure of sediment than can be obtained by any subsurface sampling technique. Additionally, stream cutbanks often afford continuous, sinuous, even serpentine exposures along an entire reach of bottomland. Used in conjunction with other sampling methods, examining such lengthy exposures frequently offers the best view of bottomland stratigraphy and is one of the best techniques for determining the presence or absence of buried surfaces and archaeological deposits, surpassing the usefulness of most other techniques in such settings. The horizontal and vertical extent of any site identified on the basis of cultural material observed within or along a cutbank should be defined by additional subsurface investigations.

Survey crews should carry one-inch-diameter Oakfield soil probes in their equipment inventory (Oakfield Apparatus Co., Oakfield, Wisconsin). These tools are useful for quickly assessing near-surface soil stratigraphy. In fact, the Oakfield soil probe is the essential tool of professional soil surveyors. Using Oakfield sediment probes can be an effective survey technique, particularly in mound or cemetery contexts. (In many jurisdictions, you must receive official authorization before initiating investigations into mounds and cemeteries; laws and procedures vary.) In known or suspected mound, cemetery, or site areas, close interval Oakfield sampling can document disturbances, which present as unnatural variations or unconformities when compared to the normal local soil profile. Atypical or disturbed profiles are characteristic of mounds, grave shafts, and other cultural features. Oakfield core sampling is among the fastest and least intrusive ways of documenting the presence of such features. But again, you must understand soils and be able to describe them in order to get the most out of Oakfield sampling as a supplemental survey technique. Also, bear in mind that soil probing is not an artifact discovery technique despite its value in soil-stratigraphic documentation.

Finally, a simple tile probe (a metal rod soldered to a handle) is also a very useful tool for subsurface investigation. This probe is most useful for following and mapping foundations, walkways, and other features that lie just below the surface at many historical period sites.

FIELD EVALUATION TO DETERMINE POTENTIAL ELIGIBILITY FOR THE NATIONAL REGISTER

Documenting the presence of archaeological sites is only half the equation of CRM-driven archaeological survey. Sites also must be evaluated to determine their potential significance based on NRHP criteria, or, in Canada, criteria for nomination to the register of National Historic Sites and Monuments or the lists of provincial heritage sites. In both countries, site identification, analysis, and mitigation are conducted in stages related to the nature and extent of information recovered.

In the United States, it is important to note the distinction between the identification of *potential* and *actual* NRHP significance. Ordinarily, at the reconnaissance survey (Phase I) level of investigation, documentation of potential significance is all that is required to recommend moving on to a more formal intensive survey or testing program (Phase II). The purpose of Phase II testing is to determine whether a site actually meets NRHP eligibility criteria. In some cases it may be obvious, based solely on Phase I evaluation, that a given site will meet NRHP eligibility criteria. In those cases, a recommendation for Phase II site testing would still be warranted to acquire additional information about the site to develop a mitigation strategy.

Properties eligible for the NRHP (as defined in chapter 2) must have *integrity* and *significance*. Minimally, Phase I survey must determine the horizontal and vertical extent of the site and its level of physical

integrity. Ideally, you will also determine the site's age, cultural affiliation, and significance.

On sites that appear as a surface scatter of artifacts under conditions of good surface visibility, horizontal site boundaries can be relatively easily determined by walkover, as discussed earlier.
Occasionally, a survey research design will call for systematic, intensive surface collection as an element of the site evaluation plan. Such
programs assume excellent surface visibility and surficial expression
of archaeological materials. A common procedure for systematic intensive surface collection is to establish a grid using lath or flags and
tapes across the site area. Unit size within the grid typically varies
from 2×2 meters to 10×10 meters, and crew members normally pick
up and bag every artifact within each unit. Provenience data are
recorded on each unit bag. Expedience sometimes warrants sampling
only every other or every fourth grid unit or employing a more elabo-
rate sampling scheme. On sites with low density of surface material,
it is often more efficient to flag and piece plot every artifact, mapping
their locations with a transit or total station. Maps of the surface collected materials often indicate features or activity areas: Concentrations of fire-cracked rock may suggest the location of hearths, or
concentrations of daub may indicate the presence of houses. Such are
the building blocks leading to a recommendation that a site is potentially significant.

For sites that afford less than ideal surface visibility or for sites that
include buried components, horizontal limits must be determined by
subsurface testing. Systematic subsurface sampling must be performed in nearly all cases to determine the depth of the site and the
physical integrity of deposits. You must dig enough holes to determine the boundaries of the site and assess its degree of integrity, but
you don't want to make Swiss cheese out of a potentially significant
site that may be the subject of further study or protection.

Identifying physical integrity is a prerequisite to a determination of
significance. Subsurface testing will allow you to determine whether
a site is deflated, as is often the case in erosional environments, or
confined to a disturbed surface layer such as a plow zone. In either
case, a determination of ineligibility for the NRHP usually would be
warranted.

Your subsurface testing program should identify evidence for in situ
cultural remains if present at the site. On historical period sites, such
remains include foundations, cellars, cisterns, privy pits, and the like.
On prehistoric sites, in situ cultural remains include pit features,

house basins, and a myriad of other feature types. The subsurface testing program should be comprehensive enough to identify buried surfaces if present and any associated archaeological components. This work is particularly important in depositional environments such as floodplains or alluvial/colluvial fans. Archaeological materials encountered on buried surfaces hold considerable potential for integrity and significance. With few exceptions, it is generally true that to be considered potentially eligible for the NRHP, a site must yield evidence of in situ, undisturbed features or other cultural materials. When Phase I evaluation procedures document the presence of such features or materials, consideration of the site as potentially eligible for the NRHP would be warranted at that stage.

So, just as when conducting your reconnaissance survey, your intensive survey must employ subsurface testing methods that are appropriate to the landscape (figures 5.11 and 5.12). Appropriate methods might be systematic, relatively close-interval shovel testing for near-surface archaeological sites, or bucket auger testing for more deeply buried sites. Your evaluation program should be systematic; units should be placed at relatively close intervals and unit levels should be screened.

Figure 5.11   The archaeologist defines an Archaic period feature within a shovel test unit during site evaluation. This feature provides excellent evidence of the site's physical integrity, a prerequisite to a determination of National Register of Historic Places eligibility.

Figure 5.12   Sometimes site evaluation requires excavation of larger, deeper test units.

One of the most difficult questions concerning site evaluation is the level of testing that is sufficient at the Phase I level. The answer depends on whether your survey is intended to evaluate the significance of each site or merely to locate the sites that are present and leave the evaluation to a later stage. Many CRM surveys are designed to identify all sites *and* to distinguish between those that are NRHP-eligible—or potentially so—and those that are clearly not eligible. Generally speaking, if you know the horizontal and vertical extent of the site, have documented the presence of in situ features or materials, and have enough information about the site to develop a testing strategy (Phase II), that is enough. If you're fairly sure of the site boundaries and believe that the site retains integrity, you can recommend further evaluation or (if consistent with your research design) conduct it yourself. If you have clearly demonstrated that the site lacks physical integrity, that is usually enough to recommend no further work. Ordinarily, you will know what your recommendation will be for any given site before you leave the field. If you aren't sure what your recommendation for the site will be, chances are you haven't done enough.

6

INDIRECT
EXPLORATION TECHNIQUES

Circumstances may preclude direct subsurface exploration and testing. For example, excavations in known or suspected cemeteries, mounds, or ossuaries may be prohibited in some regions. Fortunately, many types of sites and landscapes can be productively surveyed and evaluated in minimally invasive ways. Archaeologists find geophysical methods of site prospecting to be viable complements to pedestrian and subsurface survey. This chapter presents a general introduction to some of the most useful techniques for non-invasive, indirect subsurface exploration.

Archaeological prospecting by indirect methods of subsurface exploration has been a long-featured element in European archaeological research, and North American archaeologists also are using remote sensing and geophysical techniques more frequently. As technologies have matured, these methods have become increasingly cost-effective for archaeological survey. It is certain that they will be used more, not less, in the coming decades.

Remote sensing using aerial photography has a long history in archaeology and is useful in many CRM contexts (e.g., Avery and Lyons 1981; Camilli and Cordell 1983; Limp 1989; Lyons and Hitchcock 1977; Maxwell 1983; Scollar et al. 1990; Weber and Yool 1999). However, the focus in this chapter is on geophysical methods—those that assist archaeological survey through on-the-ground detection of subsurface anomalies.

The science of geophysics as applied to archaeology can be described in one word: *contrast*. The reason geophysical methods work well in archaeology is that cultural influences disrupt magnetic and electrical fields, creating measurable contrasts (figure 6.1). There are limitations on all geophysical techniques, and lack of sufficient contrast is a fundamental limitation. In some cases, instrument sensitivity may not be adequate. Background noise is a real problem in some areas. Noise that might disrupt the ability of instruments to measure contrasts may come from the instrument itself; the operator (e.g., metal buttons on clothes); geological bodies or layers; or nearby features such as overhead power lines, railroads, and microwave transmitters. Yet, geophysical and remote sensing techniques can be used on a variety of scales to identify individual features within a site or to examine phenomena that occur on continental scales. In the context of archaeological surveys, these techniques can be used for both discovery and evaluation. A common scenario encountered by the survey archaeologist is the historically documented but long-forgotten cemetery that exhibits no visible surface expression. Certain geophysical techniques are useful in locating grave shafts associated with such cemeteries. As an evaluative technique, geophysical methods can help document the physical integrity of sites you discover during your survey.

Applying geophysical techniques in support of archaeological survey always requires site-specific planning. At what resolution will you expect to find features? Will you target individual artifacts, hearths, grave shafts, or stockades? How do you pick a method? Is the

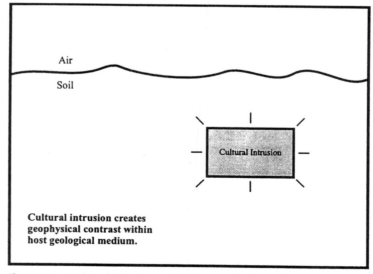

Figure 6.1 Cultural intrusion within host geologic medium.

cost/benefit ratio warranted based on your research design and scope of work?

Although more archaeologists are developing their own expertise, you will probably hire or contract with a consulting geophysicist to perform or direct the fieldwork and to provide you with a formal report of the investigation. Your geophysical contractor will consult with you about the central questions just noted, and together you will come up with an appropriate plan of action. It remains your responsibility to make sure your consultant knows exactly what you want to learn. Before even contacting a geophysical contractor, you must have a good idea of the local geology, geomorphology, soils, topography, depth to water table, weather, site access, potential maneuverability of equipment on site, what the target features will be, the contrast you expect and what signals there will be, the presence of noise-producing features such as power lines or railroads, knowledge of previous geophysical work in the area, and how much time and money you can expend on geophysical methods. Given that information, you and your consultant will be able to develop a workable, site-specific survey strategy.

Always do site-specific survey by design. How do you develop a survey design for geophysical archaeology? Determine what questions you want to answer and what data are available. Think about of what your targets are and what size they are apt to be. Use appropriate equipment for the anticipated target. For instance, you don't want to use electromagnetic equipment to find a nail, although you could.

Once you determine your anticipated target size, think in half-scale terms; that is, use a line and station grid that is half the size of the smallest feature you are targeting. Conveniently for archaeologists, the standard grid for geophysical methods is 1 × 1 meter. Make sure your geophysical data are collected in sufficient quantity and quality to be representative of the material and features present. If you have the time and money, a combination of methods may provide complementary data because of their differential ability to locate various types of targets.

Does a geophysicist have to collect the data, or can an archaeologist do it? Experience with the instrumentation is key. Some archaeologists possess limited experience with the instruments, which gives a feel for the equipment, but you will probably want to hire a geophysical consultant who really understands what's going on. Would you want a geophysicist to run an archaeological excavation?

As when working with any specialist, scheduling is critical. If possible, get in touch with your contractor a month or several months before you expect him or her in the field. Weather can be a real concern, so schedule contingency dates.

Costs of geophysical consulting are site-specific and contingent on transportation to and from the site, shipping costs for instruments, and the consultant's time. Similar to an old rule of thumb for archaeology, one full day in the field usually requires at least two days interpreting the data. Costs for your consultant can run up to $100 or more per hour when dealing with large geophysical consulting firms, but independent contractors usually run a fraction of that. You may want to negotiate an explicit agreement about billing for downtime due to equipment failure. Make sure you are paying for, and dealing with, experienced people who are familiar with archaeological problems and are comfortable working with archaeologists.

For comprehensive reviews of geophysical methods and equipment as they are applied to archaeological problems, see Clark (1990) and Bevan (1998). Heimmer and De Vore (1995) have authored a very useful complementary volume, and Weymouth (1986) and Wynn (1986) provide significant reviews of archaeological applications of geophysical methods. Techniques and equipment in common use by North American archaeologists are briefly described here. These techniques can be divided into active and passive methods. Active methods induce a measurable reaction from the host geological medium, and utilize a variety of electrical and electromagnetic instruments such as metal detectors, resistivity meters, conductivity meters, and ground-penetrating radar. The most commonly used passive method (i.e., one that measures existing geophysical conditions within a host medium—the soil), is magnetometry.

METAL DETECTOR

The metal detector is a generally underrated survey tool for archaeologists. It has had to overcome a bad reputation, derived from its use by treasure hunters to plunder sites for artifacts. But the metal detector is a very good tool for defining the boundaries of historic sites as well as activity areas within them (e.g., Connor and Scott 1998).

The sole purpose of the metal detector is to find objects. Metal detectors normally consist of a single or double coil, forming part of a tuned oscillator circuit. The presence of metal artifacts upsets this circuit, producing an out-of-balance signal (Clark 1990:121). Anomalous signals are registered by either audio (beep) or digital readers.

The equipment detects the resistivity of both ferrous and nonferrous metals, and the better instruments can be set to discriminate certain metals, such as brass, silver, or aluminum.

Metal detectors can be used as random or systematic survey tools. As always, it's best to work systematically on a grid. Transect intervals at three to five meters, resulting in about a 35 percent sample, are most common, but make your own site-specific decisions. Metal detectors are usually used in combination with a total station instrument. The standard procedure is to use a flag to mark each target, then to excavate as necessary to expose and recover the target. The total station is used to piece-plot the identified artifact. The total station data can then be downloaded into a CADD or GIS program to produce a site map. If you don't have access to a total station instrument, you can do the same thing a little more slowly using a transit and stadia rod.

The use of metal detectors has several advantages. Detectors are fairly inexpensive as geophysical instruments go, running from about $250 to $2,000. It is also a fairly fast survey technique. The 780-acre Little Bighorn battlefield was surveyed with eight metal detectors in ten days. On most projects you will be able to recruit volunteers among local hobbyists who are willing to help with their own equipment. The underlying physics and practical methods are easily comprehended by the average archaeologist, so specialized consultants are not needed.

The major limitation of the equipment is depth. Relatively unsophisticated equipment will detect objects only to an average depth of twenty to thirty centimeters. However, that depth is usually sufficient for preliminary work, as material on most historic sites is located within twenty centimeters of the surface.

Analysis of metal artifact distribution patterns can lead to sophisticated anthropological interpretations. A classic example of the archeological survey potential of metal detectors is the work of Scott et al. (1989) at Little Bighorn Battlefield National Monument. At many sites, though, metal artifacts are either so rare or so abundant that other survey techniques are more appropriate.

ELECTRICAL RESISTIVITY

This method measures the electrical resistance of the material properties of cultural intrusions vis-à-vis a surrounding matrix. These properties are measured by introducing an electrical current through current electrodes (C1, C2) into the subsurface medium and measuring reductions in current density near features and measuring the increasing potential gradient that is sampled by potential electrodes (P1, P2). The distortion of voltage resulting when a resistant object is encountered is measured by a voltmeter.

Results depend on the electrode configuration. Most archaeological applications are based on the principles of the Wenner configuration (Clark 1990; Wenner 1916) where two current electrodes (C1, C2) introduce current into the ground setting up a potential gradient, and two potential electrodes (P1 and P2) placed between the current electrodes measure the difference between the expected and actual potential. Clark (1990:37–48) reviews a variety of resistivity arrays, most of which are variations on the Wenner configuration.

The resistivity equipment most commonly used by North American archaeologists is a twin-electrode configuration, the RM-15, which was developed specifically for archaeological applications by Geoscan Research. The RM-15 includes two electrodes (C1, P1) attached to a voltmeter mounted on a single portable housing. A remote electrode (C2, P2) placed at a distance of thirty meters acts as a control (figure 6.2). An onboard data logger automatically records readings at each station along a grid.

Figure 6.2   RM-15 resistivity meter and twin electrode array.

With the RM-15, electrons enter the ground through the current electrodes, causing voltage to course through the soil in an electron scatter that exhibits radial geometry similar to the inside of an onion. These concentric rings are voltage contours that develop in a perpendicular plane relative to the introduced electron scatter (figure 6.3, left). When material or a feature with high resistivity is encountered, the feature distorts the introduced current and the distortion is read as the variance from 90 degrees, or the distortion from perpendicular between voltage contours and the introduced electron scatter. The surface contour is similarly distorted. These distortions (figure 6.3, right) are read according to the formula: Resistivity equals Volt measure over Injected Current (R=Vm/I). The variance is usually read as parts per hundred, read in ohms.

The depth of your investigation is governed by the distance between the twin electrodes. A horizontal probe (electrode) distance of one meter will provide readings to a depth of one meter. If you wish to investigate deeper features, you must move the electrodes farther apart. But if you go much deeper, you will encounter the limitations of the equipment. For deeper surveys, consider an alternative geophysical method such as electromagnetic conductivity.

Resistivity survey has many advantages. It is especially useful for identifying near-surface anomalies with high resistivity, such as

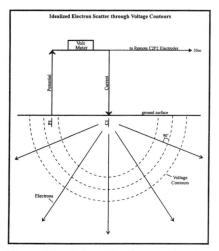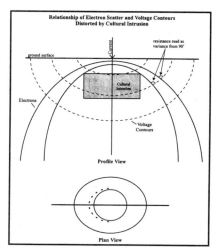

Figure 6.3   Schematic diagram showing idealized electron scatter through voltage contours, and relationship of electron scatter and voltage contours as they might be distorted by the presence of cultural intrusions.

fire-cracked rock features, hearths, stone walls, and filled excavations such as pit features or houses. The technique requires a
straightforward systematic grid that maintains spatial integrity and
is easily incorporated into existing archaeological baselines. The
method is speedy and easily understood. With minimal basic training and adequate supervision, most archaeological crew members
are capable of using the equipment and recovering field data. Under
proper conditions, data can be recovered from a 20×20–meter grid
in about thirty minutes.

Equipment built specifically for archaeological applications, such
as the RM-15 with its onboard current source, voltmeter, and data
bank, has made resistivity survey quicker, more cost-effective, and
more straightforward in terms of analysis. Stored data can be downloaded at the end of the day, and the data can be converted into
graphic formats such as profiles and contour maps using relatively inexpensive software. Your geophysical contractor usually prepares
these graphics for you as part of his or her report of investigations.
The data can then be used to guide management decisions or future
site investigations. For these reasons, resistivity survey is becoming a
relatively common component of CRM work.

ELECTROMAGNETIC CONDUCTIVITY

Conductivity is the opposite of resistivity: When electrical resistance
is high, conductivity is low, and vice versa. Electromagnetic conductivity provides a measure of porosity. The electromagnetic (EM) array
includes a transmitting antenna and a receiving antenna that measures introduced amps over resistance. That is, whereas Resistance
equals Volts over Introduced Amps, Conductivity equals Introduced
Amps over Resistance ($C = I/R$). Conductivity meters measure the
conductivity of an electrical current through the subsurface medium,
recording the measurement in units of millisiemens per meter
(mS/m) (Bevan 1983:51).

The most common EM induction instruments used for archaeological work in North America are the EM-31 and EM-38 conductivity
meters made by Geonics Limited of Mississauga, Ontario. Unlike the
resistivity array, EM instruments do not have to come in contact with
the ground. They are carried a few centimeters above the ground
along established grid lines, and measurements of conductivity are
recorded by an onboard data logger at either timed or stationed inter-

vals. The EM-31 (figure 6.4) has a boom length of about four meters (between transmitting and receiving antennas) allowing investigation of subsurface anomalies that are at least one to two meters wide and within six meters of the surface (Bevan 1983:50). The EM-38 is more compact, with a boom length of about 1 m, and is handier for investigation of anomalies situated within a meter or so of the surface (figure 6.5).

Both instruments work on the same geophysical principle (figure 6.6). Simply described (following Bevan 1983:51), antenna (coils of wire) are situated at both ends of the instrument's boom. Current in the transmitting antenna creates a fluctuating (sinusoidal) magnetic field. The magnetic field penetrates into the ground causing electrical

Figure 6.4   Electromagnetic survey using the Geonics EM-31 conductivity meter.

Figure 6.5   Electromagnetic survey using the Geonics EM-38 conductivity meter.

currents to flow through underground conductors. The more porous the conductor, the higher the rate of current. In general, the ground itself is a good conductor. When a resistant or magnetic feature is encountered, it creates eddy currents that distort the transmitted field, generating a second magnetic field. The receiving coil (antenna) at the other end of the boom senses the second magnetic field. The magnetic field at the receiving antenna represents a weighted average of the conductivity of the ground near the instrument. Circuitry attached to the antenna distinguishes between buried conductors and buried magnetic objects. "This distinction is possible because the received signal from magnetic objects is proportional to the amplitude of the transmitted magnetic field, while the signal from conductors is proportional to the rate of change of the transmitted field" (Bevan 1983:52). As further explained by Dalan (1989:44), "The equipment divides the signal measured by the receiver into two components differing in phase by 90 degrees; one component is in phase with the signal generated in the receiving coil by the transmitter in absence of the secondary field, and the other is out of phase (the quadrature-part of the signal) by 90 degrees." EM conductivity meters can therefore be used in two ways (Clark 1990:34). When operated at high frequencies (e.g., forty kilohertz), they measure conductivity by examining the quadrature component that will respond to the conduction of moisture. This is useful for identifying sump features such as filled ditches, pit features, or pit houses. However, when operated at low frequencies (e.g., four kilohertz), they examine the in-phase component that responds to the magnetic susceptibility of ferrous objects, like a glorified metal detector.

Electromagnetic conductivity surveying is well suited to archaeological exploration in many of the same situations where resistivity survey is viable. Advantages of the EM technique include relatively high resolution of subsurface features and speed of data recovery. Because the instruments require no direct contact with the ground and no external wiring for remote electrodes, EM surveying is sometimes more practical than resistivity, particularly in brushy areas. EM surveying also requires less time and personnel than are generally required by resistivity surveying. Disadvantages are that the equipment is considerably more expensive and more susceptible to outside sources of interference, such as metal pipes, fences, and incidental

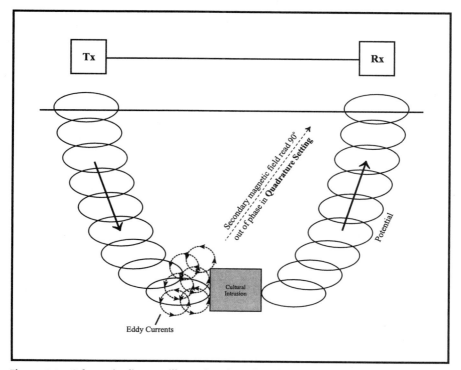

Figure 6.6 **Schematic diagram illustrating the principles of electromagnetic conductivity surveying.**

metal on the person conducting the survey (zippers, jewelry, nose rings, etc.).

Like modern resistivity equipment, EM conductivity instruments now include onboard data loggers, the contents of which can be downloaded at the end of the day. Software packages can then convert the data into conductivity profiles, or you can use various plotting programs to produce contour maps of sensed subsurface anomalies. Dalan's electromagnetic work at the Cahokia site provides excellent examples of successful applications of the technique (Dalan 1989, 1991; Holley et al. 1993).

GROUND PENETRATING RADAR

Although everyone is generally familiar with the concept of radar, Ground Penetrating Radar (GPR) is a rather complicated technology. Under ideal conditions, GPR can be a very useful technique for the archaeologist because it can detect a wide range of buried features and items (Conyers and Goodman 1997). Unfortunately, ideal conditions are rarely encountered in the real world. Of all the geophysical techniques, GPR data may be the most difficult to interpret. Ironically, GPR is often the first geophysical method many archaeologists think of using, but GPR really isn't justified in many situations. It is also a comparatively expensive method.

GPR equipment consists of a low-power antenna mounted on a chassis that can resemble a vacuum cleaner. Pulses of electromagnetic energy are transmitted into the ground at a frequency within the range of one to one thousand megahertz. A receiving antenna, also mounted on the chassis, measures reflections from subsurface interfaces and from objects that produce electrical or magnetic contrasts. Depth of objects is determined by the measurement, in nanoseconds, of the time it takes for the reflection of the transmitted wave to arrive at the receiving antenna (figure 6.7). The chassis is pulled across the surface of the site along a known baseline or grid traverse. As this is done, a continuous, real-time record of the subsurface readings is produced. A graphic plotter is attached to the antenna chassis by an electronic umbilical cord, generating an almost instantaneously gratifying scaled profile of the subsurface (figure 6.8). Under the best of circumstances, any archaeologist can see features in the GPR profiles. More frequently, however, the profiles can be virtually indecipherable to all but experienced geophysicists.

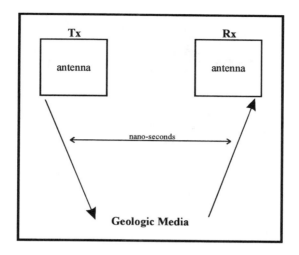

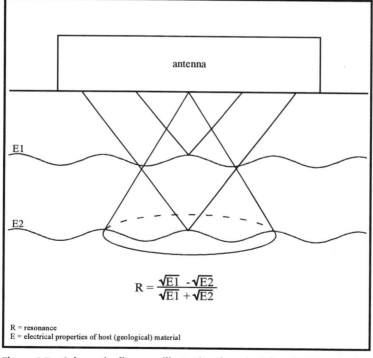

Figure 6.7   Schematic diagrams illustrating the principles of GPR surveying.

Figure 6.8   Subsurface profile emerging from graphic plotter during GPR survey.

Anticipated target depth, the electrical properties of the target(s), and the three-dimensional geometry and electrical properties of the host geological material are considerations that will determine what size antennas are required. Generally, radar will work well when conductivity is below thirty millisiemens per meter. Low-frequency antennas will penetrate deeper but yield poorer resolution. The amount of local ground moisture will affect results. Wet conditions will produce a more focused scan, which is sometimes good, but very wet or saturated conditions can render the equipment almost totally ineffective. A host matrix of predominantly clay or saline soils is also a serious handicap for GPR.

GPR works best when applied to the problem of finding subsurface voids such as pipes and, in archaeology, features such as mounded tombs or historical period cemeteries. Foundations and other belowground disturbances also can be detected. GPR is good at documenting the presence of grave shafts and especially coffins, because coffins represent a classic subsurface void (Bevan 1991). Only the best examples of GPR applications to archaeology find their way into the literature (e.g., National Center for Preservation Technology and Training 1998). The failures are rarely published. Use your geophysical dollar wisely.

MAGNETOMETRY

In North America, magnetic survey probably has the longest and strongest tradition of all the geophysical methods used in support of archaeology. Magnetic survey is effective because there is a magnetic field everywhere. The earth's magnetic field has a magnitude and direction that in the United States and southern Canada is approximately 70 degrees vertical and toward north (this is why compasses function the way they do). Cultural conditions or intrusions alter, distort, and modulate local magnetic fields by chemical, thermal, and mechanical processes. In prehistoric sites, it is the magnetic fields of the soils that are of interest. Distortions in these magnetic fields are measured at the surface with a magnetometer.

The most commonly used instrument for measuring magnetic fields on archaeological sites for many years was the proton, or total field, magnetometer. The magnetometer measures the Earth's total magnetic field in units called nanoteslas (nT). The Earth's magnetic field can range from seventy thousand nanoteslas in the polar regions to twenty-five thousand nanoteslas near the equator (Heimmer and De Vore 1995). In the Central Plains of North America, the Earth's total field varies from fifty-five thousand to sixty thousand nanoteslas (Weymouth and Nickel 1977:106). Against the background magnetic field, archaeological features may produce anomalies in a range from less than one to several hundred nanoteslas. An anomaly must exhibit at least 0.1 nanotesla of contrast to be detected by the most sensitive of magnetometers.

The background or total magnetic field can change through time, even during the course of a day. Magnetic distortion within a given project area can change by tens of nanoteslas throughout the day. This phenomenon is known as *diurnal variation*. Magnetic storms, which produce much higher variations, occasionally occur, rendering magnetic survey fruitless at those times.

Proton magnetometers are normally used on an established grid, with magnetic readings recovered at intervals of about one meter. No contact with the ground is required, and data can be automatically logged at each data point. At every data station, it takes about five seconds to read the immediate magnetic field. So essentially, it is a halt-and-go procedure. Random (diurnal) variations, intrusions (e.g., a passing train), and other "noise" must be controlled and removed from the data in order for magnetic surveys to produce desired results. Therefore, when doing a magnetic survey, you actually need two magnetometers. The second magnetometer is placed off-grid, normally within visual distance of the grid magnetometer, and acts as a control to measure the local magnetic noise. The noise is subtracted from the survey data, and, ideally, the remaining variations from the total magnetic field represent the cultural features for which you are looking (figure 6.9).

Another type of magnetometer, the fluxgate gradiometer, now is commonly used for magnetic survey in archaeology. The fluxgate gradiometer enjoys a major advantage over the proton magnetometer in speed of data recovery. With the fluxgate gradiometer, data sensing is accomplished in about one-thousandth of a second, so operation is virtually continuous (Clark 1990:69). The investigator can simply walk along established grid lines carrying the instrument. Instrument sensitivity is comparable to that of the proton magnetometer, and data are automatically logged as the surveyor walks (figure 6.10). Gradiometers measure the immediate magnetic field using two sensors mounted in a vertical mode. This array minimizes strong gradient influences and solar or diurnal effects, providing

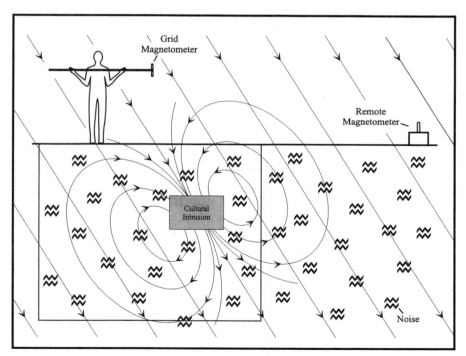

Figure 6.9   **Schematic diagram illustrating general principles of magnetic surveying.**

Figure 6.10   Magnetic survey using a fluxgate gradiometer. The archaeologist walks along an established site grid while the instrument automatically records data.

greater resolution of features and clarification of anomalies with greater precision (Heimmer and De Vore 1995).

A minor disadvantage of the fluxgate gradiometer is that it is highly directional. It measures only the component of the Earth's magnetic field parallel to its axis or along its length. The instrument must be held in a consistent direction as the operator traverses the grid. The proton magnetometer, by contrast, measures the total field without regard to direction (Clark 1990:69).

Geoscan Research has developed a line of fluxgate gradiometers that share characteristics of high sensitivity, compactness, and relative simplicity. These instruments include built-in data loggers and digital displays of grid, line, and measuring points.

As in many other geophysical exploration methods, data are stored in the field for later downloading. At the end of the day, the data can be dumped into a preprocessing program (you can use ASCII text files to edit data) and then transferred to a mapping program. During preprocessing, you can select for or against trends by using data filters. You may wish to use a high-pass filter for extreme contrasts or a low-pass filter for smoothing. You will end up with a plotted graph, gray-scale map, or contour map of your site showing magnetic anomalies that hopefully represent cultural features.

Weymouth's (1986; Weymouth and Huggins 1985; Weymouth and Nickel 1977) work on Plains Village sites provides a compelling advertisement for the use of magnetic surveying in support of archaeology.

MAGNETIC SUSCEPTIBILITY

Unlike most of the other geophysical sensing techniques, magnetic susceptibility does not sense the presence of subsurface objects or features. Instead, it measures magnetic conditions near the surface of the ground. Organic matter and bugs, worms, and other burrowing creatures create measurable magnetic conditions in the topsoil. These introduced magnetic conditions decrease with depth and are generally confined to the A soil horizon. Magnetic activity in the topsoil is conveniently increased by cultural processes, such as fires, that add organic material to the A horizon. Magnetic susceptibility therefore is useful for determining the presence and limits of surface anomalies that might be representative of midden or habitation areas within sites, rather than a method of identifying the location of individual features.

Clark (1990:99-105) reviews the complex marriage of chemistry and physics on which magnetic susceptibility is based. Suffice it to say here that in this type of survey, you are interested in measuring magnetic concentrations and the mineralogical signature of the topsoil. The standard instrumentation, currently a unit called the Bartington MS2, consists of a small electronics box, carried by the field surveyor, that is connected by cable to a canelike apparatus with a sensor attached to the bottom (figure 6.11). Power is supplied to an oscillator circuit at the sensor that generates an alternating magnetic field in the sensor coil. A probe at the instrument's distal end is inserted into the ground surface, and soil within the influence of the magnetic field (a few centimeters) will change the frequency of the oscillating current (Clark 1990:102). The magnetic susceptibility bridge coil measures alternating current frequency as it changes according to the magnetic susceptibility of the soil. The instrument is capable of data point or continuous data logging. Data processing and presentation are similar to that of the other geophysical methods discussed in this section.

Figure 6.11 Photograph showing a Bartington
MS2 magnetic susceptibility bridge coil.

CONCLUSION

Geophysical prospecting techniques are used on a small but growing percentage of archaeological survey projects. There will come a time in the career of most archaeological surveyors when one or more of these methods will be appropriate and useful. If you have reason to believe you might encounter a cemetery or other site containing human remains, a geophysical survey program should be considered as part of your research design. In most instances, geophysical methods will be most useful during the site evaluation phase of your survey project.

Select your geophysical method carefully on the basis of anticipated targets. Consider what limitations your project area will place on types of equipment you can use. Budget realistically to account for your chosen method's rate of data recovery, effort needed in interpretation, and cost. Refer to Sidebar 6.1 for a quick summary of the comparative strengths and weaknesses of each geophysical method.

6.1. RELATIVE STRENGTHS AND WEAKNESSES OF GEOPHYSICAL EQUIPMENT

	Potential Targets	Rate of Data Recovery
Metal detector	Metal objects, historical period sites, battlefields	Fast
Resistivity	Near surface features, rock features, hearths, pits, houses, mounds	Moderate
Electromagnetic conductivity	Sump features, pits, houses, trenches, metal objects	Fast
Ground Penetrating Radar	Voids, grave shafts, tombs, coffins, foundations, cellars, cisterns	Moderate
Magnetometry	Subsurface anomalies, pits, houses, trenches, foundations, wells	Moderate
Magnetic susceptibility	Middens, hearth areas, habitation zones	Moderate

With a little work, it is easy to understand and use geophysical methods in support of archaeological survey. The process is straight-forward, from field acquisition of data through download, processing, and visual representation (figure 6.12). Many archaeologists are becoming trained in these techniques. Skill in interpretation remains the key, and in most cases it is very important to interpret your results in consultation with a geophysical specialist. Colleagues can recommend geophysical contractors with successful archaeological track records in your region.

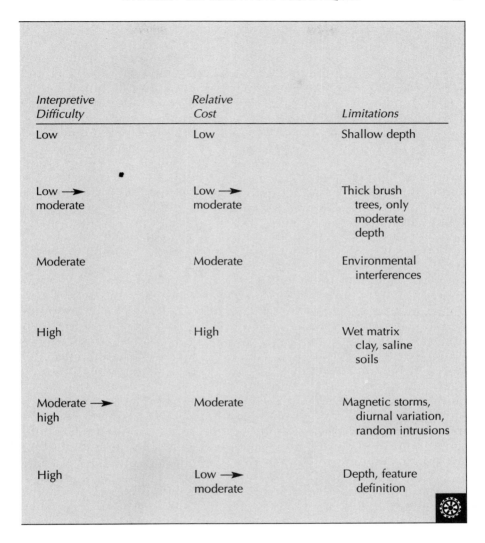

Interpretive Difficulty	Relative Cost	Limitations
Low	Low	Shallow depth
Low → moderate	Low → moderate	Thick brush trees, only moderate depth
Moderate	Moderate	Environmental interferences
High	High	Wet matrix clay, saline soils
Moderate → high	Moderate	Magnetic storms, diurnal variation, random intrusions
High	Low → moderate	Depth, feature definition

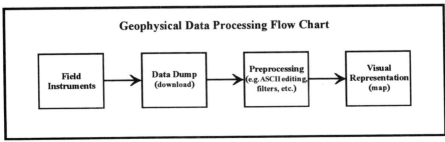

Geophysical Data Processing Flow Chart

Field Instruments → Data Dump (download) → Preprocessing (e.g. ASCII editing, filters, etc.) → Visual Representation (map)

Figure 6.12 Flow chart depicting typical path of geophysical data from field recovery through graphical representation.

7

RECORDING AND MAPPING

READING MAPS AND AERIAL PHOTOGRAPHS

A map gives us an image of the world that we can never get from the ground. It reduces a vast and complex environment to a set of symbols in a manageable paper space, something we can fold up and throw into our field pack. Some maps of the terrain, compiled from satellite images or aerial photographs, can even take the place of a ground-level survey if you are looking for large features such as field systems, trails, or architectural remains. A map can be limiting, too. CRM archaeologists know a world of engineering drawings, of narrow survey corridors that bear little or no relation to the terrain, where the project area is an absolute boundary. We all carry a map in our heads, a vague but important aspect of our thinking about what we know as meaningful space. This is important because the people whose sites we seek had their own ideas of the landscape and their own ways of remembering and recording. We have to be careful not to impose our understandings of what might be a good place for a site on people with an entirely different way of life. Reading and mapping the landscape is therefore a practical and intellectual task. Maps and aerial photographs—and, increasingly, satellite images—are essential tools in every aspect of a survey, for preliminary research and planning, for field navigation, and for recording your results.

While you are planning the survey, you need to learn all you can about the land you'll be walking through. Understanding the terrain, vegetation, animal life, drainage features, soils, and bedrock geology of a place over the last ten thousand years helps you visualize how native and immigrant cultures may have used it. With this background knowledge, you can manage survey resources more effectively, as you can identify areas with greater site potential. You may even be able to identify sites before you set foot in the field!

Aerial photographs provide the most detailed view of the land surface. As noted in chapter 6, aerial remote sensing has a long and distinguished history in archaeology. Air photos using false-color infrared (IR) film may reveal the presence of buried features and sites. IR films detect variation in reflected heat (infrared radiation) and are especially effective in detecting shallow subsurface features that retard or enhance the growth of vegetation above them. Healthy vegetation is a strong reflector of infrared, appearing bright red on a photograph. Damaged or stunted vegetation will stand out, too, often as yellowish hues.

Photogrammetric mapping based on air photos also is an important archaeological survey tool (Creamer et al. 1997; Eddy et al. 1996; Fowler 1997). Even if you will not use them to make maps, air photos are useful tools to familiarize yourself with new landscapes. Chapter 4 discusses the importance of air photos in helping you understand your study area's physical setting. At first, air photos may appear to depict a flat and rather unfamiliar world. Where photographic images partly overlap, however, you can take two consecutive pictures (a stereopair) and view them with a binocular magnifier that will give you a three-dimensional image. With practice, you will be able to see what the actual ground surface looks like along with the general land use and features you want to know about in a survey, such as rock outcrops, eroded areas, buildings, and other structures. The 3D images often enhance the subtle changes in terrain produced by buried foundations, abandoned roads, and other cultural features not visible at ground level.

Satellite imagery captures whole regions in a single image ideal for use in large-scale regional studies of topography and ecology and for the detection of trail networks, settlements, and other large archaeological features. Multispectral images produced by the Landsat 7 satellite provide views of virtually all of North America at a resolution of three meters. The Canadian satellite RADARSAT-1, carrying a synthetic aperture radar (SAR) sensor that can penetrate clouds, darkness, smoke, and fog, produces stereographic images at resolutions as high as eight meters. RADARSAT-2, to be launched in 2003, will increase the resolution to a maximum of three meters. The U.S. company Space Imaging sells color images of North America that have a resolution of one meter.

Chapter 4 notes the importance of topographic, soils, geological, and plat maps. Use these maps to obtain further background on your study area and to help you make your own maps. The essential map is the topographic quadrangle. It shows basic natural and cultural features, including drainages and physical relief, tree cover, transportation features, and buildings. An area with closely spaced contours suggests a rugged landscape with steep slopes and deep gullies; farther apart, contour lines indicate a more gentle terrain. Note any conspicuous landmarks in your survey area. You may need them once you are limited to your ground-level view.

Soil maps give a close-up picture of the land's history because soils developed in specific environmental situations. Each soil type is a product of original matrix (e.g., glacial till, alluvial sediment, bedrock), vegetation, slope, and relation to drainage (upland, slope, river bottom). Geological maps may lead you to potential lithic sources, and county plat maps and other property maps preserve local settlement history. As humans are much the same in terms of their basic material needs whatever the millennium, don't be surprised if the ideal prehistoric site locality was, or is, the site of more recent occupation.

Once you begin fieldwork, your navigation skills come into play. It looks easy on a map. On the ground, however, your view is limited, and you may have a problem figuring out exactly where you are. Surveyors in much of North America thoughtfully marked the land in one-square-mile units, as you can tell from the checkerboard pattern you see from an airplane. Yet one square mile of featureless terrain can look like the next square mile, and there are dusty, unmarked roads from the Arctic to the tip of South America. If you are in forested or mountainous terrain, the problem may be that you cannot see anything but trees. Of course, you have a compass with you, and perhaps a GPS unit, so you may not get truly lost, but to know where you are, you need to be able to translate the scale of features on a map or air photo to the same features in the real world.

Here is the problem: If someone wished to mark your exact location on a map and he gave you the space of a real-world meter to occupy, it would be represented as one twenty-fourth of a millimeter, one of the standard 1:24,000-scale topographic maps published by the U.S. Geological Survey (USGS). This is the problem of scale. So what looks like a small, easily visible gully on a map may in fact be a broad valley quite unlike what you imagine. It takes practice to change your way of seeing. In difficult terrain, follow the map carefully, as one landform may look like the next. Your aerial photographs can help you find clearings or other distinctive features that can keep you on track. The terrain looks awfully easy to traverse when it is simply rows of contours on paper. Because USGS 1:24,000 maps are drafted to be accurate to within a twelve-meter range, don't rely on the map to locate anything or any place with greater precision.

Once you have found a site, you need to locate it on the topographic map. This can be difficult, unless you are next to features already marked on the map—once again, because of the problem of scale. Imagine you have found a small lithic scatter, about ten meters square. On a 1:24,000 map, this site would occupy a space of less than one-half millimeter square. Put a dot on the map to mark the site. An average HB pencil dot is a millimeter, and that equals about twenty-four meters, or almost eighty feet. But now that basic GPS units (discussed later) are priced for virtually anyone's budget, all you need to find yourself and your site is to take a reading, and you will have a location accurate to about ten or twenty meters (one pencil dot). With GPS error correction through real time or postprocessing, you can achieve accuracy of less than a meter. This is great for site mapping, but you can tolerate a less accurate unit for locating sites on the topographic map, as you have that twenty-four-meter pencil dot to work with.

Even with electronic equipment, you still need to read the landscape and know where you are on the map, as you may not be able to get a reading because of the terrain or positioning of the satellites. It is also good practice to locate the sites on aerial photographs. With air photos and quads in hand, revisiting the sites should be no problem.

DRAFTING MAPS

Once you have identified a site, it is time to draft your own map. What kind of survey are you doing? If it is a basic inventory, a quick sketch may do if you plan to return. You will need this map anyway for the site form that you submit for every site you find. A sketch map should include enough detail to convey a basic impression of the site in its setting, so you can find it again. You might be tempted to make a highly detailed map, using a transit or other precise surveying instrument, but you must remember the purpose of your survey. If the site will be revisited anyway, your main goal is to get the location right. This is relatively easy if you have a GPS unit, as you will be able to navigate back to very close to your original reading. If you don't, you will need to map to landmarks such as geological survey benchmarks, buildings, or permanent natural features. If you shovel tested or otherwise disturbed the site, you will also have to include these data (see chapter 5). It is especially important to record additional detail at this stage if the site is small and does not appear to be archaeologically significant because this may be the only time an archaeologist ever sees it. Your record will be the only record.

How you map the site depends on your survey goals. Most archaeologists learned at field school to lay out grid systems, oriented north, with squares anywhere from one to twenty meters a side. This type of arrangement makes sense in a survey if you are trying to study intrasite variations in artifact density or if you have a research design built around a systematic sampling technique. It may be less practical if you are simply trying to determine site boundaries and collect a small sample of material as a prelude to additional work. Remember that the main goal of survey mapping is to locate the site and map its general features and your subsurface testing accurately and to scale. You could place the squares randomly and superimpose a grid later—as long as you have the squares oriented consistently. Alternatively, why not simply establish a datum and record the bearing and distance (and, perhaps, the elevation) from that datum to the objects you want to map (whether natural or cultural features, or test pits), ending up with a pattern of rays? You can easily reconstruct the map back in camp or in the lab.

Surveying instruments range from simple compasses and tapes to electronic theodolites (total stations) and GPS units. The fastest and most precise field mapping today relies on the advanced electronic capabilities of GPS units and GIS computer programs. For a more than three-hundred-mile survey project along the Cheyenne River valley in South Dakota and Wyoming, the University of South Dakota (USD) Archaeology Laboratory used a GPS unit with real-time differential correction, accurate to less than a meter; a total station that gave azimuth, horizontal distance, and relative elevation readings at the touch of a button; and laptop computers with a GIS incorporating electronic versions of topographic maps and aerial photographs. Computer software automatically transformed the field data into electronic maps, and the field crew transmitted these (via e-mail or ftp) to the lab at USD, where they were added to a master GIS that produced all the paper maps for the project report.

Does this high-tech equipment make other methods obsolete? Not at all. You may not need submeter accuracy, especially if you are simply conducting a reconnaissance survey. One traditional solution is the Brunton pocket transit, combining a compass, sights, a level bubble, and a sighting mirror. If it is mounted on a tripod, it will help you make a suitably accurate field map. If you have the luxury of time, you may carry a plane table and alidade (basically a telescope mounted on a protractor sitting on graph paper on a flat board and tripod) and produce your finished map on site. The value of this nearly obsolete though real-time method is that you avoid recording errors, a tragedy if you only discover them when you are reconstructing a map from your data in the lab. A good compromise for work requiring more speed and less accuracy is a sighting compass. You look through a sight at your target, and the azimuth appears superimposed in the view. If you think the angle or degree of slope may be important, bring along a clinometer. The same goes for altitude. You can now buy a small, electronic altimeter with an LCD display that gives you the altitude, the current barometric pressure, a visual readout of the barometer over the previous twelve hours, symbols predicting the weather over the next twelve hours, the temperature, the date and time, a timer, and an alarm to wake you up in the morning! Perhaps the most effective way to create a simple map by hand in the field is to locate the site on an aerial photograph, as you can then easily translate this to a topographic map or GIS in the lab.

Sometimes you may adjust your mapping system for historic sites, if you are dealing with standing structures or foundations. It makes sense to record these in the English system, as that is the system used to build them. Jumping from metric to English systems is something you need to be comfortable with anyway, as most of your topographic maps still have contour intervals in feet. For prehistoric sites, it depends entirely on what you, or future archaeologists, plan to do with the information you collect.

Greater precision does not necessarily produce better understanding of the phenomena you are studying. Archaeology will always be a subtle intertwining of science and imagination. You need to produce a map that will bring life to both your analysis and your interpretation.

GLOBAL POSITIONING SYSTEMS

The essence of Global Positioning Systems (GPS) is triangulation, just like ground-level surveying, but instead using one terrestrial position and three or more satellite (or SV—space vehicle) positions. There are twenty-four SVs orbiting the Earth to provide these positions. Each satellite has an atomic clock that broadcasts a continuous signal of the time. The handheld GPS unit has an antenna (either built-in or external) that receives the time signal and compares it to its own internal time clock. The difference between the two is then calculated as distance, through the old Velocity × Time = Distance formula. Following the principles of triangulation, if you get directional data from at least three positions (ideally, four or more), you can compute the position of the GPS unit, rendered by the software into the coordinate system of your choice. Archaeologists tend to work with Universal Transverse Mercator (UTM) coordinates, because you can easily compute and mark your locations on a topographic map.

Giving precise locations is fantastic enough, but the GPS can do even more. As it is able to take positions approximately every second, the unit does not have to be stationary. You can use it to record linear features and areas, and, most important, you can instruct the unit to give you readings in relation to a predetermined point. This means you can record a site in the midst of a featureless plain and then navigate back to it easily in the future.

That's basically it—a matter of pushing a few buttons. If you are going to make effective use of the GPS as a mapping tool, however, you must know two important things about how the system works so you don't get into trouble in the field.

First, the system relies on access to satellite signals. You can't take readings any time you want, because the level of accuracy depends on the positions of the satellites relative to each other and to you, holding the GPS. Sometimes there are not enough satellites in view—usually because something blocks part of the sky. You have to have a direct, unobstructed path to at least four satellites.

The second point is accuracy of the signal. Sometimes, the available satellites are simply in bad positions—they may be too close to each other in relation to your antenna's ground position—so the accuracy of the readings will be low. This measure of position accuracy is rendered numerically in your GPS unit as a DOP (dilution of precision). Of several DOPs, PDOP (position dilution of precision) provides the most general estimation of potential accuracy. When the PDOP is too high (e.g., a value over 6), you'll just have to wait until the SVs move into better positions. Fortunately, as the orbits of all the SVs are known, you can (with appropriate software) obtain an hourly readout of the measurement conditions for any day in the future—even many months ahead. This way you can plan your observation times strategically.

When the time is right, however, you have another problem to deal with: If you take a single position with your GPS, all but the most expensive single-frequency instrument may give you an accuracy of no better than five to ten meters. You can improve accuracy by taking multiple readings at this position and averaging them, but you still may not achieve accuracies below several meters. The problem is errors in satellite signal transmission. These may be related to the satellites (clock timing and orbit errors), receiver noise, or signal interference caused by conditions in the ionosphere, storms and other atmospheric disruptions, or multipath effects caused by buildings or other obstacles that can influence the direct transmission of radio waves.

The solution: If you take your reading from a known point on the Earth's surface (e.g., a benchmark), you can calculate the error for that reading—simply the difference between where you know you are and where the instrument says you are. This is practical only if you have two GPS instruments reading simultaneously, one you are using to map (the rover) and another stationary in a known location (the base station). With two sets of readings taken at the same time, in roughly the same geographic area (up to three hundred miles, actually), you can calculate the degree of error for every second of observation time and correct your instrument accordingly, a process called *differential correction.* This is how it works: When you begin to record a set of positions, the GPS unit creates a file and names it with a set of numbers that indicate the year, date, and hour of the file creation. The data for each position also include the time, to the second. While you are busy taking readings, the base station is also creating files and recording positions every second. When you have obtained your readings and downloaded both the rover and base station files into the computer, a postprocessing program automatically matches the second-by-second readings, calculates the error, and makes the correction.

If you don't have the luxury of two suitable GPS units, you can still correct your readings by obtaining base station data from a separate source. Various governmental agencies and commercial outfits maintain their own base stations. They offer (free or for a subscription price) base station files to public users, either by ftp or, increasingly, from the World Wide Web. As long as the base station is within three hundred miles of your project, you should be able to obtain files with sufficient accuracy for differential correction.

The best GPS units have a built-in receiver that is capable of detecting the signals of base stations that broadcast the error correction continuously. If you are in range of a base station beacon or subscribe to the radio frequency of a commercial differential correction satellite (e.g., Landstar, Omnistar), you can obtain real-time differential correction. Using such instruments, you know where you are to a meter, right on the spot. This is clearly a great advantage when you are using the GPS to navigate back to a site.

Once you have the planning out of the way, you can get down to the mapping. All but the cheapest GPS units allow you to record data as points, lines, or polygons (areas). Recording a position is rather easy. Once you initiate a reading, the GPS will record positions (normally, one per second) until you stop it. With averaging, you can refine your accuracy by taking more readings, but unless you have time to burn, one or two minutes at a very important location, such as a datum, is enough. Lines and polygons are different, as the unit records positions while you are moving. Hence, all positions are individual and they cannot be averaged. If you have an expensive unit, this is not much of a problem, as the accuracy with differential correction will be less than a meter. If you don't, it may be better to take a series of single points along a line or around a boundary. Each of these can be averaged, and you can connect the dots when you make the map.

As the spatial accuracy of GPS is coarse compared to transits and other surveying instruments, choose carefully what spatial features to map via GPS, so that the information required suits the accuracy of the unit. GPS is ideal for plotting site locations and for work on sites where features are more than a couple of meters apart and absolute precision is not important. You may think that this eliminates much archaeology, but think about what precision means. If you are doing a basic inventory survey and shovel-test a site, and your readings are off by two to five meters, will this dramatically misrepresent your work effort or your interpretation of the site? It may, but only if your research design uses the precise location of these tests for some analytical purpose. If this is so, limit the GPS to locating your datum, and use surveying instruments to map your site.

Agencies see the world in terms of fixed boundaries, so you are always required to determine archaeological site boundaries. A GPS with the capability to record polygons is ideal, as the boundaries of most archaeological sites are fuzzy enough that the error is meaningless. One cautionary note: If the sky is blocked on part of your site, resulting in a loss of signal, the GPS automatically joins the first and last points you take. This can cause a great problem if the points are widely separated, as you will end up with a straight line between them. In such circumstances, using the line function is better, as it is open-ended. In both cases, always remember to mark the position that you started from. It is easy to forget to do so after you have trudged around in a big irregular circle.

If a GPS allows you to locate a feature to within a meter and return to this point at any time in the future, guided by its navigational program, what is the point of a much less accurate paper map? Well, you can make notes much more easily on a sketch map—important for discussion of the site environment—and a paper map can reside safely in your backpack, unaffected by battery failure or file corruption.

GEOGRAPHIC INFORMATION SYSTEMS

Another major innovation in mapping is the suite of computer-based Geographic Information Systems (GIS). A GIS is, essentially, a tool for displaying spatial data and fostering the analysis of those and related data.

The advantage of a GIS is obvious. Rather than being stuck with a pile of paper maps, each with a separate theme—history, topography, vegetation, elevation, physical relief, geology, hydrology, and so on—you can incorporate all the information in individual databases and define them as layers in the GIS. You might have a basic topographic map as your foundation, and layers of relief, drainage features, and the other desired map information above them.

The most powerful aspect of a GIS is its analytical capability. You can apply all the operations of a database, such as selecting records with a certain condition (e.g., in a field containing a count of artifacts in a test unit, selecting all the test units with more than five artifacts), and these will be distinguished by color from records lacking the conditions. Because the information is tied to geographic position, you can do more complex operations related to the spatial relationships of features. For example, you can select all the sites within a certain distance from water and above a certain elevation, in your project area or drainage. With such capabilities, the GIS is an immensely powerful visualization tool.

The most relevant aspect of GIS for survey mapping is that GPS systems will convert their locational data to the formats of the major GIS software, so that you can seamlessly incorporate the results of your own GPS survey directly into a GIS. In 1997 and 1998, for example, a Trimble Pro-XR GPS unit was an essential part of the USD Archaeology Laboratory Phase I survey of Devils Tower National Monument, Wyoming. During the survey, we took locations on every site datum, test unit, and linear feature and on a number of site boundaries. Back in the lab, we set up a GIS with a digital elevation model (DEM) of the USGS Devils Tower, Wyoming, quadrangle as background, contoured it at ten-meter intervals, and quickly translated all the differentially corrected Trimble files into the GIS format. In a matter of minutes, the entire season's work appeared in its precise geographic location within the National Monument boundaries. To this map we added a digital orthophoto quarter quadrangle (DOQQ), which is an electronic version of an aerial photograph, and a digital raster graphic (DRG), which reproduces a standard USGS 7.5' quadrangle. Finally, using the DEM, we constructed a three-dimensional model of the tower environment. With locational uncertainty gone, now all we had to worry about was what all these hard-won data really meant!

TOMORROW'S TECHNOLOGY

It is hard to look more than a year into the future of mapping technologies. Remote sensing satellites continue to be launched, each more sophisticated and sensitive than its predecessors, so we gain access to an increasingly diverse range of imaging products. In October 2001, DigitalGlobe, a commercial earth information company, launched Quickbird, a satellite that provides the highest-resolution imagery of any current space vehicle: 61 centimeters in panchromatic (grayscale) and 2.44 meters in multispectral (color and near-infrared) forms. Significantly, this information is freely available commercially—too costly at this point, perhaps, for most individual archaeologists, but certainly within the means of larger institutions and CRM firms.

Five months later, the European Space Agency launched a gigantic satellite, ENVISAT (ENVIronmental SATellite), designed to retrieve atmospheric and terrestrial data and to enable monitoring of changes in these systems. Archaeologists should benefit as this information helps earth sciences gain better understanding of environmental and climatic changes.

GPS units continue to get more precise, smaller, and cheaper. Many have detailed topographic base maps built in, making paper maps virtually obsolete in the field (as long as you have lots of batteries and a backup system!). No archaeologist can claim today that the price of a good GPS survey unit is beyond his or her means.

Also, GIS is expanding exponentially. While it has its roots in geography, GIS is becoming indispensable in such widely divergent fields as crime mapping and land use studies. Working archaeologists in the future will ignore GIS at their peril!

Of course, no matter how beautiful and seductive all this technology is, it cannot free us from the essential dilemma: We are still stuck between the earth and sky, trying to make connections between places and cultural landscapes that have long since disappeared. So, while it is always good to dream about the future, do it with your feet planted firmly on the ground!

8

THE SURVEY REPORT

You have had a great field project, found lots of neat sites, and enjoyed your crew, and all concerned wouldn't mind doing it again. But for you, the job isn't even half finished. In from the field, you may find yourself directing a laboratory team as large as your field crew. They might be the same people. There are artifacts to be washed and cataloged, analyses to be done, tables to be made, graphics to be drawn or created, and curation standards to be met (topics covered in Toolkit, volume 4, *Artifacts*, and volume 6, *Curating Archaeological Collections*, and therefore not considered in detail here). Finally, though, you must find a way to translate all the data you've assembled, from the beginning of your background research through your field, laboratory, and analysis programs, into a coherent statement of the effects your client's project will have on cultural resources.

The culmination of every field survey project is the report of investigations. This is the product you will supply to your client. Your client will pass it on to the SHPO or provincial archaeologist for review. In the United States, it may be passed on to the Advisory Council on Historic Preservation if the SHPO and your client disagree about management decisions based on your data or recommendations. It may even be entered as evidence in a court case. Therefore, you must present the results of your survey in the clearest, most concise way possible. No review and compliance officer likes to wade through pages and pages of fluff. There is no reason to wax eloquent in your background research section about any subject unless there is a compelling reason to bring up that topic for contextual, analytical, or other reasons. Cite existing literature, if necessary, to guide you and your readers to important background material. But focus on the most effective possible presentation of *your data*. That way, the over-worked reviewers can make real-life judgments in the most expedient manner possible as to whether the project's legal mandates related to cultural resources have been fulfilled.

This is not meant to imply that you should not explore to the fullest any serious anthropological or archaeological problem to which your data are germane. Indeed, you would be negligent if you did not. Your client and the review agency need this information to make appropriate management decisions. Just don't fluff up your report. Your client and the reviewer will recognize unnecessary report padding for what it is—an expensive irritation.

The quality of reports that reviewers receive is uneven. Strive not to be among those who submit obtuse, even incomprehensible reports. Such reports are rarely accepted without further clarification, which invariably requires a time-eating, three-way dialogue. Such discussions often lead to delays and bad feelings. On the other hand, if you do the job correctly the first time, by presenting your data clearly and competently, the reviewer can quickly check off on the project or enter into timely consultation with your client regarding further work. Your report will have armed both your client and the reviewer with a clear understanding of all relevant archaeological facts regarding the project or site. Competence demonstrated in this way will make your client happy and willing to send you more work.

Volume 7 in the Toolkit, *Presenting the Past*, focuses on communicating archaeology to broad audiences of colleagues and the public. The present chapter therefore stresses preparation of the survey report to document an entity's compliance with cultural resources requirements—a necessary springboard for any further use of CRM-generated data and interpretations.

STRUCTURE AND CONTENT

Be systematic and organized when you prepare the project report. While certain fundamental content is needed for the document to move smoothly through the bureaucracy, there remains plenty of room for personal innovation in your analytical style, data presentation, and interpretive synthesis (given an interesting and productive project area).

The level of effort required for report preparation varies widely depending on the scope and results of the survey. No template can adequately express the range of variability encompassed by all survey projects, and sections of your report may be rearranged to better fit your data set, so what follows is a working formula. Many scopes of work and contracts specify the report's format, and most states and provinces have issued report guidelines, too. Discuss report organization and content with your sponsor and reviewer if you're receiving mixed signals form these sources.

TITLE PAGE

The title of your report should explicitly state the type of investigation and identify the project and its location. Identify the author by name and title. Most CRM enterprises have a numbered sequence to identify each of their reports (e.g., *XYZ Consulting Report #798*). As this will be one of the easiest ways to identify the report for future reference, the report's number and date of release should be provided on the title page. Also identify the sponsoring agency (your client) and, if applicable, the contract, job, or permit number of the project. The principal investigator, if other than the author (normally your boss), should be identified on the title page, along with your company's name and address. Some states and provinces may require a governmental review and compliance number on the title page of the document.

If you have a graphic in the report that quickly identifies the project, it may be appropriate to put that figure on the cover of your report. This is entirely optional and is rarely if ever done for small or negative surveys. However, if you have located a significant site or if the project is regional in scope and you feel your report may be frequently cited, a cover illustration is useful to future users of the document because it makes the report easier to locate on a shelf full of otherwise achromatic examples of "gray literature." If your cartographic skills are good, it doesn't hurt to occasionally show them off on the cover of your report.

FRONT MATTER

Substantial survey reports should include front matter including a table of contents that identifies page numbers for report headings, subheadings, individual site discussions, references, and appendices; a list of figures with page numbers identified for each; and a similar list of tables. Short documents (generally less than fifteen pages or so) reporting small or negative surveys may not require these pages.

ABSTRACT

The abstract is a very important component of the report and should always be included. Often, agencies will require a management summary at the beginning of the report, and that is essentially the same as an abstract. The idea of the abstract is to boil down all of the report's essential information, conclusions, and recommendations from the pages of your report into a brief synopsis. Reduce the content of each major section of the report into a sentence or two. Taken together, these sentences comprise your abstract.

Your client may never read beyond the abstract before shipping your report to the SHPO or provincial archaeologist. The abstract will be the first thing the reviewer will turn to in the report, so it should encapsulate the substantive issues covered in the project. Make the abstract a straightforward and credible summary of your report and the project.

The abstract should identify the undertaking, the type of project, and the purpose of the study. You should summarize the area surveyed in acres and hectares (2.47 acres = 1 hectare) and briefly summarize field procedures. Summarize any historic properties identified by the survey, their significance, and your recommendations for the sites. If you are recommending project clearance from an archaeological perspective, so state; if further work is recommended for any historic property, state that, too.

INTRODUCTION

The introduction should identify the contractor (your company) and the project sponsor (your client). It should specify the purpose of the study, the date(s) on which it was accomplished, and principal personnel (you, if you were in charge of the fieldwork). Your client may ask you to add a statement that the opinions and recommendations are yours (or your company's) and not necessarily theirs. Also state where materials and field records generated by the project are curated.

The introduction must include a detailed description of the undertaking—a clearly worded summary of the development project or other reason for the survey. Include a concise legal description of the project area (section or quarter section, township, range, and county), total project length (for corridor surveys), or total area (acres/hectares) surveyed. Provide a map, referenced in the text, that shows the general location of the project. Normally, the location map is drafted at a scale of 1:100,000 or smaller. Your second, larger scale map details the project location and area surveyed in relation to the surrounding topography. Site locations are also typically included on these larger scale maps. The USGS 7.5′ quadrangle, printed at the scale of 1:24,000, is used almost everywhere in the United States as a base map. Most reviewers require that you depict your project area on a 7.5′ USGS, NTS, or provincial quadrangle (figure 8.1).

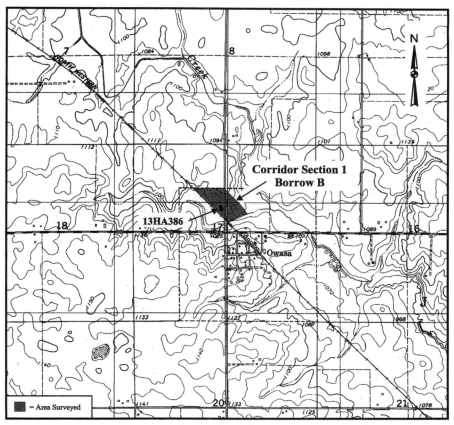

Figure 8.1   Typical large scale map (1:24,000) showing location of project.

Describe the project area and any ancillary construction in the area of potential effect, such as borrow areas or stream channel modifications. The reviewers will want to know how you defined the limits of the project, so indicate whether you worked from detailed project plans, aerial photographs, or a verbal description of the project area in relation to existing landmarks. Some reviewers and agencies require UTM coordinates for the project area. As noted earlier, UTM readings can be obtained from your GPS; also, UTM grid lines are shown on the USGS 7.5', NTS, and provincial quadrangles.

PROJECT AREA DESCRIPTION, A.K.A. ENVIRONMENTAL CONTEXT

Since all culture groups must adjust to the physical environment they occupy, and archaeological deposits inhere in the natural landscape, environmental processes that form the landscape determine the conditions of the archaeological record and influence our perception of the human past. Therefore, a discussion of the environmental conditions relevant to both the past and present of your project area is an essential component of your report.

In this report section, reiterate what you learned about the project area's physical setting during your background research and what you determined about the physiography of the project area during fieldwork. Under a subheading such as "Regional Context," provide a brief discussion of regional landforms. The regional description includes a concise summary of bedrock geology, Quaternary landforms, topography, drainage patterns, and surficial deposits. This review can be followed by a general discussion of lithologic, stratigraphic, and age-specific relationships of Holocene Age valley fills in the area.

With this background established, you can move on to a more detailed, project area–specific consideration of physiographic conditions. You can use a subheading such as "Local Context" to distinguish this relatively detailed discussion from the more general, regional data provided earlier.

SMALL PROJECTS

For small projects in uncomplicated landscapes, the project area discussion might be a fairly simple description of local topography and terrain. If applicable, you can discuss hydrologic factors; for example, does water sit in closed depressions on the landscape, or is it drained by dendritic stream patterns?

Project area soils should be described and compared to typical profiles mapped in the county soil survey. What is the parent material for local soils? Till? Loess? Residuum? Did local soils develop under prairie, savanna, forest, or something else? You should attempt to explain any discrepancy between your field data and that published in the soil survey. Mapped boundaries of soil series are not always accurate at the site-specific level, and soil profiles might have been badly eroded since the survey was published.

Discuss recent and modern cultural and natural factors that bear on the physical state of the project area. The area may have been disturbed by processes such as earth moving, stream channeling, construction, or agriculture. Soil horizons of the upper solum (i.e., the A and B horizons) are often missing from upland settings, especially in agricultural areas where plowing has exacerbated erosional processes. In such circumstances, you may find artifacts representing the location of site, but they often appear only as lag deposits, in secondary rather than primary context. Such information will influence your recommendations about site significance.

Finally, you should discuss current project area conditions. Is the area plowed, in crops, sagebrush, fallow grasses, forested, or in some other kind of cover? What is the surface visibility, described as a percentage? Because ground cover influences your investigative strategy (see chapter 5), reviewers need details on ground conditions in order to determine the adequacy of your survey methods for all parts of the project area.

LARGE PROJECTS

Large projects that encompass several physiographic zones generally require more extensive discussions of environmental contexts. The more complex the physiography of a project area, the more complex may be the human adaptations to the landscape. Large survey projects can contribute important new data about any region. For these data to be presented most usefully, a thorough discussion of the physical context of the project area is necessary. Our advice is to view research and writing about the physical environment not as a chore but as a great opportunity to learn the physiography of the area. By understanding the environmental contexts of your project area, you will acquire information necessary for interpreting human adaptations to those contexts—subjects about which large, regional surveys can provide a great deal of essential data. Do this research for your own edification and so you can serve your client and the discipline more competently. Your report will be better for it.

Start with a discussion of the basic geology of the project area. Subsections under this heading should cover the bedrock and the Quaternary geomorphological processes responsible for the current landscape. You will have source material for these topics from having done thorough background research on the physical setting of the project area before you started fieldwork (see chapter 4).

Does the local bedrock contain culturally useful minerals? Are there chert-bearing outcrops where you might expect a concentration of short-term resource procurement sites? How might the Quaternary record affect human settlement patterns? Would inhabitants of the area have enjoyed life in a settlement on the edge of an oak grove, or would they have had to manage the challenges and opportunities of a wetland setting? How has the Holocene geomorphological record affected the visibility and preservation potential of sites in valley settings? Have relatively stable floodplain surfaces been destroyed by lateral stream migration, or are they merely invisible because they are buried by historic period alluvium? These and other important questions must be answered in this section of the report.

If you contracted with a consulting geomorphologist, this section is the place to incorporate his or her information. Incorporate the specialists' expertise as usefully as possible into the fabric of the survey and the report. Most consulting geomorphologists will provide you with a report of their investigations. You can attach the report as an appendix to your archaeological reports, but often when this is done, there is no attempt to integrate the geomorphological data with the archaeological interpretations. The archaeologists and the geomorphologists were simply talking past each other. One wonders, in such cases, why bother? The disciplines should work hand in glove. To get the best out of both, the geomorphologist's data must be fully integrated into the "Environmental Context" section of your report.

Use high-quality illustrations liberally to help clarify important points. Such graphics can enhance your narrative presentation immeasurably (figure 8.2). Be as creative with visuals as you like, as long as they augment your discussion. Poor graphics are both pitiable and the mark of inexperience. Don't try to cram too much information onto any one illustration. It is better to make two maps that clearly support the ideas you want to express than to give the reviewer a

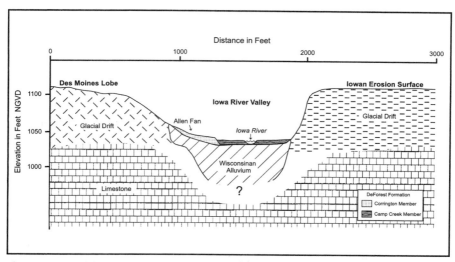

Figure 8.2 Schematic representation showing the relationship of Quaternary and Holocene deposits along an Iowa River valley transect.

headache by forcing him or her to distinguish among several data categories squeezed onto a single map.

After laying the environmental groundwork in the geology section, you can move to subsections on hydrology, soils, climate, vegetation, fauna, and the modern environment. The sections on climate, vegetation, and fauna are particularly important. Changes in climate and vegetation are frequently synchronous or nearly so. Culture groups that occupied the region at different times may have experienced and adjusted to starkly different climatic and biotic patterns. It can be useful to map these patterns diachronically because they provide excellent clues to long-term changes in settlement patterns (e.g., Collins 1991; Warren 1982). A solid discussion of environmental contexts is not fluff; as noted earlier, survey data are extremely useful for settlement pattern studies and in identifying changes in human responses to environmental variability.

In summary, the "Project Area Description" or "Environmental Context" section of your report will fix the physical background against which you will apply your data. The larger the scale of your project, generally the greater the detail you should present in this section. You should learn and present these data so you can make informed judgments and interpretations of your survey data, not because it is a bureaucratic requirement or a rote exercise. Pay attention to what you are doing. This is the essence of research, even in a CRM environment.

PREVIOUS ARCHAEOLOGICAL INVESTIGATIONS

A formal heading for this topic may not be required for most small archaeological survey projects. Generally speaking, and there are exceptions, the smaller the project, the less likely the need to discuss a large body of previous literature in detail.

For the large survey project, the opposite is the case. Just as you should provide a detailed environmental review for a large or complex survey area, a review of previous archaeological work in the region will set the stage for your new data. Your project should supplement, expand, or modify existing knowledge about the region, but it can't do this unless you know what has already been learned.

If you did a good job in your background research on the cultural setting (chapter 4), this is the place to reiterate what you found in the literature and archives. Depending on your project area, pertinent literature may go back one hundred years or more. A review of nearby sites that are recorded in the official state or provincial site file may be warranted. Who recorded the sites? Are temporal or cultural parameters for these sites secure, approximate, or negligible? Check the National Archaeological Data Base and state and provincial bibliographies for lists of relevant CRM reports. Read those reports and cite them here. Also review any other unpublished manuscripts such as theses and dissertations, as well as all relevant published archaeological literature and unpublished records and archives you consulted. Finally, discuss any local properties listed on the National Register of Historic Places, Historic Sites and Monuments register, or lists of state or provincial heritage sites. Often it is useful to supplement your discussion of the literature and previous archaeological investigations with a summary table.

RESEARCH DESIGN

Small projects are routinely conducted without the benefit of a formal, explicitly defined research design. Therefore, a separate heading to address the topic would not necessarily be found in all project reports. Still, your research design is an essential element of your project (see Toolkit, volume 1), so be sure it is presented in the report's introduction, at least.

For large survey projects, a formal section outlining the research design should be included. In this section you reiterate the research design that governed the project. State what questions or problem domains the project was to address and your assumptions about the data. If you used any kind of predictive models to guide a sampling strategy, identify them. Describe how your sampling strategy intended to obtain data pertinent to the identified problem domains. If your research design was modified during the course of the project, discuss that here.

METHODS

All reports must include a "Methods" section. For many small survey reports, it is convenient to subsume "Previous Archaeological Investigations" and "Research Design" sections within the "Methods" section. Regardless of whether the project is large or small, your "Methods" section must explicitly describe what you did to accomplish the survey. Make clear each method used during every step of the project. You will realize how important it was to have used systematic methods throughout the project, as it is always easier to write about systematic methods than those that are not.

Review the historical documents and other resources you checked, whom you consulted for background information (e.g., your landowner interviews, or discussions at the local historical society), photo collections or map libraries consulted, and any other pertinent methods used in conducting background research. If you sent mailings to landowners, discuss the particulars here.

Describe all of the field methods you used and the circumstances under which you used them. Discuss your pedestrian survey techniques, shovel tests, posthole tests, bucket augers, backhoe trenches, and how you investigated cutbank exposures. How did you define site limits? Report your artifact collection strategy. Did you recover all artifacts or a sample? Why? Define the strategy you used for site evaluation. Did the strategy differ for prehistoric and historic period sites? If so, how?

Provide details on your laboratory and analytical methods. Did you size-grade your material categories? Weigh them? Why? Discuss the classification and technological parameters used for analysis of prehistoric and historic artifacts. Did you attempt to identify the sources of the lithic material you found? How did you accomplish this? On what did you base your ceramic classification? Published sources? Comparison with extant collections? Spare no details on your methods and techniques—these are essential data for follow-up studies locally and in the general region.

Define the categories you use to organize your data on artifacts, features, and sites. Cultural categories may derive from temporal or developmental frameworks standard in your region. Functional categories can include a wide range of classifications based on any of numerous systems (see Toolkit, volume 4). The fact that you will normally be dealing with data from surface collections and limited subsurface testing often renders your interpretations tentative, but this should not deter you from describing the taxonomies you use.

Finally, state the criteria used for determining the eligibility or ineligibility of sites for the National Register of Historic Places or Historic Sites and Monuments register. Criteria applied to particular sites are discussed on a case-by-case basis in the "Results" section of the report.

RESULTS

This is where you finally get to write about what you actually found during the course of the survey. Begin with a discussion of any previously known sites in the project area. Did your examination of GLO records or other historical documents identify cultural properties in or near the project area? If so, discuss these sites. Provide illustrations keyed to the text that indicate the spatial relationship of the project area to previously recorded sites and to properties identified from historical sources. Discuss any pertinent information gleaned from local residents or from other interviews. Essentially, start this section by covering any significant information you gleaned about the project area while doing your "cultural setting" background research (chapter 4).

After that, simply present the field results—what you found on and in the ground. If the survey found no historic properties, this should be clearly stated, and you can skip to the "Summary and Recommendations" section of your report.

Under separate headings, discuss each site recorded by the survey. In the United States, headings should correspond to the site's designation as provided to you by the curator of your state's official site file. A trinomial designation used in most states identifies the state's alphabetical rank (e.g., 13 = Iowa), the county abbreviation (WA = Warren), and the order in which that site was recorded in that particular county (532). If there is reason to associate a name with the site, you may include the name in the heading of the site discussion (e.g., 13WA532, the Townsite of Wheeling). In Canada, you must number all sites according to the Borden System, a grid system based on geographic coordinates. The country is divided into coordinate blocks identified by two uppercase alpha characters, forming a grid sequence that runs from south to north and from east to west; following each uppercase alpha is a lowercase alpha that designates a subdivision based on latitude and longitude. Sites within each lowercase block are assigned sequential numbers by the Canadian Museum of Civilization or the responsible provincial ministry (e.g., AdHk-1, the Hind site).

In the first paragraph of each site discussion, identify the legal location of the site in reference to section, township, and range wherever that system is used (e.g., S½, SW¼, SW¼, SE¼ of Section 32, T77N-R21W; or NW¼, and in the NW¼, NE¼, and N½, SW¼, NW¼, NE¼ of Section 5, T76N-R21W). Provide a figure reference to a map showing the site in relation to the project area on the appropriate USGS 7.5', NTS, or provincial quadrangle. Provide specific UTM zone, easting, and northing coordinates for the site (e.g., Zone 15, E474940, N4585240). You may provide UTM coordinates for the site's center or perimeter, as your scope of work, sponsor, or reviewer may require. Also provide the site's elevation in relation to mean sea level.

Next, specify the basis on which you identified the site. For example, did you observe a surface scatter of prehistoric or historic artifacts? Was the site designated on the basis of positive shovel tests? Perhaps a local resident told you about the site. Or did you determine the presence of a deeply buried site through excavation with bucket augers? Describe the site's specific physical setting, and the condition and ground cover encountered at the time of the survey. Identify the procedure by which you determined site limits. Clearly state the spatial relationship between the site and the project right-of-way or boundaries. Is the site entirely within the project boundaries, partially within, or outside the right-of-way?

State whether or how you evaluated the site. Describe your collection strategy, and refer to a data table that summarizes the materials you collected. Did you perform an intensive, systematic surface collection? Artifact distribution maps generated from any such collections should be included and referred to in the text. Identify your subsurface sampling methods and show the location of your units on a detailed map of the site. If the site-specific geomorphological situation is complex, include plan view and cross-sectional figures showing the geological context of the archaeological materials.

Discuss the soils at the site and whether they are typical of the mapped soil series. Sites in upland settings often exhibit eroded profiles that reflect disturbance to the physical integrity of the site and its assemblages. This is often the critical factor in terms of significance determinations. If you can demonstrate that the soil profile is relatively intact and that the artifacts or features are relatively undisturbed on the surface or within the A and B soil horizons, the site retains a degree of physical integrity and a higher level of significance. If you can establish that the site retains physical integrity, it likely warrants serious consideration for potential National Register or national or provincial heritage site eligibility. For this reason, it is especially important to document any features you were able to define at the site. The presence of intact features is a clear indication that the site retains some degree of physical integrity.

Ordinarily, the site's cultural affiliation will be determined through analysis of its diagnostic artifacts or features. Be sure to cite the sources on which you base your interpretations. Significance is not necessarily precluded for sites that you are unable to assign to a particular cultural or temporal period, but it is more difficult to make the case when you cannot do so. Occasionally, cultural or temporal affiliation can be inferred from the geomorphological context of the archaeological material. For instance, if you know that the alluvial sediments containing the site are early- to mid-Holocene in age, then the artifacts themselves are also very likely to be that old. Historical records may be more reliable than features or artifacts for determining the age and significance of many historical period sites. Make the best case you can based on all lines of available evidence.

Ultimately, every archaeological evaluation in the United States should include the author's opinion of the site's eligibility or ineligibility for listing on the National Register of Historic Places. This recommendation must be made based on the significance, potential significance, or lack of significance according to National Register criteria (chapter 2). Criterion D, most frequently applied to archaeological sites, is that the site has "yielded, or may be likely to yield, information important in prehistory or history." Certain properties also may be eligible under criteria A through C. For sites that you are recommending as potentially eligible, be sure you refer to the site's significance in relation to the relevant State Plan or Historic Properties Plan (see chapter 4). Generally, these planning documents will discuss pertinent cultural contexts within which the site's significance can be considered.

Many of the sites you encounter during your survey career will not be eligible for national, state, or provincial recognition. The most common reason is that the site retains neither physical integrity nor significance. Wherever this is the case, so state, and justify your conclusion. If you have done a competent job of establishing that a site lacks secure physical context, or that the site is not likely to yield significant information or otherwise fails to meet eligibility criteria, then this should be a fairly easy thing to do.

Your individual site discussion should conclude with a paragraph summarizing the site. Reiterate the physical relationship of the site to your client's project. State concisely the temporal and cultural affiliation of the site. Include a definitive assessment of pertinent factors such as physical integrity and site significance. State whether the site does or does not have the potential for inclusion on the National Register of Historic Sites or the Historic Sites and Monuments register. Finally, recommend further appropriate action (e.g., additional testing) or, alternatively, no further work.

Repeat this process for every site discovered during your survey. For many sites, the information you provide will constitute the only record that they ever existed. Give each site the benefit of your best effort.

ARCHAEOLOGICAL SYNTHESIS

Typically, a synthesis section does not appear in reports for small survey projects. However, large survey projects can add to, modify, or change the perception of what is known about a state or a region. For this reason, a section of your report devoted to bringing all of your data together can be extremely useful to readers and researchers. An archaeological synthesis can be personally gratifying to write, as well as edifying to future readers of your work. In this section, you should bring the data together into an interpretive synthesis that addresses the problem domains set forth in your research design. Topics such as culture history or site location modeling can be approached in an integrated manner that will provide a better understanding of the archaeology of the project area than was possible before you conducted your survey.

Existing state plans or regional historic properties contexts may provide baseline data on what was known or suspected about the project area's culture history prior to your investigation. This information

can serve as a point of departure for the synthetic interpretation of
your data. Contrasts between the findings of your project and the
baseline data can both illustrate and validate the contributions of the
CRM process. Along with the identification and protection of significant resources, CRM aims to gain useful knowledge for society. So
enjoy writing your synthesis section—this is real archaeology. A job
well done will enhance your reputation as both a solid archaeologist
and a reliable CRM practitioner.

SUMMARY AND RECOMMENDATIONS

Your report must conclude with a summary of the survey and your
clearly stated management recommendations. Briefly recap the nature of your client's project and the objectives of the survey. Restate
the total area surveyed in acres and hectares.

If no sites were identified and you are confident of your survey
coverage, no further work should be recommended. If you found
sites but none are considered eligible or potentially eligible for the
National Register of Historic Places, Historic Sites and Monuments register, or provincial list of heritage sites, you should state
this and recommend no further work for those sites. Still, summarize basic data including the size of each site and whether the entire site, or only a portion, lies within the area of potential effect.
If you could not determine eligibility at the Phase I level, recommend additional survey, testing, archival research, geomorphological studies, or other types of investigation as appropriate,
explaining why in each case. Outline the types and scopes of these
additional studies.

Include a short summary of each site, with recommendations. If
you have carefully constructed the summary paragraphs in each individual site discussion within your report, you can simply cut and
paste these paragraphs into your "Summary and Recommendations"
section. All of the pertinent management recommendations should
be included (e.g., no further work, avoid site if possible, Phase II testing, etc.).

A table summarizing survey results will be useful to you, your
client, and the reviewers. This table should list the sites recorded by
the survey, along with information on landform position, site size,
cultural affiliation, range of occupation, site function, NRHP (or
HSM) potential, and recommendations.

ACKNOWLEDGMENTS

Depending on the size and complexity of your project, you may be indebted to a great number of people who helped you. It is proper to acknowledge those individuals in an acknowledgments section. This section can appear at the beginning or end of the report, but here, between the summary and the references, is often a convenient placement. Give credit to whom it is due.

REFERENCES CITED

The "References Cited" section should list all reference materials cited in the body of the report. Most archaeological and CRM reports follow the *American Antiquity* style guide for references (www.saa.org/Publications/Styleguide/styframe.html). It is very important that your references are complete and cited correctly. Nothing shouts "beginner" more clearly than an incomplete or improperly structured references section. If the "References Cited" section does not contain references that were actually cited in the text, it is impossible for the reader to examine the works you had deemed important enough to mention. A shoddy references section leads the reader to wonder whether you actually read the cited literature or merely regurgitated information and ideas out of someone else's report. Do your own research; extend the discipline. You'll be better served in your career by doing so. The better command you maintain of the literature, the more successful you will be.

FIGURES

Figures can either be collated into the body of the report (usually a good idea for large reports) or appended in order after the references section. Figures for most small survey reports are gathered at the back of the report.

TABLES

Tables also can be collated into the body of the report or appended in order after the figures. As is the case with figures, tables in most small-project reports are typically printed at the back of the report.

APPENDICES

Attach any other necessary materials at the end of your document in an appendix or series of appendices. Appended material may include the project scope of work, relevant correspondence, copies of permits, review comments on the draft report, any other pertinent forms or documents, and reports from subcontractors.

9

TRYING TO MAKE IT REAL, COMPARED WITH WHAT?

A classic jazz tune, recorded most famously by Les McCann and Eddie Harris on their *Swiss Movement* LP (Atlantic Recording Corporation, 1969), asked the question that is the title of this chapter. It seems an apt question with which to close this volume. Just what realities do we address by conducting an archaeological survey?

Archaeology is constantly changing. We use technologies today that were unthinkable even a decade ago. We also deal with social and political issues that have had a deep effect on archaeological method and theory, issues that today are perhaps as profound as the debunking of the Moundbuilder myth was a century ago.

What will the future hold? Will the North American public continue to support the ideals of historic preservation? Constantly increasing demands for more intensive levels of survey, and the development of new and better, but also more costly, techniques, offers the promise of technically more efficient site finding. Simultaneously, there is resistance from many agencies, and the public at large, concerning the costs of this technical efficiency. County officials, for instance, occupy a pragmatic world and deal with hard issues of infrastructure maintenance and generally parsimonious budgets. They are accountable to a demanding yet tax-intolerant public. It can be difficult to explain to a county engineer why the costs of archaeological surveys for their bridge replacement projects continue to increase, consuming ever larger percentages of their project budgets, while the return to the public may not be apparent. Can the archaeologist's typical response—a shrug of the shoulders and a vague reference to higher agency demands—carry water for CRM in the twenty-first century? Doubtful.

The discipline will have to do a better job of explaining the social benefits of archaeology to its patrons—the public. CRM archaeologists, including those of us who survey, can support such a movement in many ways. Once a project report is written, it doesn't take much effort to edit the manuscript, remove the professional jargon, and distill its interesting conclusions into a public-oriented, nontechnical publication or pamphlet. Some may argue that the consultant is not paid to do this. Really? If you are not providing a tangible product for your constituency, the interested public, exactly for whom do you presume to be working? All CRM archaeologists also should feel an obligation to make public presentations, especially when invited to do so by archaeological and historical societies and local project area groups. If you are unwilling to do so, it just seems very difficult to justify your work. (See Toolkit, volume 7.)

When you do media interviews, make an effort to clearly explain the meaningful archaeological or anthropological context of your project. Don't assume that the reporter will understand: Help him or her understand what you are doing and why. It is up to you to ensure that when Jane Q. Public reads the piece, she says, "Gee, that's interesting!" Otherwise, the alternative might be "What a waste of money!"

You also have obligations to your peers to present the results of your work at professional meetings and through publication outlets. If your work has resulted in something interesting, get it out there. Few professionals working outside your region will ever read the gray literature you produce. Most regional and interregional networking and information exchange occurs at conferences. Attend them. The Internet also is helpful for data exchange, and Internet publishing will no doubt increase in the future.

Throughout this book an ideal relationship has been assumed between you, the archaeological contractor, and the government archaeologist. This ideal assumes that the agency archaeologist is a partner in making a better archaeology. Many archaeologists have experienced this ideal. However, for some consulting archaeologists, the relationships with governmental review and compliance officers have been more adversarial. Keep cool, stay professional, and you'll find that nearly everybody wants to promote high-quality work despite the compromises that are often necessary.

Whatever methods we use in archaeological survey, we are often, figuratively, trying to find a needle in a haystack. Imagine a scatter of lithic artifacts, a handful of flakes, that we find in an open patch

of ground on a grassy knoll above a river. Do these artifacts represent a moment's knapping along a hunting trail used millennia ago?
A single day's occupation? Or are they a tiny bit of a large, multi-
component site that is spread over a large portion of the bluff?

Consider this example: Suppose our project area encompasses 2,500
square meters—a little over a half acre or a quarter hectare. Shovels
and augers at the ready, we set up a systematic testing strategy and
start to move dirt. Each of our eight-inch-diameter bucket auger units
explores a little over four hundred square meters of surface, or about 4
percent of a square meter. Our shovel tests, at 50 × 50 centimeters, expose 25 percent of a square meter. Since we suspect that aeolian deposits cover the bluff, and we can investigate more easily to depth
with the bucket auger than we can with the shovel, we decide to combine both methods of subsurface investigation. To test 4 percent of the
project area would require 2,500 bucket-auger units. A 25 percent sample obtained by shovel testing would provide a fair evaluation of our
site but would virtually destroy it (and take a very long time to complete). Our compromise is to sample every ten meters, instead of every
one meter, thereby excavating about thirty-six shovel test units. Our
shovel tests sample nine square meters, less than 0.4 percent of the
site. With the bucket auger, we'll sample a little over one meter of surface area on the site, or about 0.04 percent of any near-surface or
buried components that may exist. Therefore, even "intensive" survey
often opens only tiny windows into the archaeological record.

Keep your perspective. No matter how systematically we plan our
methods or how scientific they appear, we don't always know what
we're getting into when we survey and evaluate sites.

Will new technologies change the way we evaluate sites? Remote
sensing gives us a representation of the subsurface without digging.
Geophysical techniques work best when distinctive contrasts are
present—buried metal, an abrupt change in soil moisture, an inter-
ruption in the pattern of magnetic fields—so they are effective for
documenting disruptions produced by historic structures; trenches;
and the more obvious prehistoric pits, hearths, or houses, particularly
when they occur within a relatively uniform geological matrix. If the
technology continues to develop at the present rate, however, it
might not be long before our ability to detect subsurface features will
significantly curtail the need to excavate for site assessments.

At the same time, we are now able to view and analyze three-
dimensional models using computers. More than a decade ago,
researchers such as Dr. Paul Reilly at IBM in England began to

construct experimental archaeological sites in which all artifacts were positioned within a transparent, three-dimensional matrix. If, in the future, we combine remote sensing and three-dimensional imaging technologies, similar to the way GPS and GIS are now combined, we may find that archaeological survey will be as much a computer visualization skill as it is a matter of physical labor.

Such technological progress may have ancillary benefits. By limiting physical testing, especially when investigating sensitive sites (e.g., cemeteries, mounds), we may assuage some of the concerns held by descendant communities about our work. We may never agree on how the past should be represented, and for what purposes, but we may be able to come to terms on how it might be investigated.

With all the promise of higher technology, however, field archaeologists do what they do because of their fascination for discovery and the love of the land. These emotional forces may lurk behind the protective masks provided by jargon and professionalism, but they are always present. We will always survey, no matter what government policies are in effect, or what issues are relevant to special interest groups, or what the new technologies have to offer. As long as there remains among people an inherent interest in who they are and where they have been, archaeologists will continue to seek the past's silent remnants, which remain hidden, buried beneath our feet.

 **REFERENCES**

Abbott, Larry R., and Craig A. Neidig
  1993   Archaeological Postholing: A Proposed Subsurface Survey and Site-Testing Method. *Illinois Archaeology* 5:38–45.
American Anthropological Association
  Issued yearly   *The AAA Guide.* American Anthropological Association. Arlington, Virginia.
Avery, Thomas E., and Thomas R. Lyons
  1981   Remote Sensing: Aerial and Terrestrial Photography for Archeologists. Cultural Resources Management Division, National Park Service, U.S. Department of the Interior, Washington, D.C.
Baker, Craig, and George J. Gumerman
  1981   *Remote Sensing: Archeological Applications of Remote Sensing in the North Central Lowlands.* Cultural Resources Management Division, National Park Service, U.S. Department of the Interior, Washington, D.C.
Bettis, E. Arthur III (ed.)
  1992   Soil Morphologic Properties and Weathering Zone Characteristics as Age Indicators in Holocene Alluvium in the Upper Midwest. In *Soils in Archaeology*, edited by Vance T. Holliday, pp. 119–44. Smithsonian Institution Press, Washington, D.C.
  1995   *Archaeological Geology of the Archaic Period in North America.* Special Paper 297. Geological Society of America, Boulder, Colorado.
Bettis, E. Arthur III, and Edwin R. Hajic
  1995   Landscape Development and the Location of Evidence of Archaic Cultures in the Upper Midwest. In *Archaeological Geology of the Archaic Period in North America*, edited by E. Arthur Bettis III, pp. 87–113. Special Paper 297. Geological Society of America, Boulder, Colorado.

Bevan, Bruce
    1983   Electromagnetics for Mapping Buried Earth Features. *Journal of Field Archaeology* 10:47–54.
    1991   The Search for Graves. *Geophysics* 56:1310-19.
    1998   *Geophysical Exploration for Archaeology: An Introduction to Geophysical Exploration.* Special Report No. 1. U.S. Department of the Interior, National Park Service, Midwest Archaeological Center, Lincoln, Nebraska.

Camilli, Eileen L., and Linda S. Cordell.
    1983   *Remote Sensing: Applications to Cultural Resources in Southwestern North America.* Cultural Resources Management Division, National Park Service, U.S. Department of the Interior, Washington, D.C.

Clark, Anthony
    1990   *Seeing Beneath the Soil: Prospecting Methods in Archaeology.* Batsford, London.

Collins, James M.
    1991   *The Iowa River Greenbelt: An Archaeological Landscape.* Office of the State Archaeologist, University of Iowa, Iowa City.

Connor, Melissa, and Douglas D. Scott
    1998   Metal Detector Use in Archaeology: An Introduction. *Historical Archaeology* 32(4):76–85.

Conyers, Lawrence B., and Dean Goodman
    1997   *Ground-Penetrating Radar: An Introduction for Archaeologists.* AltaMira Press, Walnut Creek, California.

Creamer, Winifred, Jonathan Haas, and Thomas Mann
    1997   Applying Photogrammetric Mapping: A Case Study from Northern New Mexico. *American Antiquity* 62:285–99.

Dalan, Rinita, A.
    1989   *Geophysical Investigations of the Prehistoric Cahokia Palisade Sequence.* Illinois Cultural Resources Study No. 8. Illinois Historic Preservation Agency, Springfield.
    1991   Defining Archaeological Features with Electromagnetic Surveys at the Cahokia Mounds State Historic Site. *Geophysics* 56:1280–87.

Deuel, Leo
    1969   *Flights into Yesterday: The Story of Aerial Archaeology.* St. Martin's Press, New York.

Eddy, Frank W., Dale R. Lightfoot, Eden A. Welker, Layne L. Wright, and Dolores C. Torres
    1996   Air Photographic Mapping of San Marcos Pueblo. *Journal of Field Archaeology* 23:1–13.

Fowler, Melvin L.
    1997   *The Cahokia Atlas Revised: A Historical Atlas of Cahokia Archaeology.* Studies in Archaeology, Volume 2. Illinois Trans-

portation Archaeological Research Program, University of Illinois, Urbana.

Gourley, Kathryn
1995 The Section 106 Process. Unpublished manuscript in possession of the author. Office of the State Archaeologist, University of Iowa, Iowa City.

Green, William, and John F. Doershuk
1998 Cultural Resource Management and American Archaeology. *Journal of Archaeological Research* 6:121–67.

Heimmer, Don H., and Steven L. De Vore
1995 *Near-Surface, High Resolution Geophysical Methods for Cultural Resource Management and Archaeological Investigations.* Interagency Archaeological Services, National Park Service, Denver, Colorado.

Holley, George R., Rinita A. Dalan, and Philip A. Smith
1993 Investigations in the Cahokia Site Grand Plaza. *American Antiquity* 58:306–19.

King, Thomas F.
1998 *Cultural Resource Laws and Practice: An Introductory Guide.* AltaMira Press, Walnut Creek, California.
2000 *Federal Planning and Historic Places: The Section 106 Process.* AltaMira Press, Walnut Creek, California.

King, Thomas F., Patricia Parker Hickman, and Gary Berg
1977 *Anthropology in Historic Preservation.* Academic Press, New York.

Kintigh, Keith W.
1988 The Effectiveness of Subsurface Shovel Testing: A Simulation Approach. *American Antiquity* 53:686–707.

Krakker, James J., Michael J. Shott, and Paul D. Welch
1983 Design and Evaluation of Shovel-Test Sampling in Regional Archaeological Survey. *Journal of Field Archaeology* 10:469–80.

Lightfoot, Kent G.
1986 Regional Surveys in the Eastern United States: The Strengths and Weaknesses of Implementing Subsurface Testing Programs. *American Antiquity* 51:484–504.
1989 A Defense of Shovel-Test Sampling: A Reply to Shott. *American Antiquity* 54:413–16.

Limp, W. Frederick
1989 *The Use of Multispectral Digital Imagery in Archeological Investigations.* Research Series No. 34. Arkansas Archeological Survey, Fayetteville.

Lyons, Thomas R., and Robert K. Hitchcock (eds.)
1977 *Aerial Remote Sensing Techniques in Archeology.* Chaco Center, National Park Service, U.S. Department of the Interior, Albuquerque, New Mexico.

McManamon, Francis P.
  1984   Discovering Sites Unseen. In *Advances in Archaeological Method and Theory*, Volume 7, edited by M. B. Schiffer, pp. 223–92. Academic Press, New York.
Maxwell, Gordon S. (ed.)
  1983   *The Impact of Aerial Reconnaissance on Archaeology.* Research Report No. 49. Council for British Archaeology, London.
Merry, Carl A., and John G. Hedden
  1995   Excavation Safety Plan for the Iowa Office of the State Archaeologist. *Journal of the Iowa Archeological Society* 42:5–7.
Mickle, Jack L.
  1995   Occupational Safety and Health Administration Regulations on Excavation Safety. *Journal of the Iowa Archeological Society* 42:1–4.
Nance, Jack D., and Bruce F. Ball
  1986   No Surprises? The Reliability and Validity of Test Pit Sampling. *American Antiquity* 51:457–83.
  1989   A Shot in the Dark: Shott's Comments on Nance and Ball. *American Antiquity* 54:405–12.
National Center for Preservation Technology and Training
  1998   Ground Penetrating Radar: New Developments in Data and Image Processing Techniques. *NCPTT Notes* Number 26. National Center for Preservation Technology and Training, United States Department of the Interior, National Park Service, Washington, D.C.
Schoeneberger, P. J., D. A. Wysocki, E. C. Benham, and W. S. Broderson
  1998   *Field Book for Describing and Sampling Soils.* National Soil Survey Center, Natural Resources Conservation Service, United States Department of Agriculture, Lincoln, Nebraska. (Online at www.statlab.iastate.edu/soils/nssc/field_gd/field_gd.htm)
Scollar, Irwin, Allain Tabbagh, Albert Hesse, and Irmela Herzog
  1990   *Archaeological Prospecting and Remote Sensing.* Cambridge University Press, New York.
Scott, Douglas D., Richard A. Fox Jr., Melissa A. Conner, and Dick Harmon
  1989   *Archaeological Perspectives on the Battle of Little Bighorn.* University of Oklahoma Press, Norman.
Shott, Michael J.
  1985   Shovel-Test Sampling as a Site Discovery Technique: A Case Study from Michigan. *Journal of Field Archaeology* 12:458–69.
  1989   Shovel-Test Sampling in Archaeological Survey: Comments on Nance and Ball, and Lightfoot. *American Antiquity* 54:396–404.
Soil Science Society of America
  1987   *Glossary of Soil Science Terms.* Soil Science Society of America, Madison, Wisconsin.

Squier, Ephraim G., and E. H. Davis
   1848   *Ancient Monuments of the Mississippi Valley.* Smithsonian Contributions to Knowledge, Volume 1. Smithsonian Institution, Washington, D.C.
Thomas, Cyrus
   1894   *Report of the Mound Explorations of the Bureau of Ethnology.* Twelfth Annual Report, Bureau of American Ethnology, Smithsonian Institution, Washington, D.C.
Trench Shoring and Shielding Association
   1994   *Excavation Safety Guide.* Trench Shoring and Shielding Association, Tarrytown, New York.
Warren, Robert E.
   1982   Prehistoric Settlement Patterns. In *The Cannon Reservoir Human Ecology Project: An Archaeological Study of Cultural Adaptations in the Southern Prairie Peninsula,* edited by Michael J. O'Brien, Robert E. Warren, and Dennis E. Lewarch, pp. 337–68. Academic Press, New York.
Weber, Scott A., and Stephen R. Yool
   1999   Detection of Subsurface Archaeological Architecture by Computer Assisted Airphoto Interpretation. *Geoarchaeology* 14:481–93.
Wenner, F.
   1916   A Method of Measuring Earth Resistivity. *Bulletin of the United States Bureau of Standards* 12:469–78.
Weymouth, John W.
   1986   Geophysical Methods of Archaeological Site Surveying. In *Advances in Archaeological Method and Theory,* Volume 9, edited by Michael B. Schiffer, pp. 311–91. Academic Press, New York.
Weymouth, John W., and R. Huggins
   1985   Geophysical Surveying of Archaeological Sites. In *Archaeological Geology,* edited by George Rapp and J. A. Gifford, pp. 191–235. Yale University Press, New Haven, Connecticut.
Weymouth, John W., and Robert Nickel
   1977   A Magnetometer Survey of the Knife River Indian Villages. *Plains Anthropologist* 22(78), part 2:104–18.
Whitley, David S.
   2001   *Handbook of Rock Art Research.* AltaMira Press, Walnut Creek, California.
Wobst, H. Martin
   1983   We Can't See the Forest for the Trees: Sampling and the Shapes of Archaeological Distributions. In *Archaeological Hammers and Theories,* edited by James A. Moore and Arthur S. Keene, pp. 32–80. Academic Press, New York.

Wynn, Jeffrey C.
    1986   Review of Geophysical Methods Used in Archaeology. *Geoarchae-ology* 1:245–57.
Zeidler, James A.
    1995   *Archaeological Inventory Standards and Cost-estimation Guidelines for the Department of Defense.* USACERL Special Report 96/40. U.S. Army Corps of Engineers, Construction Engineering Research Laboratories, Champaign, Illinois. (Online at www.denix.osd.mil/denix/Public/ES-Programs/Conservation/Legacy/AISS/usacerl1.html)

INDEX

map: soil, 28, 101; topographic, 25, 26, 101–2, 109, 115; uses of, 99–100
mapping/recording: aerial photograph, 5, 28–29, 77, 100, 102, 104; drafting survey map, 102–4; future of, 109–10; Geographic Information Systems, 8, 28, 103, 108–9, 110; Global Positioning System, 8, 102–3, 104–8, 109; photogrammetric mapping, 100; as prefield strategy, 25–26; satellite imagery, 8, 100; strength/weakness of, 99–100
metal detector, 80–81, 96–97
Moundbuilder, origins of, 3–4

NAGPRA. *See* Native American Graves Protection and Repatriation Act
nanoteslas (nT), 91
National Air Photo Library, 28
National Archaeological Data Base, 30, 120
National Environmental Policy Act (NEPA), 11
National Historic Preservation Act (1966), 10, 11, 12–13, 17
National Historic Sites and Monuments, 72
National Institute for Occupational Safety and Health, 71
National Park Service, 38
National Register Bulletin 38, 50
National Register of Historic Places (NRHP), 10, 12, 33, 72–75, 120, 124–25, 126
National Topographic Service of Canada (NTS), 25, 26
Native American, 3–4, 11, 49–50
Native American Graves Protection and Repatriation Act (NAGPRA), 11

NEPA. *See* National Environmental Policy Act
New Archaeology, 6
nonarbitrary unit, 21
nonsite survey, 7–8
NRHP. *See* National Register of Historic Places
NTS. *See* National Topographic Service of Canada

Oakfield soil probe, 71–72
Occupational Safety and Health Administration (OSHA), 70–71

PDOP. *See* position dilution of precision
pedestrian survey: basic method for, 57–58; of cave/crevice/shelter, 55–57; to determine National Register eligibility, 73; flagging artifact, 59; inspecting stream cutbank, 60, 61; mapping/describing soils, 60; as preferred method, 55; recording rock art, 57; shoreline observation, 61–63; viability of, 54–55
personnel, 36–38
petrograph/pictograph, 56–57
photogrammetric mapping, 100
planning documents, 29–30
plat book, 43–44
plat map, 31, 33
position dilution of precision (PDOP), 105
posthole testing, 69
postprocessualist archaeology, 7
probabilistic survey, 21, 22
"Procedures for the Protection of Historic and Cultural Properties," 10
project area description: for large project, 117–19; for small project, 116–17

ABOUT THE AUTHORS
AND SERIES EDITORS

James M. Collins is an archaeologist on the staff of the Office of the State Archaeologist, University of Iowa. He has been engaged in Midwest and Plains archaeology since 1974. In addition to hundreds of archaeological survey and excavation reports, recent publications include articles in *American Antiquity, Illinois Archaeology, Plains Anthropologist, The Minnesota Archaeologist, Midcontinental Journal of Archaeology,* and the *Journal of the Iowa Archeological Society;* chapters in *Mississippian Communities and Households* (University of Alabama Press, 1995) and *Cahokia: Domination and Ideology in the Mississippian World* (University of Nebraska Press, 1997); and four monographs: *The Archaeology of the Cahokia Mounds ICT-II: Site Structure* (Illinois Historic Preservation Agency), *The Iowa River Greenbelt: An Archaeological Landscape, The Archaeology of the Dolomite Ridge Site,* and *Prehistoric Archaeology of the Marriott Site* (Office of the State Archaeologist, University of Iowa). Among his interests are the prehistoric and protohistoric archaeology of the Midwest and Plains; the archaeology of settlements and settlement systems; the social, economic, and political parameters that define territories; the psychology and structure of complex societies; geoarchaeology; geophysical prospecting; and cultural and natural resource management. Most recently, his attention has focused on the Woodland tradition of the Upper Mississippi River Valley, ongoing research in the Iowa River Greenbelt, and the iconography and distribution of late prehistoric shell masks on the Prairie Peninsula and Plains.

Brian Leigh Molyneaux is an archaeologist, writer, and photographer. He is a specialist in prehistoric art and society, the human use of the landscape, and computer-aided applications in archaeology. He is director of the University of South Dakota Archaeology Laboratory, codirector of the Missouri River Institute, and a research associate of the Royal Ontario Museum, Toronto. He received his M.A. in art and archaeology from Trent University, Peterborough, Ontario, in 1977 and his Ph.D. in archaeology at the University of Southampton, England, in 1991. His extensive fieldwork includes many years of travel in northern Canada, studying Algonkian rock art, ritual, and religion, and archaeological research in the northern Great Plains. He recently conducted a two-year archaeological survey at Devils Tower National Monument, Wyoming. Dr. Molyneaux has published several books: *The Presented Past* (coedited with Peter Stone, Routledge, 1994), a study of archaeology, museums, and education around the world; *The Sacred Earth* (Little, Brown, 1995), a study of spirituality related to the landscape; *Native North America* (with Larry Zimmerman, Little, Brown, 1996), a detailed survey of Native North American culture, past and present; *The Cultural Life of Images* (editor and contributor, Routledge, 1997), a study of pictures and other visual representations of the past in archaeology; a new edition of *Native North America* (Oklahoma University Press, 2000); *Sacred Earth, Sacred Stones* (with Piers Vitebsky, Laurel Glen, 2001), a compilation dealing with spirituality in landscape and architecture; and *Mythology of the Americas* (with David M. Jones, Lorenz Books, 2001), a general encyclopedia. His rock art photographs have been exhibited in the National Gallery of Canada and featured in the PBS/BBC series *Land of the Eagle,* and he is an active contributor to web-based symposia on art, technology, environment, and culture (e.g., The Anthology of Art, www.anthology-of-art.net, School of Fine Arts, Braunschweig, Germany).

Larry J. Zimmerman is the head of the Archaeology Department of the Minnesota Historical Society. He served as an adjunct professor of anthropology and visiting professor of American Indian and Native Studies at the University of Iowa from 1996 to 2002 and as chair of the American Indian and Native Studies Program from 1998 to 2001. He earned his Ph.D. in anthropology at the University of Kansas in 1976. After teaching at the University of South Dakota for twenty-two years, he left there in 1996 as Distinguished Regents Professor of Anthropology.

While in South Dakota, he developed a major CRM program and the University of South Dakota Archaeology Laboratory, where he is still a research associate. He was named the University of South Dakota Student Association Teacher of the Year in 1980, given the Burlington Northern Foundation Faculty Achievement Award for Outstanding Teaching in 1986, and granted the Burlington Northern Faculty Achievement Award for Research in 1990. He was selected by Sigma Xi, the Scientific Research Society, to be a national lecturer from 1991 to 1993, and he served as executive secretary of the World Archaeological Congress from 1990 to 1994. He has published more than three hundred articles, CRM reports and reviews, and is the author, editor, or coeditor of fifteen books, including *Native North America* (with Brian Molyneaux, University of Oklahoma Press, 2000) and *Indians and Anthropologists: Vine Deloria, Jr., and the Critique of Anthropology* (with Tom Biolsi, University of Arizona Press, 1997). He has served as the editor of *Plains Anthropologist* and the *World Archaeological Bulletin* and as the associate editor of *American Antiquity*. He has done archaeology in the Great Plains of the United States and in Mexico, England, Venezuela, and Australia. He has also worked closely with a wide range of American Indian nations and groups.

William Green is the director of the Logan Museum of Anthropology and an adjunct professor of anthropology at Beloit College, Beloit, Wisconsin. He has been active in archaeology since 1970. Having grown up on the south side of Chicago, he attributes his interest in archaeology and anthropology to the allure of the exotic (i.e., rural) and a driving urge to learn the unwritten past, abetted by the opportunities available at the city's museums and universities. His first fieldwork was on the Mississippi River bluffs in western Illinois. Although he also worked in Israel and England, he returned to Illinois for several years of survey and excavation. His interests in settlement patterns, ceramics, and archaeobotany developed there. He received his master's degree from the University of Wisconsin at Madison and then served as Wisconsin SHPO staff archaeologist for eight years. After obtaining his Ph.D. from the University of Wisconsin at Madison in 1987, he served as state archaeologist of Iowa from 1988 to 2001, directing statewide research and service programs including burial site protection, geographic information, publications, contract services, public outreach, and curation. His main research interests focus on the development and spread of native agriculture. He has served as editor of the *Midcontinental Journal of Archaeology* and

The Wisconsin Archeologist; has published articles in *American Antiquity, Journal of Archaeological Research,* and other journals; and has received grants and contracts from the National Science Foundation, National Park Service, Iowa Humanities Board, and many other agencies and organizations.